THE LANGUAGE OF JUDAISM

by

Simon Glustrom

A JASON ARONSON BOOK

ROWMAN & LITTLEFIELD PUBLISHERS, INC.
Lanham • Boulder • New York • Toronto • Oxford

A JASON ARONSON BOOK

ROWMAN & LITTLEFIELD PUBLISHERS, INC.

Published in the United States of America
by Rowman & Littlefield Publishers, Inc.
A wholly owned subsidiary of The Rowman & Littlefield Publishing Group, Inc.
4501 Forbes Boulevard, Suite 200, Lanham, Maryland 20706
www.rowmanlittlefield.com

PO Box 317
Oxford
OX2 9RU, UK

Copyright © 1988, 1973, 1966 by Simon Glustrom
First softcover edition 1994
First Rowman & Littlefield edition 2004

British Library Cataloguing in Publication Information Available

Library of Congress Cataloging-in-Publication Data

Glustrom, Simon.
   The language of Judaism / by Simon Glustrom.
      p. cm.
   Reprint, with new introd. Originally published: New York, Jonathan David, 1966.
   Bibliography: p.
   Includes index.
   ISBN 1-56821-205-4 (pb)
   1. Judaism—Terminology.   I. Title.
BM50.G55 1988
296'.03—dc20   88-22281

Printed in the United States of America

⊖™ The paper used in this publication meets the minimum requirements of American
National Standard for Information Sciences—Permanence of Paper for Printed Library
Materials, ANSI/NISO Z39.48-1992.

To Helen
Jan, Beth, Aliza

CONTENTS

PART III
RESPONSIBILITIES TO GOD

PART IV
MORAL RESPONSIBILITIES TO OURSELVES

PART V
RESPONSIBLE AND IRRESPONSIBLE MEN

PART VI
THE RESPONSIBILITY TO REMEMBER

PART VII
RESPONSIBILITIES
TO THE HOME AND FAMILY

PART VIII
ASPECTS OF FAITH

PART IX
THOSE WHO PRAY
AND THE LANGUAGE OF PRAYER

PART X
SABBATH AND FESTIVALS

PART XI
LIFE CYCLE OF THE JEW

PART XII
SACRED PLACES

PART XIII
THE LITERARY HERITAGE OF ISRAEL

PART XIV
THE COMMUNITY OF ISRAEL
AND THE LAND OF ISRAEL

PART XV
JEWISH LAW AND AUTHORITY

TRANSLITERATION RULES

א	-	ל	*l*	
ב	*b*	מ	*m*	
ב	*v*	נ	*n*	
ג	*g*	ס	*s*	
ד	*d*	ע	-	
ה	*h*	פ	*p*	
ו	*v*	פ	*f*	
ז	*z*	צ	*tz*	
ח	*h*	ק	*k*	
ט	*t*	ר	*r*	
י	*y*, *i* at the end of a word	שׁ	*sh*	
כ	*k*	שׂ	*s*	
כ	*kh*	ת	*t*	

INTRODUCTION

Authors are known to agonize over the selection of an appropriate title that will succinctly summarize the message of their book. A colleague once admitted to me that he spent almost as much time selecting a title as he did preparing the volume for publication. After dismissing many suggested titles for this book I found myself most comfortable with *The Language of Judaism*. The cultural and religious tradition of Judaism consists of a uniquely rich Hebrew vocabulary indispensable to an understanding of its value system.

The language of Judaism is not identical with the modern Hebrew spoken on the streets of Tel Aviv. A Hebrew-speaking Israeli would have no difficulty reading any of the Hebrew concepts found in this volume. However, unless he learned about these concepts at home or in the classroom, he might be unable to explain their meanings.

Most of the words in *The Language of Judaism* can be found in the Bible, but they take on a conceptual meaning much later — during the talmudic period (the first through the fifth centuries). Thus, they are often referred to as rabbinic concepts. During the talmudic period these expressions became so familiar that they were imbedded in the consciousness of the people, scholars and laymen alike. Furthermore, wherever the Jewish people chose to live or were forced to live, these Hebrew concepts were incorporated into their spoken languages.

With the daily use of these expressions taken from classical Jewish sources, each generation tangibly contributed toward Jewish survival. Through this use of the selective idiom Jews were identifying themselves with former generations who used the same Hebrew expressions. Each generation acknowledged the same Jewish value system as had their ancestors, and they prepared their children to follow their example.

In addition to this vertical identification, Jews also felt a horizontal kinship with their co-religionists in many parts of the world who availed themselves of the same moral vocabulary. No one had to explain or elaborate on the meaning of these concepts since they were understood by almost all Jews. When someone asked for *rahamanut* (compassion) or complained that his child was giving him *agmat nefesh* (grief of soul), the Jewish listener instantly recognized the problem and the feeling.

These Hebrew concepts were verbalized by almost all Yiddish-speaking Jews, many of whom assumed that these were Yiddish phrases and probably were not aware that they were using Hebrew expressions taken from rabbinic literature. Little did they know that they were perpetuating the Hebrew language, which could have been lost forever were it not kept alive by the masses.

Sephardic Jews also shared many of these Hebrew concepts with their Ashkenazic, Yiddish-speaking brethren. Although the *Sephardim* did not speak Yiddish, and the *Ashkenazim* could not converse in Ladino or Judeo-Arabic, both groups understood the same language of Judaism. True, these expressions were pronounced differently within each cultural group, yet when either referred to the *yetzer hara* (evil impulse) or the *neshamah* (soul), they had little difficulty in understanding their common theological vocabulary. The language of Judaism became the code language that enabled members of the universal Jewish community to understand each other's needs and priorities.

We should not assume that all these concepts held the same meaning or importance for Sephardic and Ashkenazic Jews alike. Both were familiar with the meaning of *yihus* (family status) and *golem* (a clod), but their separate cultures, customs, and adaptations lent different shades of meaning to the same word-concepts. For the *Sephardim*, the *hakham* (wise person) was the spiritual head of the community, revered for his learning and piety. The

Ashkenazim, on the other hand, never referred to their spiritual leader by the title *hakham*. If the *Ashkenazim* wanted to describe their *rov* (rabbinical authority) as wise or perceptive, they would use the term as an adjective or noun, but never as a title. Occasionally they would even use the term satirically to convey the same meaning as "wise guy."

The Hebrew concepts were important unifying ideas that had a strong influence on the daily conduct and behavior of the Sephardic and Ashkenazic communities. Through these expressions, children were constantly being made aware of their responsibilities to God, to themselves, and to others. Expressions such as *mitzvah* (religious commandment), *shelom bayit* (peace in the home), *derekh eretz* (acceptable behavior)—all household words— were uttered so frequently that they assumed the highest values within Jewish family life. Conversely, the fear of being regarded as an *am haaretz* (ignoramus) or *apikoros* (religious skeptic) was so real that people of all ages strenuously avoided identification with these negative stereotypes.

Although most of these concepts are found in religious sources and were most frequently uttered by traditional Jews, secular-minded Jews also relied on the use of Hebraic moral concepts to express their concern for social justice and community responsibility. In their stirring speeches and essays, dating from the nineteenth and early twentieth centuries, Jewish socialists and revolutionaries—avowed secularists—made vast use of the rabbinic vocabulary to articulate their passionate concerns. What more effective way could these idealists find to express their concern for human rights and to persuade their fellow workers of the justice of their cause than by employing this built-in moral vocabulary.

In the forty years that I have been a rabbi, I have observed many dramatic changes within the American Jewish community. Along with the gradual demise of Yiddish, those Hebrew concepts that were so familiar to East European Jewry have become totally alien to most American Jews. Even the small group of

American Jews who have learned to speak modern Hebrew do not usually learn the language of Judaism that has so enriched the thought-life of generations of Jews.

I have long felt that this vocabulary can be rediscovered by people of all ages, even by those who are no longer conversant in Yiddish or Hebrew. A skilled instructor can introduce this terminology in the classroom and, through its frequent use, impress upon the student the Jewish vocabulary that so richly conveys ethical ideas. Parents can also learn to express the essential values of Judaism through the use of these time-honored Hebrew concepts.

When visiting the Soviet Union in December of 1987, I was asked to speak before several groups of teachers who were educating themselves in the Hebrew language. I was most impressed with their commitment to learning and their hunger for new educational materials to teach other adults. (Teaching children Jewish culture or religion is still forbidden in the Soviet Union.) With the exception of a few educators who were students of Talmud, most of those I met were totally unaware of Hebrew concepts, even though they were learning some of the most modern technical Hebrew terms along with the Hebrew idiom spoken in Israel. When we began to discuss some of the ancient moral concepts, I found that their appetite to learn more was insatiable. They wanted to know the origin and meaning of each expression. What affected me so emotionally was the thought that the vocabulary of Jewish life, which came so naturally to their grandparents, had become a virtually "dead language," found only in sacred books and commentaries unavailable to these courageous teachers. In learning about these concepts for the first time, these young Refuseniks were rediscovering another essential aspect of their Jewish identity found in the sounds of an old-new language – the language of Judaism.

Part I

RELIGIOUS RESPONSIBILITY

1

MITZVAH

מִצְוָה

Divine Commandment

An act performed in agreement with God's will is called a *mitzvah*. Its definition cannot be accurately conveyed in any other language because it combines so many different shades of meaning. It includes not only the commandment, but also the *law*, the *obligation* to fulfill the law as well as the *act* of fulfilling it. Next to *Torah*, it is the most basic term in the language of Judaism, serving as the general name for both positive *(mitzvot aseh)* and negative commandments *(mitzvot lo taaseh)*.

The *mitzvot* total six hundred and thirteen (called *taryag*), ranging from the commandments required of the High Priest in the Temple to a simple act of kindness or charity required of every Jew. The *mitzvot* are divided into two categories – "The commandments between man and God," which may be translated loosely as *ritual* and "commandments between man and his fellow," which are usually understood as *ethical*.

The Jew looks upon a *mitzvah* almost as if it were an object rather than a concept. He speaks of "acquiring *mitzvot*," "pursuing *mitzvot*," "adorning himself with *mitzvot* before God." Jewish tradition has allegorically compared *mitzvot* to a man's friend, his offspring, his garments.

Christianity has no equivalent of this Jewish concept. While it is true that "good works" are important in Christian thinking, greater emphasis has been placed on *faith*, as the classic sentence in the New Testament conveys: "Believe in me and you shall be saved." The emphasis is reversed in Judaism. While faith is significant, the creed is not as important as the fulfillment of a religious act. By performing righteous acts at stipulated times and seasons, or whenever an appropriate occasion arises, the Jew is also training himself to develop his beliefs and define his faith. Conversely, people who merely profess faith in certain ideals frequently fail to act on this faith when they are put to the test because they find performance more demanding than belief.

Scholars have disagreed as to which precisely are the six hundred and thirteen *mitzvot*. Maimonides, the great medieval legalist and philosopher, lists them according to his reckoning in the *Mishneh Torah*.

Some random examples of positive and negative *mitzvot* are: to permit a laborer to eat during work; to restore lost property; not to accept bribes; not to slander; not to eat milk and meat together; to remove leaven on the Eve of Passover; to fast on the Day of Atonement; to hear the sound of the *Shofar* on the first day of Tishri (Rosh Hashanah).

The first four *mitzvot* mentioned here are between man and man; the last four are between man and God.

2

AVERAH

עֲבֵרָה

Transgression

Averah is a general term used by the rabbis to express any thought or act in disagreement with the will of God. It is the very opposite of a *mitzvah*. The two terms are frequently mentioned together for purposes of contrast. For example, "One *mitzvah* leads to another *mitzvah;* one *averah* leads to another *averah.* The reward for a *mitzvah* is another *mitzvah;* the reward for an *averah* is another *averah.*"

The sages did not intend to be specific in using the term *averah.* There are other terms provided by the Torah that are more definite: 1) *het,* straying from the right path; 2) *avon,* crookedness or perversion; 3) *pesha,* a wicked act committed in defiance against God. An *averah* includes any undesirable act, be it ritual or ethical. It is an *averah* to kindle a fire on the Sabbath – or to charge an exhorbitant price for a purchase.

With the growth of Yiddish, *averah* and *mitzvah,* still opposites, were used to connote loss and gain respectively: "It is an *averah* to see a bright person waste his energy on trivial things. It is a *mitzvah* to rest when one is exhausted."

It has been suggested that modern Jews continue to stress the rabbinic concept of *mitzvah* because of its positive implications whereas *averah* should be minimized in Jewish thinking. Jews have always been trained to be more *mitzvah*-conscious than *averah*-conscious (Abraham Heschel). Nevertheless, if sin or man's sinfulness has no place in modern thought, it is questionable whether religion can continue to serve a useful purpose in our lives. How will a person recognize that he has acted immorally, that he, not his parents or his community, is primarily responsible for his actions? How will he choose to seek repentance unless he is aware of sin? True, destructiveness cannot always be attributable to sin; there are people who are incapable of controlling their actions. Others are victims of poverty, broken homes, denial of opportunity. But too many people are prepared to absolve themselves of personal responsibility for wrongdoing by conveniently placing the blame on others, when the choice was clearly theirs to make. They succumbed to evil because they were too weak or self-centered.

Perhaps a workable approach would be one that would reserve the term *averah* primarily for transgressions of the ethical code. Though we believe that following the rituals will benefit the individual and the group, failure to observe them does not necessarily constitute sin. We commit an *averah* when we steal, gossip, or dishonor our parents. To classify riding on the Sabbath with stealing – to call them both an *averah* – is confusing and unrealistic. To be sure, there are some ritual laws that, when ignored completely, do constitute an *averah*. If a Jew completely ignores the Sabbath, treating it as any other day in the week, he is in effect denying God's role in the creation of the world.

Similarly, if a person does not pray on any particular day, he has not committed a sinful act, but if he ignores prayer completely or scoffs at it, he then refuses to recognize his most important means of communication with God, which is tantamount to saying that he does not need God at all.

The most spiritual men are prone to commit *averot* (pl.) even while engaged in righteous acts, but the recognition of their inner conflict and the desire to overcome their weaknesses reflect their uncommon spirituality.

3

SIMHAH SHEL MITZVAH

שִׂמְחָה שֶׁל מִצְוָה

Joy of Fulfilling a Commandment

The rabbis coined the phrase, *simhah shel mitzvah* to emphasize that the commandments should be performed with a joyous heart and with pure motives rather than with a feeling of oppressive duty. True, at times they spoke of the "burden of the *mitzvot*," but they did not consider these two concepts to be contradictory. They felt that responsibility and privilege, duty and love, even trembling and rejoicing went hand in hand and should be felt simultaneously in performing a *mitzvah*.

Dr. Solomon Schechter describes this dual sensation out of personal experience: "I myself had once the good fortune to observe one of those old type Jews, who, as the first morning of the feast of Tabernacles drew near, used to wake and rise soon after the middle of the night. There he sat, with trembling joy, awaiting impatiently the break of dawn, when he would be able to fulfill the law of the palm branches and the willows!"

So essential was the pleasurable sensation in religious observance that one sage declared that the joy in carrying out a *mitzvah* was even more acceptable to God than the *mitzvah* itself.

It is difficult for one who does not practice the Jewish observances fully to appreciate how joy may be derived from religious discipline. For centuries non-Jews imagined that the Sabbath with all its prohibitions, its minute requirements, created more sorrow and anxiety than joy. How could one derive pleasure from deprivation? But the observing Jew felt no resentment. On the contrary, he felt privileged to be a member of a group that proclaimed at Sinai, "We will do and we will hearken." He greeted the Sabbath as one would receive a bride or a queen. He described the Festival of Sukkot as the "Season of our Rejoicing." He anticipated each new stage in the life cycle of his children with grateful appreciation, marked by rituals and ceremonies at which he invited friends and relatives to share in his joy.

Unfortunately, many Jews associate their religion with sadness because their contacts with it are limited to sad occasions. They meet the rabbi only when they have lost a relative. They enter the synagogue only to recite the *Kaddish*, to observe *yahrzeit*, or to participate in the *Yizkor* (memorial) service. But Judaism is not a sad religion.

Israel Zangwill distinguished it from other religions by calling it "a cheery creed." The Talmud reads: "When man faces his Maker he will have to give a reckoning for the joys of life that he failed to experience." True, the pursuit of pleasure as a goal in life is discouraged, but Judaism insists that life abounds with blessings of joy and pleasure that God wants man to taste.

4

HIDDUR MITZVAH

הִדּוּר מִצְוָה

Adornment of the Commandment

A fundamental attitude toward a *mitzvah* (religious commandment) is that it be fulfilled with enthusiasm, with an additional touch beyond the literal requirement of the law. This rule is based on the verse in Exodus, "He is my God and I shall adorn Him." Rabbi Ishmael questions, "And is it possible for a man of flesh and blood to make lovely his Creator? But it means I will be lovely to Him in performing *mitzvot*. I will make before Him a beautiful booth, a beautiful palm branch, a beautiful ram's horn to be sounded on New Year, a beautiful fringe, a beautiful scroll of the Torah written in His honor with the finest ink, with the best pen, by the most competent scribe, and wrapped in the purest silks."

The laws of Judaism should therefore not be performed in a perfunctory manner, but should be infused with an extra touch of concern and loving care. *Hiddur mitzvah*, like the concept *kavanah* (devotion), requires the highest degree of personal involvement in a religious act. If an individual possesses an appreciation for art, he should enhance the beauty of his home on the Sabbath and holidays. Jewish law requires that the *sukkah* merely have three walls and a cover. And yet, the conscientious Jew transforms it into a thing of beauty by elaborately decorating it with fruit and vegetables of the season. Furthermore, in the spirit of *hiddur mitzvah* the Talmud suggests: "If he has beautiful vessels, he should bring them up into the *sukkah*, beautiful divans he should bring them up into the *sukkah*."

The Sages recognized that this desire to honor God could

lead to harmful excess, such as impoverishment. Thus, a rule was formulated by the rabbis: *hiddur mitzvah* may only extend to a third of the value, i.e., only a third may be added to the normal cost in order to "adorn the commandment."

It is significant that the rabbis had to limit the giving of charity to one-fifth of a person's income or to caution against overspending in fulfilling a *mitzvah*. We are able to learn of the zeal with which some people fulfilled their religious obligations in the talmudic era. But even more significantly, we can appreciate the realism of the rabbis who discouraged neglect of the basic requirements of the family. A man cannot glorify God and simultaneously bring shame upon his wife and children by refusing to recognize their daily needs.

5

SEUDAT MITZVAH

סְעוּדַּת מִצְוָה

A Meal Accompanying
a Religious Ceremony

The quanity of meals that we choose to eat in a day is voluntary. However, there are occasions in Jewish life when we are required to participate in a meal in conjunction with a religious act. In fact, the meal is intimately associated with the act itself and is set down as a religious requirement, known as *seudat mitzvah.*

Examples of *seudot mitzvah* (pl.) are the repast served after a wedding ceremony, *brit milah, pidyon haben,* etc. Also when the study of a whole volume of the Talmud has been completed, a ritual meal of celebration is provided for the students.

In addition to the special occasions in the lifetime of the Jew, a festive meal is also required on certain days of the Jewish calendar. The meal eaten on the eve of Yom Kippur is deemed as essential as the fast on the following day. The *seudah* on Purim day is required by Jewish tradition, as is the third meal before the conclusion of the Sabbath *(seudah shlishit).*

The family dinner on the first two evenings of Passover is served in the midst of reciting the *Hallel* (hymns of praise). According to one authority, this unique arrangement of eating between prayers serves the purpose of teaching that the Passover meal is not regarded as an interruption of the *Hallel* prayer; both rituals are regarded as one continuous act of praise to God.

The concept of *seudat mitzvah* has lost much of its meaning for a large segment of American Jewry. As a result of this neglect, families see no relationship between a *bar mitzvah* or

11

wedding and the reception that follows. They have separated the formal ceremony, which conforms with religious tradition, from the collation, which they believe to be a purely social or secular activity. But the intent of our forbears is abundantly clear: no distinction should be made between the formal *mitzvah* and the festivity that follows. They are both one continuous *mitzvah*.

Part II

RESPONSIBILITIES TO MAN

6

TZEDAKAH

צְדָקָה

Love, Charity

Tzedakah is usually understood as charity, but this meaning alone does not convey all that *tzedakah* implies. Its derivation is from the biblical word, *tzedek*, meaning righteousness or justice. Helping those in need is not merely responding with sympathy or pity, but is a religious obligation to establish justice. The Torah leaves no choice but for the privileged to give as an act of social justice: "The needy will never disappear from the land; therefore I command you, open your hand to your poor and needy brother in your land" (Deut. 15:11). The Bible does not regard man's possessions as really belonging to him, but rather to God. Therefore, in helping the underprivileged, he is merely a guardian, distributing God's wealth where it rightfully belongs.

Later, the term *tzedakah* comes to mean love or charity, where giving becomes an act of compassion for the underprivileged. The poor man is not regarded as a burden, but as a brother in need. He is to be treated with warmth and sympathy; he must be spared from embarrassment.

For this reason Maimonides praises the man who dispenses charity in secret, so that the recipient does not know him. Even more praiseworthy is the man who does not know to whom he gives. "The highest form of charity is to help strengthen the hand of the poor by giving him a loan, or to join him in partnership, or to find him work. In brief, to help him out of his poverty, to help him establish himself."

Ever since talmudic times, each Jewish community established a fund for supporting the poor. The leaders of the commu-

15

nity were in charge of the collection and distribution of *tzedakah*. In the Middle Ages, when persecutions caused widespread poverty among Jews, many charitable societies, each distributing its own *tzedakah*, were formed especially to care for the helpless refugees who were constantly driven from town to town.

Giving charity through societies or organizations never absolved the Jew from personal charity. On frequent occasions he remembered the poor. Every celebration, every holiday was marked by gifts to the needy. In pre-modern Europe, every house contained tin boxes that supported institutions and individuals. Coins were deposited before the housewife kindled the Sabbath candles. The members of the household placed coins in the boxes before or after family crises occurred. Children were trained to give *tzedakah* early in life. They were often given the responsibility of distributing charity in the home when the poor would make their regular visits.

In modern times the giving of *tzedakah* through large agencies such as United Jewish Appeal has drastically changed the whole method of giving charity. Undoubtedly, the advantage of combining one's contributions into a single fund has proven to be effective in raising huge sums for legitimate causes. Nevertheless, the need for giving *tzedakah* does not end with these organizational campaigns. There are people in need who are too proud to seek aid through an agency; others are in drastic need of immediate aid beyond the limited relief that an agency may provide. In such cases the Jew is by no means morally absolved from helping individuals merely by making an annual contribution to an institutional fund. Jewish law explicitly states that it is forbidden to turn away any man who seeks help.

7

RAHAMANUT

רַחֲמָנוּת

Compassion, Pity

The origin of *rahamanut* is *rehem*, meaning "womb," which reveals a most important insight: the compassion that a mother has for her child represents the highest type of love. It is unconditional, not depending on the ability of the infant to show his love in return.

This ability to show compassion and pity not only to those who have shown the same feeling toward us but to those who may not even be aware of our presence reflects the true meaning of *rahamanut*. It includes the unique ability even to feel compassion for those who have wronged us or who have failed to develop the capacity to love others.

In short, it is the ability to mature beyond selfcenteredness, to "grow out of oneself" and "into someone else," accepting another's pain as our own, that constitutes the essential meaning of *rahamanut*.

One of the many names given to God in our tradition is *Rahamana*, "Compassionate One." One of our best-known prayers contains the request: "Our Father, merciful Father, the ever compassionate, have mercy upon us." Jews are required to be "compassionate sons of the Compassionate." Compassion is among the greatest of Jewish virtues.

Our tradition is clear in emphasizing that compassion must not be misunderstood as mere sentimentalism. Justice must not be put aside when discipline is called for. The Bible warns that a judge must not favor the poor man if he has wronged a wealthy person. If there is no justice, there can be no recognition of

17

wrong. A society cannot endure without law. At the same time, justice must be tempered with mercy if we are to expect wrong-doers to be rehabilitated.

Milton Steinberg, a well-known American rabbi, wrote this about the quality of *rahamanut:* "He is a failure as a human being, no matter what his other traits and achievements, whose heart does not hurt for his fellow man. And he is a successful human being, no matter where else he may be lacking, who is rich in compassion."

8

AGMAT NEFESH

עַגְמַת נֶפֶשׁ

Grief Caused by Others

More severe than physical pain, which may be transitory, is the inner pain or "grief of the soul" that frequently lingers indefinitely. *Agmat nefesh* ("a grief of the soul") does not refer to the grief that one experiences as the result of illness or death of a dear one. Grief that results from natural causes is usually unavoidable. On the other hand, *agmat nefesh* refers to the pain caused to a person by another's behavior—pain that could and should have been avoided.

The disappointment that parents feel when their children repudiate their way of life—despite the most strenuous efforts that parents have exerted in their behalf—may well be an example of one of the most painful instances of *agmat nefesh*. Even the most strong-hearted parents must admit, if they are candid about their feelings, that they cannot become resigned to this disappointment.

Agmat nefesh is also deeply felt when one becomes disenchanted with a friend whose sudden change of attitude has revealed a facet of his character that was heretofore unknown. It is primarily the disillusionment after years of mutual trust and admiration that contributes to the feeling of *agmat nefesh*.

When we read about the experiences of German Jews whose erstwhile friends turned against them overnight, refusing to help them in their despair or even to speak to them after years of lasting friendship, one can begin to understand the deeper meaning of this grief. Even physical torture could not produce greater grief than the bitterness of total disillusion. One could

19

possibly accept such treatment from strangers, but never from apparently trustworthy neighbors and friends.

Thus, when the Jew speaks of *agmat nefesh*, he cannot help but become passionate, for he is speaking of a bitter disappointment in his life—a disappointment that has affected his whole personality as well as his outlook on the future.

9

TZAAR BAALEI HAYIM

צַעַר בַּעֲלֵי חַיִּים

Suffering of Living Things

Though the Jews never felt the necessity to form a society for prevention of cruelty to animals, their tradition clearly insists on adopting a humane attitude toward the lower forms of life. Animals, too, were regarded as God's creation. God also hears their cry of pain when inflicted upon them unnecessarily by callous human beings.

The Bible warns against yoking together animals of unequal strength, lest the burden be too great for the weaker animal. We are forbidden to muzzle the ox, for preventing him from satisfying his natural desire is a form of cruelty. The Sabbath was instituted for the benefit of the animal as well; he, too, like man, must not be overburdened with work.

The attitude of the rabbis in the Talmud concerning prevention of cruelty to animals is reflected in a story about Rabbi Judah the Prince who was punished because he spoke unfeelingly to an animal. Once when a tender calf ran toward him for protection before its slaughter, he thrust it aside saying, "Go, that is thy destiny." Rabbi Judah learned his lesson after being punished for his insensitivity. He later observed that his servant was exterminating weasels from his home and insisted that they not be harmed, saying, "It is written: 'And His tender mercies are over all His works.' "

Our Jewish sources are filled with directives that are clearly intended to protect the helpless beast. "One may not sit down to eat until he has first fed his animals." Many Jewish authorities condemn the hunting of animals for sport; gladiator shows and

21

pigeon racing were frowned upon as unlawful exploitations of animals.

The Jewish method of slaughtering an animal for consumption is clearly intended to minimize its pain. Great care is given to the knife that it be regularly examined before and after its use to determine that it contains no defects that might rip the flesh. The cut severs the arteries to the head of the animal, and thus circulation to the head region is stopped, rendering the animal unconscious to pain. This same painless effect is not experienced by stunning the animal with a blow.

Undoubtedly a strong case could be made here for vegetarianism, which would prohibit the taking of an animal's life even by painless methods. In fact, the tradition regards vegetarianism as an ideal. That is why Adam and Eve abstained from meat in the garden of Eden. In the time of Noah, meat was permitted as a compromise with the human desire to eat meat. Generally, the Jewish tradition gives priority to the needs of human beings, keeping in mind, however, the avoidance of unnecessary pain to the helpless animal. It is in this spirit that experiments on animals are permitted as a necessary means of preventing disease and death in humans. Showing a tender consideration for animals, the tradition has a still deeper concern for mankind.

10

BAL TASHHIT

בַּל תַּשְׁחִית

The Prohibition
against Needless Destruction

Judaism is concerned with more than the protection of humans and animals. Even plant life that is useful to man may not be wantonly destroyed. The origin of this prohibition is expressed in the Bible: the Israelites who were about to enter Palestine were forbidden to destroy the fruit trees, presumably to make weapons of war. From this evolved the concept of *bal tashhit*, the prohibition against wasting or destroying all useful things. The Jew is warned against putting bread on the ground where it can be stepped upon or throwing away any food that is edible.

The Sages warn against needless damage to property; a person who tears his clothes, smashes household objects, or squanders his money in a moment of rage is severely criticized.

The underlying thought is that, in an ultimate sense, we do not own anything. Everything that we possess rightfully belongs to God—even our food and clothing. All our possessions have been given in trust on condition that we make wise use of them. We do not even have exclusive rights to our own bodies. We may not take our own life or abuse our own flesh in any way.

This prohibition has special meaning in a prosperous society such as ours, which encourages waste and which thrives on the concept of planned obsolescence. We have been misled into thinking that waste, in this sense, is a patriotic gesture. We perform a great disservice to ourselves when we destroy anything useful merely because we have enough funds to replace it.

Included in the prohibition of *bal tashhit* would be the destruction of flower-gardens, defacing of art objects, the tearing of pages from a book, or the destruction of any object from which we or other people may derive pleasure or instruction.

11

ALMANAH

אַלְמָנָה

Widow

Just as the Bible urges that the poor, the stranger, and the orphan are to receive special consideration, so must the widow be treated with extreme kindness. She was to share the gleanings of the field and to be invited to the sacrificial meals and feasts. "And you shall rejoice before the Lord your God, you and your son and your daughter . . . and the orphan and the widow." Spoils of war were given over to the widow. Her clothing was not to be taken as a pledge; to take a widow's ox for a pledge was considered an act of oppression.

In later times the rabbis extended the safeguards on behalf of the *almanah*. They were concerned that she should not "go begging at people's doors" and were anxious to protect her reputation. She was to be supported from the estate of her deceased husband. She was to have a dwelling becoming of her dignity, maintaining the servants and all the utensils she used during her husband's lifetime. Furthermore, if orphans sold her dwelling, their action was ruled illegal.

The Sages felt that it was unrealistic for a widow to remain single. She was encouraged to remarry. She could even marry a priest, though not a High Priest. Yet an ordinary priest married to a widow was not forced to abandon her if he were elevated to the High Priesthood. (In contrast to this attitude a recent Pope indicated that while Catholicism did not condemn remarriage for widows, he commended those who remained faithful to their first husband and to the "perfect symbolism of the sacrament of marriage.")

Incidents are related in our history about famous scholars and community leaders who would disregard dignity to help an unfortunate widow. One well-known rabbi of the nineteenth century observed a certain widow who was standing behind her fruit stall waiting in vain for a customer. The rabbi stood at the stand and began to sell her fruit. When news spread that the rabbi had become a salesman, people rushed to make their purchase, and the widow's cause was helped.

12

SHALOM

שָׁלוֹם

Peace

The term *shalom* is used as a greeting or farewell. It is best translated as "completeness," derived from the word *shalem*.

Tradition reveals that *shalom* is one of the names of God and should not be uttered in an unclean place. Some of our most important prayers—the Priestly Blessing, the Grace after meals, the *Amidah*—conclude with the word *shalom*.

Some of the most inspiring passages in our Bible consist of the prophetic visions of a peaceful future. Isaiah and Micah envisioned an age when nations shall "beat their swords into plowshares and their spears into pruning hooks; nation shall not lift up sword against nation, neither shall they learn war any more."

When our tradition speaks of *shalom* it does not mean merely an absence of strife. A cold war or armed truce cannot be described in terms of *shalom*. Where *shalom* exists there is a strong desire to cooperate with and to understand other nations. *Shalom* implies a striving for unity and harmony, in spite of major differences among peoples.

Shalom does not apply to peace among nations only. An individual person may often feel helpless to bring about international peace, but he is in a position to improve his relationship with other people with whom he may disagree. The peace-maker is highly regarded in our tradition. The man who loves and pursues peace is regarded as a disciple of Aaron, the High Priest.

The peace-loving man is by no means a weakling or a coward. He is prepared to speak out against injustice, indeed, to become angry when he encounters evil in others. But even in his anger, he looks upon his opponent as a potential friend who will eventually change his ways and appreciate the effort that is being made to help him.

13

VIKUAH

וִכּוּחַ

Controversy, Debate

Though the rabbis show great regard for men of peaceable nature, such as Aaron the High Priest, they do not claim that one should always shun controversy. There are times when controversy is necessary to sharpen the mind and to produce constructive results. The Mishnah differentiates between two types of *vikuhim:* "Every controversy that is for the sake of Heaven will in the end endure; but one that is not for the sake of Heaven will not endure." Then follow examples of the constructive and destructive kinds of controversy: Hillel and Shammai, the representatives of two great schools of thought, often debated, but both wanted to achieve similar ends—the strengthening of Judaism. They differed only in their approach. On the other hand, when Korah sought to upbraid Moses, his motives were personal and selfish. His goal was to deny the authority of Moses and elevate himself to a position of supreme authority. He engaged in controversy that was "not for the sake of Heaven."

Unfortunately, most controversies fall into the latter category. They are kindled by contentious people who thrive on belligerence. They find it difficult to respect the viewpoints of others, to accept authority which they wrongly identify with conformity. Organizations and communities should welcome debate on essential issues; the freedom to debate policies candidly assures democratic procedure, freedom of speech. By the same token, members or citizens should be able to differentiate a live issue from a meaningless one; they should be prepared to direct their energies to problems that affect the future welfare of an institution or community. Dissent should never become an end in itself. It stifles genuine progress and creates useless animosities among erstwhile friends.

Historically, the *vikuhim* denote a series of infamous debates or disputations in which Jews were forced to participate during the Middle Ages. Especially in the thirteenth century, Jewish scholars were called to defend accusations against the Talmud in open debate with Christian authorities. The judges were usually members of the royal family and church leaders, who prejudged the debates from the start. One of the best known of these *vikuhim* took place in Paris in 1239 between a renegade Jew, Nicholas Donin, and a group of rabbis led by Rabbi Yehiel of Paris. Donin berated the tales and legends of the Talmud and twisted some passages into attacks on Christianty. Yehiel gave the truthful interpretations of the passages cited by Donin, but his defense fell on deaf ears. The Talmud was condemned as a dangerous book, and soon afterward twenty-four cartloads of volumes were brought to the public square in Paris and burned.

14

GEMILUT HASADIM

גְּמִילוּת חֲסָדִים

Acts of Loving-kindness

Any deed of loving-kindness extended to another person, living or dead, is called *gemilut hesed*. Just as God's loving-kindness is available to all — to the fallen, the sick, the imprisoned, the dead — so are we required to follow God's merciful ways by performing deeds of piety even when no material reward may be expected. Especially in deeds performed for the dead — burying him in a proper manner, protecting his name, caring for his family — the departed cannot repay the *gomel hesed*.

Gemilut hasadim is accorded an even higher place in Jewish values than the giving of charity. Our rabbis assert that charity applies only to the living, but acts of loving-kindness apply to the living and the dead. Charity is something a man does with his wealth; acts of loving-kindness he carries out with his means and with his own person. In acts of loving-kindness the poor man's feelings are spared, as when one lends a poor man funds to help him in his hour of need; however, when he gives the poor outright charity, the recipient inevitably feels some shame. Charity is given only to the poor; acts of loving-kindness are bestowed upon the rich also. Nor is kindness to be confined to human beings: "It is forbidden for a man to eat before he has given food to his animal."

So important is *gemilut hasadim* that it was equated with the study of Torah and the Temple service. The three together form the principles on which the world stands. This claim was made before the Roman destruction of the Temple in Jerusalem (70 C.E.). After the destruction, Rabban Johanan ben Zakkai consoled his people with the thought that *gemilut hasadim* could adequately replace the sacrificial service as an atonement for Israel. His conclusion was based on the prophet Hosea (8th century B.C.E.) who proclaimed in God's name, "For I desire mercy and not sacrifice."

The most helpful charitable institutions in Jewish life were formed as a means of implementing the *mitzvah* of *gemilut hasadim*. For example, burial societies, free loan associations, orphan homes, and homes for the aged were established in most communities where Jews settled.

15

BIKKUR HOLIM

בִּקוּר חוֹלִים

Visiting the Sick

Visiting the sick is regarded not so much as an act of courtesy, but rather as one of the essential commandments of Judaism. In a talmudic passage repeated in the daily prayer book, *bikkur holim* is listed among the ten major commandments that yield reward in the present and future life. We are reminded that the visitor of the sick follows God's example, imitation of God being the primary goal of religion. "Just as He visited the sick – as it is written 'And the Lord appeared unto him (Abraham, following his circumcision)' – so shall you, too, visit the sick." The Talmud goes even further in stating that the refusal to perform this duty is likened to the shedding of blood, since visiting the sick helps to restore them to life. Maimonides, the great physician–scholar, said of *bikkur holim*, "Whoever visits a sick person is regarded as if he took away part of the disease and relieved him of it."

In light of these strong statements in traditional Jewish sources, it is understandable that Jews always took their responsibilities toward the sick with utmost seriousness. Israel Abrahams, writing about Jewish life in the Middle Ages, remarks that "this duty was incumbent on every Jew, rich and poor, and was extended toward patients of all classes and creeds." After the Sabbath morning services, the worshipers would pay regular visits to the sick before returning home to partake of their meal. The laity did not depend on their rabbi to visit the sick in their stead. The rabbi merely performed his share like other members of the community.

Jews would abide by a certain code of behavior regarding the sick. Only intimate friends called upon a patient immediately after he fell ill, in order that he might not be frightened. The visitor was careful not to stay with the patient for too long nor to visit him when he was in great pain. The patient was to be cheered—not depressed by dismal talk. A man was not expected to visit an enemy; his visit might create greater discomfort for the patient. A prayer was usually uttered for the patient's recovery.

Bikkur holim societies were prevalent in many European Jewish communities and continue to exist today. These voluntary societies provide medical expenses for the ill who cannot depend on their families for help. Members of the society visit and comfort the sick. Here we have another of the many *mitzvot* that were formalized into permanent Jewish institutions.

The tendency in recent years has been to depend on the rabbi to visit the sick in homes and hospitals. The layman feels absolved of this responsibility so long as the sick are called upon by someone. But the principle of *bikkur holim* requires every Jew to be personally involved in the needs of others, especially when an act of *tzedakah* is involved.

16

REFUAH SHELEMAH

רְפוּאָה שְׁלֵמָה

A Complete Healing

It is customary upon visiting the sick to extend the prayerful wish that the patient be granted a complete recovery from his illness. The phrase is taken from the eighth benediction in the daily *Amidah* where the worshiper petitions God to heal all who are ill. In this paragraph it is permissible to introduce a voluntary prayer for any individual whom we may choose to remember.

The *mitzvah* of visiting the sick is highly regarded as a meritorious act in Judaism. One's presence alone helps the patient in his fight for recovery. Moreover, in the presence of the patient the visitor is encouraged to petition God, "the faithful and merciful Physician," for his recovery regardless of the language in which he chooses to pray.

Jewish law also advises that when greeting a patient one should include all the sick in Israel to strengthen the effect of his prayers. The patient himself is reminded to strengthen his faith in God and seek the success of his treatment through prayer.

Though God is called Physician and prayers for recovery are advocated, we are cautioned against refusing medical care or relying solely on supernatural methods of healing. Prayer was never intended to replace the efforts of the physician. Time and again the Talmud refers to medical measures to combat illness and disease. Furthermore, in medieval times many well-known rabbis chose the field of medicine as a second career. They used the best medical methods known to them to heal Jews and non-Jews alike. Healing the sick among all religious groups was looked upon by these skilled physicians as a religious obligation, and they regarded themselves as agents of God to implement His will.

17

HAKHNASAT ORHIM

הַכְנָסַת אוֹרְחִים

Hospitality

Hospitality is generally regarded to be no more than etiquette in contemporary circles. In the Jewish tradition, however, it is elevated to one of the essential *mitzvot*. Abraham, the first Patriarch, is extolled for this virtue of hospitality. Whenever the opportunity was presented to him, Abraham gave food and drink even to idolators; he also taught them wisdom and knowledge of God to nourish their souls.

Rabbi Yonah taught: "When a poor man visits you at home, receive him cordially and serve him at once, for he may not have eaten for some time, yet he is ashamed to ask for food. . . .Console and encourage him. Attend to the poor man's needs yourself, even if you have many servants. Is any one of us superior to Abraham who served the disguised angels with his own hands?"

Sharing one's table is preferred to giving money to the needy. The first is a personal act, the second impersonal. A meal provides immediate benefit. When money is distributed, the poor man's benefit is not realized *until he has bought food with his money*.

We are advised to show hospitality indiscriminately, even to those whom we suspect do not need our help. We cannot discern at a glance between the needy and the pretender. We are exhorted not to embarrass the poor by reminding him that he is a parasite without a gainful occupation. He may appear ablebodied, but who can really determine his state of physical or mental health?

The mitzvah of *hakhnasat orhim* applies to the rich as well as to the poor guest. Even those who are self-sufficient may be unable to find lodging or may feel lonely in a strange town. Some people can only be happy when they are made to feel at home. We are required to treat such a visitor as if he were a poor guest, sharing our bread with him; his need for warmth is not unlike that of the needy for bread.

Like other *mitzvot* that were concretized into institutions, many Jewish communities established and maintained *hakhnasat orhim* societies to help visitors find comfort and hospitality in a strange environment.

18

NIHUM AVELIM

נִחוּם אֲבֵלִים

Comforting the Mourners

It is an important religious duty to visit mourners, especially during the week after the death of their relatives. This custom of offering consolation to the bereaved is very ancient. The Bible refers to it several times. In the Book of Job, however, we have the most vivid description of friends visiting the unfortunate Job in his hour of sadness: "They sat down upon the ground with him seven days and seven nights."

As in visiting the sick, the comforter of mourners is also advised to follow certain protocol according to Jewish law: he is not permitted to open the conversation before the mourner has spoken, and if he perceives that the mourner wishes him to leave, he must do so. Also, the comforter is advised not to say: "What can you do? It is impossible to alter the decree of the Creator."

It is not really necessary for one to converse at all, if either the visitor or the mourner will be uncomfortable. The mere presence of the visitor offers consolation. In fact, tradition has wisely provided the visitor with a meaningful formula of comfort—a substitute for conversation—that he addresses to the bereaved family: "May God console you along with the other mourners of Zion and Jerusalem." Participation in the daily prayers during the *shivah* period at home also gives the visitor an important function that is deeply appreciated by the mourners.

Those visitors who do converse with the mourners should remember that they are not expected to cheer them up in their time of anguish. One does not console by attempting to distract the mourner. A person finds greatest comfort in talking about his dear ones who have passed on, by recalling meaningful incidents in their lives that were not known or were forgotten by the family.

The home is the only place where mourners are appropriately comforted in the Jewish tradition. In recent years more and more families have adopted the non-Jewish custom of coming to the funeral chapel on the evening before the funeral to view the deceased and accept visitors. This practice is contrary to Jewish custom. It also is a trying experience for the mourner, who must sit with his loved ones who are being exposed to public view, while he himself is forced to make conversation. Surely at such a somber moment, it seems reasonable to assume that the mourner would prefer to give private expression to his feelings. For those acquaintances who cannot attend the funeral on the following day, there is still no need to visit the chapel before the funeral. The following seven days provide ample opportunity for sympathetic friends to console the mourners at home.

19

PIDYON SHEVUYIM

פִּדְיוֹן שְׁבוּיִים

Ransom of Captives

Ever since the rebellion against Rome, Jews have regarded the duty of ransoming captives as one of the most urgent obligations of the community. Huge sums were raised to free their brethren who had been kidnapped for the purpose of selling them as slaves. The Romans were aware that the Jews were prepared to make great personal sacrifices to redeem their fellow-Jews, and they did not hesitate to extort as much money as possible from them.

The problem of extortion became so grave that the rabbinic authorities were forced to enact laws against paying too high a ransom for captives. The Mishnah explicitly states that captives should not be redeemed for more than their value as workers, for the sake of the general welfare. Even assisting their attempts to escape was discouraged by the Talmud for fear that their captors would treat them more harshly.

Nevertheless, Jews often persisted in ransoming their brethren at all costs, unmindful of the drain on the resources of the community. In the Middle Ages, the Jews of Venice organized a society, called *Hevrat Pidyon Shevuyim*, to liberate their fellow-Jews captured by bandits. Wardens were appointed in other Italian communities to collect funds for redeeming captives. Any Jew who sold himself into slavery or was enslaved through debt was helped by the Jewish community.

During the 1940s, Jewish leaders were in contact with Nazi officials, again offering huge sums to help their fellow-Jews escape. The notorious Eichmann also offered to free a large number of Jews in exchange for trucks, but despite their heroic efforts to raise sufficient funds, the Jewish leaders found it impossible to meet his exorbitant demands.

Pidyon shevuyim represents a noble attempt to help those who cannot help themselves. Who will deny the infinite value of saving one life? But we are confronted with a dilemma in the performance of this noble act: Is it moral to negotiate with criminals, to contribute to the success of their plans, to encourage others to follow their example? There is no simple answer, especially since the saving of human lives is involved here, which is far more complicated than the general problem of whether ends justify the means.

20

DEREKH ERETZ

דֶּרֶךְ אֶרֶץ

Decency or Acceptable Behavior

The exact meaning of *derekh eretz* cannot be translated into any other language. It has been defined as etiquette, decorum, good manners, *savoir faire*, etc. But the Hebrew phrase definitely has ethical implications. As a whole it refers to a code of behavior toward one's fellow man—his community, his country, his family, and himself.

The rabbis were intent on setting rules of behavior to establish a good name for oneself and promote the welfare of society. For example, one should not enter another's house without previously announcing his coming; a guest should conform to the wishes of his host; one should spend more money on his clothes and less on his food in order to present a neat appearance.

Scholars were not exempt from the rules of *derekh eretz*. They were required to take care of their appearance. A scholar who wears soiled clothes and patched shoes destroys in those who meet him the respect for knowledge. Hillel regarded personal cleanliness as a fundamental principle of Jewish life. Hurrying home to bathe for the Sabbath, Hillel claimed he was fulfilling a commandment to care for his health and body.

Derekh eretz is closely associated with the Torah itself. They are inseparable, say the rabbis. A Midrash claims that *derekh eretz* preceded the Torah, probably meaning that there are rules of proper conduct that are derived from common sense and are not explicitly spelled out in the Torah. For example, the need to seek financial independence should be instinctively appreciated

by all intelligent human beings. What good is academic knowledge if an individual cannot support his family? "It is better to
skin dead animals for a living than to become a burden on the
community." A father must teach his son a trade; he must teach
him how to swim to assure self-preservation.

Many rules of *derekh eretz* that are formulated in the
Talmud deal with promoting a sound family relationship. Here
especially, consideration for the emotional and psychological
needs of members of the family is required. A man must make
every attempt to provide new clothing for his wife, especially for
the holidays. A man must be careful not to provoke his grown
children lest they become disrespectful and thus commit a sin.
Children must not be burdened with responsibilities too difficult
for them. A parent should develop the skill of strictness with one
hand and gentleness with the other.

The Jew is required to practice a code of acceptable behavior that goes beyond the formal observances. *Derekh eretz*,
though concerned primarily with man's decent conduct toward
his fellow man, is unquestionably regarded as a *religious* obligation that God requires of us.

21

EMET

אֱמֶת

Truth

All religions extol the virtue of truth. Without truthfulness morality cannot exist; where truth abides, there God's presence is felt. We are reminded that just as God is first, last, and ever-present, so are the three letters of *emet*—*aleph*, the first, *mem*, the middle, and *tav*, the last letter of the Hebrew alphabet. Thus God and truth, says the parable, are inseparable.

The Bible leaves no doubt about the fundamental virtue of truth: "Ye shall not deal falsely, nor lie one to another." Moses chooses "men of truth" to serve as judges over the Israelites. Bearing false witness against one's neighbor is condemned in the ninth commandment of the Decalogue.

The Talmud also is unwavering in its support of truthfulness. False speech is compared to idolatry. "God despises the man who says one thing with his mouth and another with his mind." "A liar is excluded from the presence of God." "Let your 'yes' be honest and your 'no' be honest." "This is the penalty for the liar: even when he tells the truth, no one believes him."

The Jewish tradition is concerned with more than the mere uttering of the truth when one speaks. A person is not permitted to withhold the truth by remaining silent. To protect a criminal by maintaining silence when one can assist the law is as serious a transgression as outright lying.

Likewise, to create a false impression without directly lying is distorting the virtue of *emet*. For example, to invite someone to your home when you are certain that he will refuse is a kind of insincerity that the Talmud criticizes.

45

On the other hand, truth is not to be used as a cloak for brutality or unkindness. People who, for example, criticize the physical features of another while insisting on their "sincerity" are abusing the concept of *emet*. Certainly the virtue of truthfulness was never intended to exclude tact or common sense.

People have long debated whether the "white lie" is a departure from truth. There are always dangers that the "white lie," like petty stealing, leads in time to more serious dishonesty. But there are times when even the Jewish tradition recognizes that a "white lie" is permissible—especially when the interests of peace are involved. If a separation can be prevented between husband and wife or between two friends, then for the sake of *shalom* the truth may be withheld. In other words, only when a virtue higher than truth is served may truth be set aside.

22

KAVOD

כָּבוֹד

Honor, Glory

Kavod is one of those versatile Hebrew terms that is used in many different contexts. In some places it refers to the splendor of God. He is referred to as *Hakavod,* the Glorious One. God imparts His glory and splendor to those who revere Him, especially the prophets and the righteous. Just as God bestows His *kavod,* so are we bidden to show *kavod* (honor) to worthy people.

God's glory is also manifest in the lives of parents who are privileged to give birth to children. Children in turn are bidden to honor their parents for this divine gift of creation that has been imparted to them (*kibbud av vaem*). We are likewise bidden to honor the Sabbath and festivals (*likhvod Shabbat*) because they are infused with the influence of the divine.

It is natural for us to seek honor from our fellow men. Our rabbis consistently warn us, however, that honor cannot be acquired by the man who pursues it. In fact, the more one pursues it, the more does honor elude him; only if one seeks to avoid honor will it pursue him. They offer another sound piece of advice: "Who is honored? He who honors his fellow man."

Frequently, *kavod* is employed in a negative sense. Those who seek the approval and respect of their neighbors merely because of their social or financial position derogate the value of *kavod.* People are usually able to differentiate between *kavod* that is justly or unjustly earned. Implied in the term *kavod* is a feeling of love rather than of fear for those who deserve honor. Those who insist on respect will never evoke the warmth and love that true honor brings.

23

KEVOD HABERIYOT

כְּבוֹד הַבְּרִיוֹת

Regard for Human Beings

Known also as *ahavat haberiyot*, this concept, which stresses the dignity of each person, represents one of the highest goals of the Jewish religion. A religion that would require love only for God and not for His creation ignores the constant need to improve human relationships.

It is for this reason that the statement of Ben Azzai is so highly regarded in Jewish thinking. He declared that the foundation of religion is embraced in the verse: "This is the book of the generations of man, in the day that God created man, in the likeness of God made He him." Since man is made in the divine image, he is of inestimable worth.

Since each individual is infinitely precious to God, he must be treated with the same regard and honor by his fellow man. Each person represents a world. He who saves an individual is credited for having saved an entire world; he who destroys an individual is regarded as though he destroyed the whole world.

It is precisely because of the infinite worth of the individual that God created each person in a different fashion. No two people look exactly alike, think or react in a similar way. "Man strikes many coins and they are all identical," says the Talmud, "but God stamps each man in the mold of Adam, and yet no one is identical with his fellow. The creation of Adam teaches that each human being is obliged to declare, 'For my sake was the world created.'"

The rabbis were explicit in their insistence on the divine

image in all men, regardless of race or nationality. Adam was created from the dust of the four corners of the earth so that no nation could claim him exclusively as their ancestor. Furthermore, God created one rather than many men on the sixth day in order to teach future generations that all of humankind descended from one ancestor, and that no one could later claim superiority over another, saying that his ancestors preceded those of other peoples. Since Adam was the father of the human race, all his descendants are to be regarded as brothers.

Jewish tradition proclaims that caring for the needs of one's fellow man takes precedence over communion with God. They cite the example of Abraham the Patriarch. While Abraham was communing with God, he learned of three strangers who needed hospitality; he interrupted his conversation with God and hastened to attend to the strangers.

24

SHEFIKHAT DAMIM

שְׁפִיכַת דָּמִים

Bloodshed

The shedding of blood is regarded to be the worst criminal act possible, not only because it deprives another human being of his right to live, but also because it is the most serious form of sacrilege. Since man is created in the divine image, he who sheds blood diminishes that image of God within man.

Unlike the ancient Greeks who considered murder solely as a crime against the individual, the Jews found the murderer as also having sinned against God. Hence, if a fatally wounded man forgave his assailant before his death, the Greeks barred any further prosecution. The Jews, however, who did not regard life as the personal property of the individual, could not accept the forgiveness of the victim as sufficient reason for the murderer to go free. No human being has the right to pardon a murderer for the gravest act of sacrilege.

Shefikhat damim, understood in its broader sense, also includes human negligence that permits needless death of innocent people. In Deuteronomy a strange law is set forth, but its implication is very clear: If a corpse is found on the road between two cities with no knowledge of the murderer, then the following procedure was required. The elders of the city measured the distances to the towns to determine which was nearer. The people of the nearer town were required to offer a sacrifice at which time the elders of the city proclaimed, "Our hands did not shed this blood, neither have our eyes seen it. Forgive O Lord, Thy people Israel whom You have redeemed, and permit not innocent blood to remain in the midst of Your people Israel."

The rabbis comment on these words: "Would it occur to us to suspect the elders who comprised the court to be guilty of bloodshed? The meaning of the verse is this: We did not let him depart when he came to us hungry, nor did we refrain from befriending him when we saw him." The implication is apparent that had the elders neglected this man while he was alive by permitting him to suffer hunger or depart without protection, then they would have been guilty before man and God for his death.

The Talmud also equates shaming another man publicly with *shefikhat damim,* their reasoning being that he "causes his blood to leave his face." Hence, to cause this feeling is as grievous as murder, and he who is guilty of it loses his share in the world to come.

25

LESHON HARA

לְשׁוֹן הָרָע

Slander, Gossip
(literally: Evil Tongue)

Maimonides defines *leshon hara* as speaking disparagingly of anyone, even though what he speaks be truth. "A person with an evil tongue is one who, sitting in company, says, 'That person did such a thing; his ancestors were so and so; I have heard this about him;' and then proceeds to talk scandal."

There are other forms of *leshon hara* that may be camouflaged, but are nevertheless discouraged, because they still result in defamation of character. When one initiates a conversation by saying, "I do not want to discuss what happened to an individual," he may be trying to arouse the curiosity of the listener, and in his own way plant seeds of suspicion without accusing anyone outright.

The Sages equate *leshon hara* with idolatry, incest, and murder. They further contend that to indulge in *leshon hara* is comparable to a denial of the fundamental principle of religion. They remind us that "the evil tongue slays three persons: the utterer of evil, the listener, the one spoken about; and the listener will be punished more severely than the speaker."

It is doubtful whether the rabbis meant literally this severe condemnation. They knew very well that few people commit murder during their lifetime, and that even the righteous are prone to gossip and defame in their weaker moments. Even those scholars who issued such lofty pronouncements were not always immune to the very sins that they abhorred. This was their way, however, of emphasizing an evil in the most dramatic way possible, in the hope that people would avoid participating in or listening to *leshon hara* by equating it with the gravest sins.

It is noteworthy that of all transgressions, evil talk is perhaps the easiest to commit. The great satisfaction derived from it is immediately felt; usually there is no legal penalty to deter such action. Thus the temptation is maximal, the guilt feelings incurred are minimal. It is precisely for these reasons that mortals should be reminded whenever possible of the extensive damage that can be caused by *leshon hara*. Its disastrous effects can be felt hundreds of miles away; it is potent enough to destroy an entire community, a whole people. Even the image of God can be diminished by the evil tongue. It is most appropriate that we conclude the silent *Amidah* with the supplication:

> Guard my tongue from evil,
> My lips from speaking guile.

26

NEKAMAH

נְקָמָה

Revenge

The Torah prohibits both acts and thoughts of vengeance with the explicit command: "You shall not take vengeance nor bear a grudge against the children of your people." Even though there is no specific penalty for such conduct, *nekamah* is nevertheless regarded as immoral.

The sages clarify the meaning of revenge with the following case: A neighbor says, "Lend me your axe." The other replies, "I will not lend it to you." The next day, the latter needs a similar favor and says to the same neighbor, "Lend me your axe," and receives the reply, "I will not lend it to you for you did not lend me your axe when I asked it of you."

They define thoughts of vengeance or bearing a grudge in this way: A man says to his neighbor, "Let me borrow this axe." He is refused. Subsequently the latter has need to borrow an axe from the same neighbor who replies, "I will lend it to you since I am not like you. I will not treat you as you treated me." As long as one nurses a grievance and keeps it in mind he will eventually commit an act of revenge.

The author of the Torah is probably aware that such feelings of hostility cannot be eradicated merely by biblical command. Vengefulness is an emotional reaction that one experiences after being hurt by another and is as spontaneous as the feeling of shame or envy. It is not the spontaneous reaction that is immoral, but rather the unwillingness to deal with it constructively by second thoughts, by mature reasoning. After all, thoughts and acts of revenge will never produce happy results for either party, perpetrator or victim. In fact, the perpetrator becomes victimized by his own feelings of indignation.

King David passionately denounces *nekamah* by absolving himself of evil intentions against Saul: "If I have requited him that did evil to me, if without cause I oppressed him that was my enemy, let the enemy pursue my soul and overtake it."

27

HASAGAT GEVUL

הַסָּגַת גְּבוּל

Removal of Another's Landmark

The Book of Deuteronomy warns twice against the removal of a neighbor's landmarks, which were used to show where one man's property ended and the other's began. Removing a landmark was equivalent to stealing another's land. Before the introduction of landmeasurements, removing landmarks was a crime more difficult to combat than today.

In later times, this prohibition of *hasagat gevul* was extended to include other areas of interference, especially in business affairs. The *massig gevul* was severely cautioned against unfair encroachment upon another man's livelihood. If a man held a position and another applied for the same position, this would be regarded as a violation of the biblical law. Any unfair "cutting into another's territory" was similarly forbidden.

The rabbis of the talmudic era were fully aware of the benefits of the competitive spirit in business. Some rabbis favored more control than others. For example, Rabbi Judah and the Sages debate whether a businessman may lower his prices to attract another's customers. Rabbi Judah says: "He does not lower the price." But the Sages say, "Let him be remembered for good." Again, Rabbi Judah says: "A shopkeeper may not distribute parched corn or nuts to children, for then he accustoms them to come (only) to him." But the Sages permit it.

However, when it came to the question of unfair competition, most of the rabbis felt that regulations were necessary. Unrestricted competition was opposed on economic and moral grounds. *Hasagat gevul* was clearly implied in cases of unbridled competition.

Though we are living in a vastly more complex business society today, the moral issues are not dissimilar. The competitive spirit is generally regarded as vital to American free enterprise, and yet, special government agencies are constantly on the alert against *hasagat gevul*, illegal moves to control prices, to create monopolies, to oust smaller businessmen from the competitive market.

28

KINAH

קִנְאָה

Jealousy

Kinah is frequently accompanied by the word *sinah*, hatred. And with good reason. It is difficult to separate these two emotions; even when the two are not felt together at the start, hatred usually follows jealousy.

The tenth commandment – "You shalt not covet" – is understood as a prohibition against envy or jealousy. The evil intentions that jealousy produces do not constitute a sin punishable in court, but are clearly a violation of a negative command (*mitzvah*). The Sages felt that covetousness would eventually lead to the greater transgression of robbery. Maimonides, following the view of the Sages, cites the story of Ahab and Naboth (I Kings: 21) as an example, and thus warns of the danger of covetousness: "Desire leads to coveting, and coveting to robbery. . . . Furthermore, if the owner will stand up against the coveter in order to safeguard his property or prevent him from committing robbery, it may lead to bloodshed."

Some people will question the wisdom of regarding covetousness as evil. How are people motivated to improve their status if they are not envious, if they lack desire? The Jewish tradition obviously does not extol poverty as an ideal. But in one's desires to improve himself economically, he need not feel resentment against the person who has honestly succeeded in business. It is a mark of moral weakness and indolence to begrudge another his possessions. Though *kinah* usually destroys human relationships, a sage recognized that in the academic area, at least, it may well produce beneficial results:

Raba said: "If we have a teacher who gets on with his pupils, but there is another who can get on better, we do not replace the first by the second, for fear that the second when appointed will become lazy." Rabbi Dimi from Nehardea, however, claimed that the second would exert himself still more if appointed, for "the jealousy of scribes (*kinat soferim*) increases wisdom" (i.e., the jealousy of the one who has been replaced will stimulate the second not to be removed from his position). [*Baba Batra* 21a—this talmudic proverb is freely interpreted to mean that "rivalry among scholars increases wisdom."]

29

GENEVAT DAAT

גְּנֵבַת דַּעַת

Deception
(literally: Stealing the Mind)

The Hebrew term for deception, creating a false impression, is *genevat daat*—stealing another's mind. Hence its inclusion in the prohibition against theft. The Talmud states explicitly that it is forbidden to deceive another person. Maimonides expands on the talmudic law with the exhortation: "It is forbidden to cheat people in trade or to deceive them. This same rule applies to both Jew and non-Jew. He who knows that there is a defect in his wares is obliged to notify the purchaser."

Genevat daat does not only apply to business dealings. The deceitful person may be honest in his commercial transactions and yet "steal the heart" of his neighbor. "He who urges his neighbor to be his guest when in his heart he does not mean to invite him; he who makes his guest believe that he is opening a barrel of wine especially for him when in reality it has been sold to the retailer . . . he is accounted as one who, if he could, would deceive the Most High."

The Sages have much to say on the matter of honesty in business. Both buyer and seller are duty-bound to adopt a code of honesty for themselves and to demand it of the other party. Where there is willful deceit, either party may cancel the transaction, even after it has been fully consummated. A prime constituent of commercial honesty in the days of the Sages was the accuracy of weights and measures. Thus, much attention is paid to this matter. "A wholesaler must clean out his measures monthly and a householder once a year. Rabban Simeon ben

Gamliel says: "The contrary is the rule. The shopkeeper must clean out his measures twice a week, polish his weights weekly, and clean out his scales after every weighing."

Just as the seller must be honest with the purchaser, so must the purchaser be honest with the seller. "One should not say, 'How much is this item?' if he has no intention to buy it." In other words, the deliberate wasting of a businessman's valuable time was regarded as a form of thievery—stealing the precious time and falsely raising the hopes of the seller.

In today's complex business world one finds *genevat daat* prevalent in almost every area. The advertising industry often misrepresents the real value of its products; machines and cars are "dressed up" for quick sale; packaged goods are beautifully wrapped and sold exclusively on eye-appeal; customers are constantly deceived into believing that they are getting bargains at discount stores, where they are really offered inferior merchandise. These and many other practices have been permitted in the name of the competitive spirit in our society. Only recently has the government begun seriously to investigate these fraudulent claims, especially in the advertising field.

The moral imperatives of the rabbis were undoubtedly directed to a more simple business community than we have today, but the underlying principle of their morality is eternally valid: dishonesty in business is incompatible with faith in a just God. Honesty preserves one's own reputation and assures the preservation of a society based on mutual trust.

Part III

RESPONSIBILITIES TO GOD

30

TESHUVAH

תְּשׁוּבָה

Repentance

Repentance is expressed in Hebrew not by a word like "penance," which implies self-punishment, but by the concept of *teshuvah*, "return." Man may get back on the right track if he chooses to return to God by restoring his proper relationship of love and respect for God.

This theme of returning to God was a favorite theme of the prophets of Israel. Hosea speaks to his people, saying, "*Return* O Israel, unto the Lord your God." Jeremiah warns, "*Return*, you backsliding Israel, says the Lord." Ezekiel pleads, "*Return* you, and turn yourselves from all your transgressions."

The worst sinner is encouraged to believe that he can improve his ways, his sins being merely a temporary obstacle rather than a permanent and ineradicable stain on his character. No one need sink so low that he cannot be reconciled with God by returning to Him. Even the most wicked biblical character, King Menasseh, who promoted idol worship, is pictured in our tradition as a *baal teshuvah;* he petitioned and received pardon from God. In fact, our rabbis assert that God provided the possibility for *teshuvah* before creating the world, for He knew that without such an opportunity the human race could not endure; no man could expect to survive were he to stand before a God of stern justice and without mercy.

Teshuvah requires more than an external act such as prayer or fasting. The Talmud, commenting on the repentance of the people of Nineveh in Jonah's time, reminds us, "It was not said of them that God saw their sackcloth and fasts, but that 'God saw their works that they turned from their evil way.'"

Repentance requires a determined desire and effort on the part of the sinner to break with his past. "He must give up his sin, remove it from his mind, and determining in his heart not to repeat his evil action, regret his past. . . . He must also confess with his lips and give expression to his thoughts, which he has determined in his heart." Note the order of *teshuvah* prescribed by Maimonides. Oral repentance follows the inner desire to return, enabling the sinner to reaffirm his prior determination.

The Jew is bidden to repent every day for transgressions known and unknown to him. One of the Eighteen Benedictions (*Amidah*), which is recited three times daily, deals with this theme of repentance. One should not postpone repenting until the High Holy Day season, even though these are the special Days of Repentance.

Ideally one should repent when his temptation to sin is greatest—while it is active and vigorous. Repentance in old age or immediately before death does not require the same spiritual strength and genuine humility as when it is sought by a healthy and vibrant person who is frequently too busy to make resolutions requiring change of character. Nevertheless, the doors of repentance are never closed, even when one lies on his deathbed.

31

KEDUSHAH

קְדוּשָׁה

Holiness

One of the fundamental principles of Judaism is man's aim to achieve a state of holiness. Many other Hebrew terms are closely related to this concept of *kedushah—kaddish, kiddush, kiddushin,* etc.

The Torah speaks of *kadosh*: "Ye shall be holy, for I the Lord your God am holy." It is from the Scriptures that the positive meaning of *kedushah* is derived: the duty to imitate God's ways. Just as God is frequently referred to in rabbinic literature as "The Holy One, blessed be He," so Israel may be called holy by striving to become God-like. "Just as God's way is to be ever merciful towards the wicked and accept their repentance, so be you merciful toward each other. As He bestows gifts on those who know Him and those who do not know Him and deserve not His gifts, so bestow you gifts upon one another."

Naturally, the Sages were fully aware that man could not completely imitate God's ways. Since God practices the virtues of kindness or mercy to perfection, man could only imitate these virtues in his own limited fashion. However, the more he concentrates on these God-like virtues, the more holiness man is able to attain.

The key phrase in a *berakhah* is *asher kidshanu bemitzvotav,* "Who has hallowed us by His commandments." The *mitzvot* were bestowed upon Israel by God to enable them to attain holiness. "With every new *mitzvah* that God bestows upon Israel, He adds to their holiness." The *mitzvot* then, provide us with clues and directions as to how we may effectively imitate God, thereby achieving the ideal of holiness.

Dr. Solomon Schechter observes that the concept *kedushah* has both positive and negative implications. Just as we are bidden to imitate God, so are we bidden to separate, to withdraw from anything that is impure or offensive. Idolatry, adultery, and the shedding of blood are regarded as the main sources of defilement. Other sins, too, render a person spiritually unclean. *Kedushah* then means to withdraw oneself from any offensive act or thought that tends to separate us from God.

From this idea flow the many other requirements concerning care for one's bodily health. Holiness requires special care to refrain from eating unclean food, diseased animals, eating with unclean utensils, taking one's food with filthy hands. The more care that is shown for cleanliness, we are told, the more one purifies his soul for the sake of God.

Significantly, the term *kedushah* is also applied to certain objects—a *sefer Torah, tefillin, mezuzah*—all of which are on parchment and contain the Scripture. The synagogue is also regarded as holy, essentially because it is associated with the *sefer Torah*. A *shofar, lulav* or *tallit,* important as they are, do not merit the term *kedushah* and may be eventually discarded—unlike those objects of *kedushah* that must be stored away when no longer used. The high regard and loving care that Jews have shown for books, regarding them not merely as objects but as respected friends, is partially due to the holiness attributed to scrolls in Jewish law.

32

KIDDUSH HASHEM

קִדּוּשׁ הַשֵּׁם

Sanctification of God's Name

The assertion that man, with all his limitations and faults, can hallow God, and that God requires man to hallow His name, is known in rabbinic literature as *kiddush Hashem*. Man may be sanctified by God if he chooses to follow His commandments, thus imitating His ways. It is likewise the duty of man to hallow God. "I will be hallowed among the children of Israel; I am the Lord who hallows you," proclaims the Torah.

The verse quoted from Leviticus was originally directed to the priesthood, who, as guardians of the Sanctuary, were warned in this manner to fulfill their duties to God.

Later, however, the obligation to sanctify God's name was extended to the "Kingdom of priests"—the whole Jewish people. *Kiddush Hashem* and its opposite, *hillul Hashem* (profanation of God's name), became two of the basic polarities of Judaism. The Jew was required to look upon himself as a guardian of his people's reputation. Any extraordinary act that would bring honor to the Jewish people was regarded as *kiddush Hashem*.

One of the best-known examples of *kiddush Hashem* that the Talmud relates concerns an incident in the life of Simeon ben Shetah, who found a valuable gem hanging around the neck of a camel he had bought from an Arab. His disciples urged him to keep the treasure that God had bestowed upon him. However, Simeon quickly returned the stone saying, "I purchased an animal, not a precious stone." When the Arab was given back the stone he exclaimed: "Blessed be the God of Simeon ben Shetah; Blessed be the God of Israel." Here God's name became hallowed

69

because Simeon demonstrated that his belief in God was real, so real that he did not succumb to the temptation of taking advantage of an innocent person. He caused a non-Jew (prior to Mohammedanism) to praise the God of Israel.

The most extreme form of *kiddush Hashem* is martyrdom—the instance of a Jew's faith in God being so strong that he is willing to forego the privilege of living, if necessary, to prevent the desecration of God's name. It was during the war against the Romans who imperiled the existence of the Jewish people and the Torah that *kiddush Hashem* became associated with martyrdom. Did this mean that a Jew could destroy himself if he believed that the cause for which he stood was important enough? Life was too precious for the individual to make such a crucial decision. The rabbis then decreed that only with regard to three cardinal sins—idolatry, incest, murder—should a person prefer to make the supreme sacrifice rather than be forced to commit any of these transgressions. If he were coerced to violate any other commandment, he should spare himself from death and violate the law.

But does God need to be sanctified? Can we help to improve God as He enables us to improve? Not really. Yet, He is in need of man to recognize and testify to His presence among those who are estranged from Him. *Kiddush Hashem* then means, in essence, to become God's helper by fulfilling His purpose and by furthering His cause—usually by an extraordinary demonstration of devotion to Him.

33

HILLUL HASHEM

חִלּוּל הַשֵּׁם

Profanation of God's Name

The opposite of *kiddush Hashem* is *hillul Hashem*. Just as a *kiddush Hashem* is an act that helps to encourage belief in God, *hillul Hashem* is an act that causes others to withdraw from God. For this reason both *kiddush Hashem* and *hillul Hashem* are usually associated with acts committed in public. This is not to say that a person may feel free to violate the commandments in private. Nevertheless, public violation is regarded to be a more serious offense, for it shows a complete disregard for the religious sensitivities of others and contributes to a general breakdown of religious loyalty.

Admittedly, the concept of *hillul Hashem* can be easily misunderstood by those who claim that there should be no discrepancy between private and public behavior. They claim that the moral person is consistent. If he feels that his practices are proper, he will not hesitate to perform them in public. There is no doubt that our religion requires a consistent morality. Many examples may be found in the Jewish teachings requiring truthfulness and sincerity even at the expense of public condemnation. But another kind of moral problem is involved here. Let us suppose that a man professes atheism and declares his opinions in the classroom or from the lecture platform. In the course of time, he may radically change his religious attitudes, but the opinions that he once shared publicly cannot be effectively retracted, since he was responsible for having influenced some of his students to deny belief in God. For this reason our rabbis have questioned whether repentance is possible if one has committed a *hillul Hashem*.

71

The more prominent the individual, the more vulnerable he is to committing a *hillul Hashem*. A respected scholar, for example, is required to conduct himself with greater dignity than the average man, for he bears a special responsibility to uphold the Torah. Thus, in discussing what constitutes a *hillul Hashem*, Rab, the founder of the Babylonian academy, said: "In my case, if I should buy meat from a butcher and not pay for it immediately."

Like its counterpart, *kiddush Hashem*, the concept of *hillul Hashem* also concerns itself with the impression that a Jew creates for his people among non-Jews. Any immoral act committed by a Jew that gives non-Jews an opportunity to criticize the Jewish community has been regarded as a *hillul Hashem*. True, the bigot seizes any opportunity to generalize about Jews from single instances of misbehavior. One is not concerned here with the irrational bigot, but with the impressionable masses who do not isolate individual cases of wrongdoing. Here it is the responsibility of the individual Jew to show concern for the image of his people that he creates in public. The career of the Jewish people has been closely associated with their belief in and worship of God. The individual Jew who takes his religion seriously continues to regard himself as a "light unto the nations," not by missionizing among them, but by creating an example worthy of the name that he upholds.

34

YIRAT SHAMAYIM

יִרְאַת שָׁמַיִם

Fear of Heaven

Critics of religion are accustomed to argue that obedience to God out of fear rarely improves human character. Fear of parents or of God can only result in loss of self-respect or eventual rebellion. And yet, we find many references in the Bible and rabbinic writings to this virtue of "fearing God." In fact, we pray that God instill in us *yirat Shamayim* – fear of Heaven. Normally a man pleads to be free from fear!

But the fear of Heaven should not be taken in the literal sense. It doesn't imply that God is a tyrant ready to punish wrongdoers for the slightest infraction of His laws. *Yirat Shamayim* really implies a sense of awe for God, Whose ways we cannot begin to fathom, but for Whom we have supreme regard. *Yirat Shamayim* includes the sensations of surprise and fascination when we observe those miracles that surround us daily – the miracles of nature, of human birth and development.

Dr. Evelyn Garfiel (1958) has indicated that the Bible uses the phrases "love of God" and "fear of God" interchangeably. They both imply devotion to Him. In Deuteronomy, the command to love and to fear the Lord is mentioned in the same context. For example, "What does the Lord, your God, ask of you, but to *fear the Lord*, your God, to walk in all His ways *and to love Him*, and to serve the Lord, your God, with all your soul."

In rabbinic literature, as in the Bible, we find that both expressions are synonymous, again suggesting devotion to God. However, the rabbis do sometimes distinguish between loving and fearing God. When the meaning of the two phrases is not

73

used interchangeably, then the Sages usually teach that love of God is preferable to fear of God.

In the popular idiom, to say that one has *yirat Shamayim* is another way of defining a pious Jew who is convinced that he is fulfilling the will of God in performing the *mitzvot*. His feelings of love and awe are intermingled, just as a child's feeling of love and awe for parents cannot be described separately. It is this inseparable combination that results in *yirat Shamayim*.

35

BITTAHON

בִּטָּחוֹן

Trust in God

Bittahon is seldom understood in the sense of faith in God's existence. This faith was seldom questioned in ancient times. The Psalmist contends, "The fool says in his heart that there is no God." *Bittahon* is rather a feeling of trust and reliance on God. It is the security of sensing that God will never forsake us no matter what the present predicament may be.

This steadfast trust that God is concerned with us does not imply that man merely has to believe in Him, and He in turn will relieve us of our own cares and problems. Trust in God does not replace human responsibility. If anything, it increases human responsibility, for God requires our effort and cooperation as His partners.

The Bible and prayerbook frequently caution against trusting in mortals. These warnings do not imply that men are unworthy of trust, nor that they should be regarded with suspicion. If this were the meaning of these passages, then the injunction to love one's neighbor as oneself or to regard man as created in God's image would lose all significance. We are cautioned, instead, not to allow trust in man to replace trust in God. To rely on man's scientific or technical achievements as the sole answer to human needs is an example of such replacement.

We are bidden, then, to place our trust in man, recognizing at the same time human fallibility, the possibility of accidental and even deliberate error. We may not choose to rely upon God for all our needs—especially for many material things—but with *bittahon* we are confident that God will never deceive or mislead

us. We are convinced that God offers the faithful more than
material prosperity, namely the conviction that life has meaning
and that God will not permit the good to fail in its struggle with
the forces of evil.

36

AVODAH ZARAH

עֲבוֹדָה זָרָה

Idolatry
(literally: Strange Worship)

Time and again the Israelites are warned in the Torah against the sin of idolatry, the worship of other gods. The second commandment clearly prohibits the worship of heathen gods and forbids the Israelites from making any visible representation of the one God.

The elimination of idolatry among the ancient Israelites was regarded to be the most formidable task with which Moses was confronted. First, the Israelites had to free themselves from the religious influences of the Egyptians. They also came into contact with idolatrous nations during their sojourn in the wilderness. Then they had to be cautioned against the influence of the new nations with whom they were to live once they entered the new land.

In the era of the Judges and Kings, the Israelites often lapsed into the idolatrous ways of their neighbors, frequently ignoring the stern warnings of their religious leaders. Even their kings found the worship of foreign gods irresistible. Only a few of the strong-willed and devout kings such as Josiah and Hezekiah resisted the attractive religion of neighboring peoples.

Especially under Greek and Roman influence, monotheistic Judaism was under threat of extinction by the religious practices of these culturally advanced civilizations. The Maccabean war was largely a protest against the Grecian influence on the Jewish religion. Greek gods were placed in the Temple. Jewish Hellenists had accepted polytheism as a way of life. The Maccabees were aware that their religion would soon disappear unless an all-out effort were made to free Judaism from alien religious influence.

The rabbis in talmudic times were vitally concerned with the danger of *avodah zarah*. They were not unmindful of the many cultural advantages that could be gained from contact with the Romans. Many rabbis were on friendly terms with influential Romans. And yet they were most vehement in their protests against adopting the heathen practices of Rome. The Jew was advised to accept death rather than to be forced into idolatry. "He who commits idolatry denies the Ten Commandments and all that was commanded to Moses, to the Prophets, and to the Patriarchs." "He who renounces idolatry is as if he professed the whole Law." A whole volume of the Talmud was devoted to the immorality of idolatry.

Ancient idolatry no longer exists to seduce modern man. But modern man is presented with idolatry's modern manifestation. When we idolize ourselves or other people, we remove God from the center of our existence. Will Herberg, author of *Judaism and Modern Man*, defines idolatry in its present form as "absolutization of the relative." When science, which admittedly has much to offer mankind, is held to be the only truth, the ultimate truth—this, says Herberg, is idolatry. The same can be said about other relative goods that may be elevated to absolute goods—race, nation, class, state, or party. These have become the dominant idolatries of our time.

37

APIKOROS

אַפִּיקוֹרוֹס

Religious Skeptic

Since there are few dogmas in Judaism, there is no original Hebrew term to designate a heretic. The Jews, therefore, borrowed the word *Apikoros* from the name Epicurus, a fourth-century Greek philosopher who taught, among other ideas, that the soul was composed of material substance and thus destructible. One of the earliest meanings of *Apikoros* found in the Mishnah defines him as one who, like the followers of Epicurus, refuses to believe in life after death.

Later, however, the term was extended to include a larger group of religious skeptics. The *Apikoros* shows disrespect for the authority of the rabbis; he permits what is forbidden and forbids what is permitted; he does not believe in the divine origin of the Torah. In later Judaism, *Apikoros* was applied to those who mocked the miracles stated in the Talmud or who denied the existence of God. It is apparent that the term was used very widely to designate general lack of belief in any of the essential doctrines of Judaism.

Today, large numbers of Jews would be termed *Apikorsim* (pl.) if the belief in specific doctrines of Judaism were still the criterion of Jewish loyalty. There are vast numbers of dedicated American Jews, among them religious leaders and educators, who cannot accept some of the traditional doctrines that their ancestors accepted unflinchingly. A significant group of those who are wrestling with their ancestral beliefs are intimately involved in synagogue life. Referring to this group as *Apikorsim* would be an insult to their strong Jewish convictions and their intellectual integrity.

If the term *Apikoros* is to have meaning today, then it should be applied to those who have ceased to be concerned with their religious doubts. They have closed the door to further religious inquiry because they categorically deny the reality of everything that does not come within the purview of science or reason. Those who never question their doubts, like those who never question their faith, fear most of all the pain of possibly admitting to error.

Part IV

MORAL RESPONSIBILITIES TO OURSELVES

38

TOKHO KEVARO

תּוֹכוֹ כְּבָרוֹ

A Sincere Person

Commenting on the biblical verse that prescribes the Ark to be inlaid with gold inside and out, the rabbis deduce that a man's inner self, also, should be no less fine than his outward appearance. They caution against saying one thing with the lips and another with the heart. Intentions and actions must be consistently good; otherwise one does not qualify as a sincere person.

In the past as well as the present, the charge of hypocrisy has been leveled against religious observers who do not believe what they practice. Even the prophets rebuked those who publicly observed the Sabbaths and holidays but privately schemed to exploit their neighbor after their periods of rest. More often, however, the charge of religious hypocrisy was unjustly leveled against the sincerely observant. To this very day, the term "Pharisee" is still associated with the hypocrite, despite the efforts by Jewish and Christian scholars to show that such an accusation was unfounded.

Inconsistency in religious observance is also called hypocrisy — often unjustly. A person may sincerely question the bases for religious observance, but nevertheless continue to observe the religious laws out of respect for his tradition, until he shall have come to a mature decision about his feeling. Sometimes it takes years of painful self-evaluation before a person is prepared to modify his religious observances. He is in no way insincere if he continues to observe, even though his thought may temporarily be inconsistent with his deeds.

By the same token, one can still be sincerely religious even if he chooses to observe less than the entire law. It is unfair to brand a person insincere, if he makes an effort to observe the Sabbath or dietary laws only partially, so long as he does not delude others into thinking that he is totally observant.

In brief, the value of *tokho kevaro* expresses what in modern language is known as the "integrated personality"–a human being who is at odds neither with himself nor with society.

39

GAM ZU LETOVAH

גַּם זוּ לְטוֹבָה

This Too is for the Best

One of the most outstanding features of Jewish thought is its consistent optimism in the midst of adversity. The devoted Jew always found great comfort in Rabbi Akiba's favorite slogan, "Whatever God does, He does for the best." It is told of him that he was compelled by the Romans to leave his home. He wandered about, his main possessions consisting of a lamp by which he would study Torah at night, a rooster that would awaken him at the break of dawn, and a donkey on which he rode. Akiba suffered a series of misfortunes. He was refused lodging in a village; a wind blew out his lamp; a wolf snatched the rooster away; a lion then carried off his donkey. And yet, after each crisis Akiba merely accepted his misfortune with the words, "Whatever God does, He does for the best."

In the morning, Akiba set out to the village to find another beast of burden. To his horror, he found that no one was alive. Robbers had plundered the village during the night and killed the inhabitants. Then Akiba exclaimed, "Now I know that men are wrong who regard as evil what is intended for their good. Had not the hard-hearted people driven me from the village, I should have shared their fate. If my lamp or my animals had betrayed my presence to the robbers, I too should have been attacked. All that God does, He does for the best."

Although we cannot substantiate the facts of this story, the value it teaches appears to be consistent with Akiba's attitude that God does nothing without a benign purpose. When he was about to be executed by the Romans, it was said of him that, to the dismay of his pupils, he smiled. Again his answer was one of happy submission: "All my life I was perplexed about the meaning of the biblical verse, 'You shall love the Lord your God with all your soul.' It means, 'Even if He take your soul.' I have wondered when I would have the opportunity to fulfill the command. Now that I am able, should I not fulfill it?"

Akiba was not alone in his faith that God always does things for man's ultimate good. That is why the Talmud prescribes praise of God for evil as well as for the good that befalls man.

Although the original meaning *gam zu letovah* may have implied complete submission to God's will, it has been used to express varying attitudes of faith in the presence of misfortune. Only the extremely pious are willing to assert that every instance of misfortune is intended by God to serve a useful purpose. Generally, we are willing to accept the belief that misfortune is the price that humans must pay for the privilege of living. *Gam zu letovah* is a way of expressing that man is willing to accept tragedy and misfortune as essential to God's world; if there were no tragedy, life could not be possible. It is better to live with misfortune than not to live at all.

Furthermore, it expresses an awareness that our misfortune could have been worse. When we think that we have experienced the supreme tragedy, we later realize that the predicament of others has been even more tragic. *Gam zu letovah* is an antidote to self-pity. It is an assertion that there are still more reasons to be grateful to God than we presently realize, and that we will seize each opportunity to overcome despondency and depression.

40

HAVEL HAVALIM

הֲבֵל הַבָלִים

Vanity of Vanities

This phrase, taken from the opening verses of Ecclesiastes (Kohelet) describes the classical attitude of the skeptic. Life is futile; there are no real goals for which man can strive. Everything that appears to be important is an illusion.

What prompted Kohelet, the author, to express this conclusion about life? All of life fails to satisfy his vain search for meaning. Even the world of nature is a changeless cycle with no novelty or progress. The four elements of the universe—the earth, sun, wind, and sea—repeat their monotonous courses. So does man race interminably in circles. Furthermore, he had experimented with wealth, which he found meaningless. Truth, he concludes, is unattainable, and wisdom causes misery. Physical pleasure offers only temporary satisfaction.

To add further skepticism, Kohelet observes that human actions are preordained. All activity is therefore useless. He condemns the lack of justice in the world, where the weak are the victims and the unjust the powerful. Furthermore, Kohelet shows little faith in the character of men and especially women. He questions the loyalty of children to parents. He concludes that in the final analysis, the only valid goal in life is the pursuit of joy. Joy is a gift, a command from God. Failure to obey the command is a sin before God.

We wonder how such a skeptical view of the world and of man could have been included in the sacred literature of the Bible. The rabbis heatedly debated the question before and after its acceptance in 90 C.E. Undoubtedly, decisive factors in the final acceptance were the attribution of the work to King Solomon, as well as the distinctly religious note of its concluding section.

Whatever the motives of the rabbis in accepting Ecclesiastes, it is hard to reconcile *havel havalim* with a religious outlook. If man's striving has no meaning, then there is no reason to believe that God has created a purposeful universe. If all is predetermined, then man has no need or capacity to make moral decisions. If man is not basically good, then suspicion and distrust must prevail over love and respect. The optimism of the Jew amidst the most tragic conditions has stood in direct opposition to the *havel havalim* view of life. Had the Jew adopted such a personal philosophy of nihilism and hopelessness, he would undoubtedly have lost the battle for survival centuries ago. Though exposed to the reading of Kohelet every year at Sukkot, and undoubtedly fascinated by its profound message, nevertheless, the Jew chose to adopt a philosophy that would sustain his faith and give him hope in God and man.

41

TZNEEUT

צְנִיעוּת

Modesty

Tzneeut usually refers to modesty in dress, but also implies other virtues—chastity, humility, dignity. Especially worthy of praise is the woman, the *tznuah*, who does not seek attention by her provocative appearance but who unobtrusively gains the respect and admiration of men and women for the dignity with which she conducts herself.

According to Genesis, the first garments that Adam and Eve wore were presented by God. No other product of civilization was presented to man by God. He did not teach him how to make fire, how to till the soil, how to build a house. Adam had to discover these all by himself; but garments were divinely provided for him. Even the act of putting on the garments was not left to man, for the text explicitly states that "the Lord God made for Adam and his wife garments of skin, *and He clothed them.*" Hence, clothing is not just a social convention but an addition to the work of creation—a kind of second skin given to man.

Benno Jacob (1974) in his book on Genesis explains, "Clothing is not merely a protection against cold or ornamentive. It constitutes the primary and necessary distinguishing mark of civilization. In the moral consciousness of man it serves to set him higher than the beast."

Rashi, the great biblical commentator, also indicates that modesty and morality are synonymous. He observes that God made garments for Adam and Eve, for they were not ashamed of their nakedness, ". . . for they did not know the ways of modesty (*derekh tzneeut*), even as they could not distinguish between good and evil."

Tzneeut does not necessarily imply prudishness. In fact, students of the Talmud were introduced to the study of sex at a very tender age. Discussions on the human anatomy were conducted without shame or restraint. George Eliot correctly observes that Judaism emphasizes "reverence for the human body, which lifts the need of the animal life into religion." It is significant that one of the preliminary morning prayers praises God ". . . Who has formed man in wisdom and created in him many passages and vessels. It is well known before Your throne, that if but one of these be opened or closed (contrary to the laws of nature), it would be impossible to stand before You."

And yet, with all their frankness and realism, our forefathers were vitally concerned with dangers of immodesty in dress or in speech. Every attempt was made to discourage aggressiveness or seductiveness that would lead to intimacy before marriage or an adulterous relationship after marriage.

With the exception of the ultra pious, the great majority of American Jews no longer observe the social restrictions that were at one time generally acceptable. Yet, the need for emphasizing a code of *tzneeut* has not diminished. In fact, the need for modesty becomes greater as our conventional codes of morality become weaker.

42

SHEM TOV

שֵׁם טוֹב

A Good Name

The author of Ecclesiastes was the first to use the expression *shem tov* as an ideal for man to pursue. Playing on two words with similar sounds, *shem* (name) and *shemen* (oil), he declares, "A good name is better than precious oil." Material wealth cannot be compared to the achievement of a good name (reputation) among one's fellow men.

Rabbi Simeon boldly takes the position that the crown of a good name is superior to the crown of the scholar, the priest, or the king. The crowns of priesthood and royalty are automatically conferred upon men who are privileged at birth. The crown of scholarship is likewise placed upon the head of those gifted with unusual intelligence. But the crown of a good name can be achieved by any person possessing character and desire to serve the needs of the community.

Is it not possible for a person to be more concerned with his reputation than with his personal convictions? Should he be willing to ignore his own conscience in order to serve a cause that will help him win public esteem? Rabbi Judah the Prince dealt with the problem when he asked: "Which is the right course that a man ought to choose for himself?" He answers: "Whatever is deemed praiseworthy by the one who adopts it and for which he is also deemed praiseworthy by men." First, he must be convinced himself that his course of action is worthy. Only then may he seek the approval and esteem of his fellow man.

To be sure, a *shem tov* is not always or necessarily a valid index of a man's true worth. Many a person is beloved by the public and accorded distinction—yet the public may be acquainted with merely one facet of his character. Many a person popular with his friends may be unable to relate properly to his wife or children. Who will deny that he should have attempted to gain the respect of his family before attempting to contribute to the larger community? He begins his work at home; he does not end it there.

All men do not agree on a belief in personal immortality. But few will question that a good name survives long after a person has passed away. More valuable than any tangible gift that he leaves to his family or community is the character and reputation by which he is long remembered.

43

HESHBON HANEFESH

חֶשְׁבּוֹן הַנֶּפֶשׁ

Soul-searching

One of the main functions of prayer is to encourage the worshiper to take stock of himself, to search the inner recesses of his soul. The very essence of the expression "to pray" in Hebrew means to judge oneself. Especially during the solemn Days of Awe the Jew is expected to undergo a rigid self-examination. He should train himself to look inwardly, to ask himself basic questions: Where have I sinned? Have I lived selfishly during the past year? Have I shirked my moral responsibility to myself and my fellow man?

Though the term *heshbon hanefesh* is used for the first time in medieval Jewish philosophy, self-examination as a deterrent to sin is implied throughout the Bible. Nowhere does God "make" a person change his ways. Change can only come from within, where there is realization through rigorous self-appraisal that one has failed to live up to his moral commitments. *Heshbon hanefesh* is implied in the story of Jacob's fierce struggle with the angel from which he finally emerges victorious.

Scholars have interpreted this passage allegorically – Jacob is actually struggling with himself, his doubts. Only *after* his painful inner struggle, his soul-searching, does he become worthy of a new name. Similarly, with Joseph who was thrown into the pit by his brothers, the reader senses that the days spent in isolation provided Joseph with the opportunity to take serious stock of himself – of his immature brashness and his vanity that so incensed his brothers.

Self-appraisal cultivates humility; through humility one becomes aware of himself as he really is, without embellishment. Akabya ben Mahalalel says: "Reflect on three things, and you will not fall into the clutches of sin. Know from where you come, where you are going, and before whom you are destined to give an account and reckoning.

     — From where do you come? — From a putrid drop.

     — Where are you going? — To a place of dust, worms, and maggots.

     — Before whom are you destined to give an account and reckoning? — Before the King of Kings, the Holy One, Blessed be He."

Heshbon hanefesh also cultivates a sense of gratitude together with humility. Both are powerful antidotes to sin. The famous Jewish moralist of eleventh-century Spain, Bahya ibn Pakuda, related *heshbon hanefesh* to gratitude in his *Duties of the Heart*:

> A person should take account with his soul and reflect on God's great goodness to him in having bestowed upon him the advantages of intellect, power of perception, and many other desirable faculties. . . . He should consider that if he were void of understanding and perception and another man like himself supplied him with these faculties, and he realized the superiority of his present condition over his former state, would the whole of his life be sufficient for continuous thanks to his benefactor for what he had done? How much greater is the duty of gratitude to the blessed Creator, whose benefits bestowed on us are endless and whose kindnesses are unlimited . . . .

Part V

RESPONSIBLE AND IRRESPONSIBLE MEN

44

TZADDIK

צַדִּיק

A Righteous Person

As early as biblical times the term *tzaddik* was applied to a person who devoted his life to *tzedek* (righteousness). He was known for his just dealings with his fellow man and his regard for God's commandments. Though he possessed qualities of excellence greater than those of most men, he was by no means considered to be without faults. Nor did he choose to live a life removed from the challenges and temptations of society. Our tradition has never regarded the hermit as an ideal, and the *tzaddick* was in no sense a hermit.

Basing itself on the biblical verse, "The righteous is the foundation of the world," the Talmud asserts that the world exists only through virtues of the *tzaddik*. The *tzaddik* is in such close communication with God that he can make special requests for the welfare of the community.

In time, the term *tzaddik* became a title conferred upon the leader of the hasidic community. He was usually a member of a dynasty of *tzaddikim* that traced its ancestry to the founder of Hasidism – the Baal Shem Tov – or to one of his original disciples. The *tzaddik's* chief task was to help people who needed advice or charity. He would often comfort them in their sorrow and promise them miraculous relief from their misery. In turn, his simple followers attributed superhuman powers to their *tzaddik*. They believed in his infallibility and were convinced that he possessed the power to grant prosperity, forgive sins, and cure physical ailments. Some of these *tzaddikim* were indeed righteous men; others merely inherited their title but felt no qualms about exploiting the ignorance of their followers. This blind devotion to the *tzaddik* undoubtedly contributed to the eventual decline of the hasidic movement as a great spiritual force in Jewish life.

The term also has been used in a negative sense to describe the self-righteous individual who would like to be regarded as a *tzaddik* by his contemporaries but whose actions actually indicate the contrary. His very striving for recognition negates a basic attribute of the *tzaddik*, as the genuinely righteous person is not aware that he is regarded as a *tzaddik*. He is, on the contrary, the first humbly to recognize his own defects and shortcomings.

45

LAMED VAV TZADDIKIM

לָמֶד וָו צַדִּיקִים

Thirty-six Righteous Men

According to an old talmudic source, the existence of the world depends on thirty-six saintly men for whose sake God extends His mercy to all mankind. The two Hebrew letters, *lamed* and *vav*, represent the numerical equivalent of thirty-six. Part of the essence of the saintliness of these thirty-six men is their anonymity. Often they are poor workmen, and their special holiness and mission (if not their goodness) remain unknown to their most intimate friends, as well as, usually, to themselves.

Legend relates that occasionally a *lamedvavnik* will come forth from his self-imposed concealment and, by virtue of his special powers, avert an impending disaster. Once he has accomplished his task he will return to his former obscurity. It happens on rare occasions that one of these righteous men is accidentally detected, in which case the secret must not be revealed.

Some of the *lamedvavniks* experienced great personal tragedy. Their suffering, we are told, was at times excruciating—especially the suffering of those who remained unknown to themselves. In the seventh century, Andalusian Jews venerated a rock shaped like a teardrop, which they believed to be the petrified soul of an unknown *lamedvavnik*. A hasidic legend relates that when an unknown just man rises to Heaven he is so frozen that God must warm him for a thousand years before his soul can enter Paradise. Some remain forever inconsolable because of their misery, so that God Himself cannot warm them. But instead God sets forward the clock of the Last Judgment by one minute.

Because of their alleged anonymity, any suggestion that well-known personalities were among the *lamedvavniks* was always subject to suspicion. Yet, many legends about the "Thirty-six" include such popular figures as the Baal Shem Tov, father of Hasidism, and Elijah Gaon of Vilna, the greatest talmudic scholar of his age.

One example of a typical story taken from Yiddish literature relates the heroic exploits of a saint living in Cracow, Poland. Disguised as Hayyim, a tailor, he frustrated a plan of the Polish king to extort a huge sum of money from the Jews and by his special powers forced the king to abandon it. The minister to the king who originated the scheme fled and was converted to Judaism.

46

GER TZEDEK

גֵּר צֶדֶק

A Sincere Convert to Judaism

The very term *ger tzedek* indicates that sincere conversion was respected and welcomed by the Jewish community. To be sure, the *ger tzedek*, the righteous convert, was warned not to expect the easy life, and it was incumbent on his teachers to warn him of the hazards of his new commitment. The Talmud requires a rabbi to caution a prospective convert with these solemn questions: "What induces you to join us? Do you now know that in these days the Israelites are troubled, oppressed, despised, and subjected to countless sufferings?" Moreover, all the religious duties must be clarified to a candidate, and only if he insists on following through is he accepted.

Once the convert is accepted as a Jew, he is entitled to all the privileges that Jews born into the faith enjoy. He may be called to the Torah to recite the appropriate blessing, be included in a quorum necessary for public worship, and he may participate in all religious ceremonies. Maimonides responds to a question directed to him by a convert with the assurance, "You are to say '*Our* God and the God of *our* fathers,' because Abraham is your father . . . you may certainly say in your prayers 'Who has chosen *us*, Who has given *us* the Torah.' Let not your heritage be deemed insignificant. If our heritage is from Abraham, Isaac, and Jacob, your heritage is from God Himself."

Converts to Judaism were numerous before the rise of Christianity. Within Palestine and outside, wherever Jews came into contact with pagans, Judaism held a strong attraction. Converts came from every level of Roman society—from the slave classes as well as the aristocracy. Christianity, however, offered the attraction of monotheism and at the same time imposed fewer restrictions on its new adherents than did Judaism. Commencing with the fourth century, when Christianity became the official religion of the Roman Empire, Jews were no longer permitted to continue their missionary activity. In spite of the peril to Jews and proselytes alike, we read of various instances where Christians joined the ranks of the oppressed Jews. Some died as martyrs for accepting the new faith.

47

MESHUMAD

מְשֻׁמָּד

An Apostate

Jews have always distinguished between their brethren who were compelled to adopt another religion and those who voluntarily sought conversion. The former were known as *anusim*, forced converts, and the latter as *meshumadim*.

Especially during the Spanish Inquisition, hundreds of thousands of Jews were given the alternative of conversion or death. Significant numbers who accepted conversion publicly practiced their religion in secret. They were helped by their brethren to maintain contacts with their ancestral faith. Jewish books were secretly smuggled into their homes; their children were given private instruction; they even joined together in worship wherever possible. Others among the forced converts maintained no contact with their original faith and eventually became indistinguishable from the Christians. Generally both groups of *anusim* were looked upon with compassion for the shame and misfortune that they endured.

The *meshumad*, on the other hand, frequently renounced his religion to gain personal advantage. He either sought a "passport to society" with its social and economic advantages, or was attracted to the customs and beliefs of another religion. In either case he was severely criticized by his former brethren for having forsaken his ancestral ties.

But why, we may ask, should anyone feel compelled to remain a Jew? Why may he not choose to affiliate with another religious body? Is religion not a matter of personal choice? Is it not moral to follow one's convictions? Actually, in a voluntary

community every individual does have this choice. The oppro-
brium that the tradition attaches to the *meshumad* reflects the
suspicion that he is indeed not acting morally and that he has
made his decision without a thorough examination of its principles and ideals. Judaism is not "caught" merely by intuition. Only
through study can its insights be fully appreciated. Unfortunately, most converts have not devoted the time nor taken the
trouble to find the answers to their perplexing religious questions.

Furthermore, the tradition maintains there is a moral responsibility to help maintain a heritage that has managed to
survive amidst the most adverse conditions primarily because of
the courage and loyalty of its devoted men and women who
resisted every conceivable kind of pressure to renounce their
faith. Does a contemporary Jew not owe an obligation to perpet-
uate this unbroken heritage by contributing to its survival and
passing it on to a future generation of Jews? These are the
questions that Jews ask when they pass judgment on their
brethren who seek the security of another religious faith.

48

HASID

חָסִיד

A Pious Man

Coming from the word *hesed* (lovingkindness), the *hasid* was most highly regarded in the Jewish tradition. If any word in Hebrew approximates the term saint, it is the *hasid*. He is placed on an even higher scale of virtue than the *tzaddik* – the righteous man – because of his godly nature.

Unlike the man who seeks merely to observe the law, the *hasid* is anxious to go beyond the requirements of the law. He does not wait until he is asked to perform a *mitzvah*. He says, "Mine is thine, and thine is thine." "He is hard to anger and easy to pacify."

The *hasid* is not satisfied to wait until the appointed time for prayer. Because of his religious enthusiasm, he prepares for public worship with serious deliberation and individual prayer; he continues to pray long after the other worshipers have fulfilled their religious duty.

The *hasid* delights in exercising self-discipline. He is careful to control his speech, to measure his words. He never permits himself the luxury of overeating and excessive drinking. He fears the possibility of degrading himself to the animal level. He endeavors to control his emotions and actions, if he is to serve God.

Most important to him, the *hasid* seeks to love all God's creation – Jew and non-Jew, friend and foe, human being and beast. We read in the *Little Book of Saints:* "Refrain thy kindness and thy mercy from nothing that the Holy One, blessed be He, created in this world. Never beat nor inflict pain on any animal, beast, bird, or insect; nor throw stones at a dog or cat; nor kill flies or wasps."

In time the term *hasid*, like *tzaddik*, came to be associated with a sect of Jews. Their way of life was called Hasidism. The *hasidim* in some ways patterned their lives after the original type of *hasid* we have described. They, too, prayed with deep religious fervor, not confining their prayers to appointed times. Among their devotees, they encouraged humility and love for all God's creation. They often went beyond the confines of religious law to experience an extra measure of spirituality. As their movement became more highly developed, however, their way of life, their mystical beliefs, their emphasis on miracles, their unquestioning devotion to their leadership created a different emphasis, far removed from the way of life espoused by the original *hasid*.

With all the luxuries and pleasures that are offered to modern man and with all the secular demands that require his attention, it becomes exceedingly difficult to pattern one's life in the image of the original *hasid*. Yet, one cannot help but admire his religious devotion and appreciate his spiritual goals. Even if this generation of Jews can keep a vivid picture of the *hasid* in mind as it deals with its own day-to-day problems, if it learns the value of self-control or goes beyond the requirements of the law in its religious enthusiasm, it shall have paid lasting tribute to the *hasid* in Jewish tradition.

49

ANAV

עָנָו

A Humble Person

The modest man is God's greatest ally, for he recognizes his limitations and readily admits to error and fallibility. Unlike the *baal gaavah*, who is too proud to admit that he has much to learn, the *anav* seeks God's counsel and direction. God in turn is drawn to him because he is receptive.

Moses, we are told, was "the most modest man on the face of the earth." It was this spiritual quality that enabled Moses to show such patience with his people, for he was painfully aware of his own short-comings. Moses never considered himself too great to learn from others—from Jethro, his father-in-law, or from Aaron, his brother. Furthermore, Moses was willing to recognize the special gift of prophecy in other gifted men and expressed the wish that all Israel would be endowed with similar divine inspiration. It was primarily this unique spirit of genuine humility that qualified Moses to be chosen as leader of his people.

Like Moses, the *anav* is modest but by no means fearful of challenge. He regards it his duty to face danger, if necessary. He does not hide from society and his responsibility toward his fellow man. He recognizes the talents and abilities that God has given him and puts them to good use, recognizing at the same time that his successes and accomplishments have been given to him for a purpose. He is God's *shaliah*, messenger, on Whose behalf he must act.

People frequently play the part of the *anav* by berating themselves in front of others. They will belittle their performance after giving a public speech or playing a musical rendition.

However, they betray their real feelings of arrogance under the guise of humility when they say, "I performed terribly today." They are saying in effect, "I'm really great! Recognize me as such." The truly humble man sees no need to draw the attention of others to himself; he has no need to impress others with his *anivut* (humility). True feelings of humility do not require that he walk around with his head bowed.

The story is told of a king who wanted to learn the secret of humility. He tried wearing sackcloth, putting ashes on his head, depriving himself of food and water. He even left his palace to live among the poor; he employed men to beat him. He failed in his efforts, however, for he felt more arrogant now than before. A sage then offered him counsel: "Dress like a king, live like a king, act like a king, but let your *heart* be humble."

50

BAAL GAAVAH

בַּעַל גַּאֲוָה

An Arrogant Person

The Hebrew language contains several expressions, each signifying different shades of arrogance. In the morning service we petition God to be saved from *azei panim*—insolent men, hardened and shameless people who ignore the feelings of others. We also ask that we ourselves be delivered from *azut panim*, that same "boldness of face," the insolence that corrupts so many human beings. Then there is the incisive expression, *hutzpah*, which has even been incorporated into the English language, denoting outright impudence—the epitome of arrogance. *Hutzpah* is also used in a positive way to express nerve or boldness, but it still expresses a form of arrogance that leaves little room for restraint or regard for another person's feelings.

Gaavah is a general term for pride or conceit. The *baal gaavah* is the greatest adversary of God. He places himself in God's stead. He seeks to play the role of God. The Book of Deuteronomy cautions against his spiritual blindness.

> Beware lest you forget the Lord your God in not keeping His commandments, and His ordinances, and His statutes, which I command you this day; lest, when you have eaten and are satisfied, and have built goodly houses and dwelled therein; and when your herds and your flocks multiply, and your silver and gold is multiplied, and all that you have is multiplied; then your heart be lifted up, and you forget the Lord your God who brought you forth out of the land of Egypt, out of the house of bondage . . . and you say in your heart: "My power and the might of my hand have gotten me this wealth."

109

The problem of arrogance is the oldest and most essential problem of religion. No human failing is condemned so vigorously as the sin of the arrogant man. The Talmud says of him: "The proud man's sin is as if he had committed every kind of unchastity. It is as if he had denied God. Pride is equivalent to idolatry. Concerning such a person God declares, 'He and I cannot dwell together in the same world.' "

The primary function of our religion is to enable man to overcome the sin of self-centeredness. Through genuine prayer, he removes himself from the center of his limited universe, recognizing God alone as worthy of adoration. When he partakes of food or drink he recognizes God and not himself as the *real* provider. He is constantly reminded that he owns nothing in this world. His children are merely entrusted to his care. He is not even permitted to do what he wishes with himself; he may not neglect his health, abuse his body, take his own life. All the commandments dealing with *tzedakah* (charity) remind him of his debt to society, his responsibilities to his fellow man. He is trained to regard himself as a social being—not an "island unto himself."

51

HAKHAM

חָכָם

A Wise Man

Generally, a *hakham* is a cultured and insightful person, be he Jew or non-Jew. One is not born with *hokhmah;* it is accumulated by varied experience and sound education, which enable the individual to apply his learning to practical problems.

In ancient times the Jews, like the Greeks, had special schools of Wisdom to train young students to develop *hokhmah* – practical Wisdom – so that they could successfully cope with the problems of their society. The Book of Proverbs, for example, was written by teachers of Wisdom whose primary task was to prepare young men for the world before them. These teachers sought to inculcate in their students the virtues of hard work, moderation, seriousness, loyalty to authority – these and other elements of morality necessary for worldly success. The Bible then regards the *hakham* as a cultured person who knows how to deal successfully with life's problems. He is wise enough to understand that virtue and morality are not abstract ideals but rather highly practical approaches to life. They lead to success and happiness, just as vice leads to poverty and disappointment.

In the talmudic era *hakham* became an official title. We are not certain just what his duties were. It has been suggested that the name was given to the directors of academies of learning in Palestine. The Talmud also uses the term *hakhamim* (pl.) to designate the majority of scholars who agree on a viewpoint of law, in contrast to a single authority.

The rabbis also refer to a *hakham* in the general sense, not necessarily as an outstanding rabbi. Though their emphasis is

111

more on scholarship, they continue, in the biblical tradition, to stress the value of moral insight and worldly wisdom as hallmarks of the *hakham*. Ben Zoma said, "Who is a *hakham?* He who learns from all men; as it is said, 'From all my teachers I have acquired understanding.' "

When referring to a *hakham*, one frequently thinks of another Hebrew expression, *sekhel*–common sense, or the ability to be relevant. Dr. Louis Finkelstein, in a letter addressed to the Rabbinical Assembly of America, writes: "Trained judgment–what our parents and grandparents called *sekhel*, and the Bible calls *hokhmah*–is needed to find one's way in the uncharted seas of a changing world." In sum, the *hakham* holds a unique reputation in Jewish life; over the years he has trained his mind to apply his knowledge to the practical problems of living; he is constantly seeking knowledge from all available sources–from books, from people, from personal experience–so that he may cope more effectively with the complex issues of contemporary life.

52

TALMID HAKHAM

תַּלְמִיד חָכָם

A Scholar, Disciple of the Wise

That there are so many terms denoting "the scholar" in the Hebrew tongue is in itself indicative of the honored position he earned in Jewish life. There is *ben Torah*, son of the Torah; *baal Torah*, master of Torah; *lamdan*, erudite one; *matmid*, diligent student; *harif*, the acute mind; *iluy*, genius; *oker harim*, uprooter of mountains; etc. The *talmid hakham* is more than a scholar. He is, as the Hebrew signifies, a perpetual student *(talmid)*; despite his superior knowledge, he is eager to learn from all sources, even from those who are less scholarly than he.

Traditionally, Jews have given greater respect to scholars than to men of wealth who are unlearned. In eastern Europe the learned men would be given seats of honor along the eastern wall of the synagogue; the most learned of all would sit next to the Ark where the Torah was kept. Budding scholars were considered the most desirable husbands for daughters of the elite, and, on the other hand, were encouraged to marry daughters of scholars.

The Hebrew scholar is not only respected for his sharp mind or his ability to store knowledge. More important, he is expected to apply his learning to all current problems that may arise. He can demonstrate the vitality of Torah in dealing with social and economic problems as well as the moral problems of the day. Furthermore, the *talmid hakham* is not content to keep his knowledge locked up inside. He is a perpetual teacher, even as he is a perpetual student. He raises disciples, imparts his wisdom and scholarly technique to them, for they will carry on after him, thereby assuring continuity of the cultural and religious tradition. So vital are scholars to the perpetuation of our way of life that on every Sabbath and the High Holy Days a special prayer is recited in the synagogue asking for their long life and good health.

53

AM HAARETZ

עַם הָאָרֶץ

An Ignoramus
(literally: People of the Soil)

Over the course of years, the term *am haaretz* assumed various shades of meaning. (Such a process can be seen with English words also. For example, the word *pagan* originally meant countryman, *boor* meant farmer, *villain* was understood to be a freeholder.)

In the days of Abraham, the natives of Palestine, the Hittites, for example, from whom he purchased the cave of Machpelah, were called *am haaretz*.

In a later period, the term *am haaretz* denoted the rural population of Palestine, in distinction to the urban Pharisees. Probably because they lived as farmers in the rural areas and had little contact with the centers of Jewish life, they neglected the laws of purity and believed in superstitious practices. It is believed by some scholars that the *am haaretz* were among the early Christians. They were relieved to be accepted by this new group that did not require observance of the rituals of Judaism.

After the destruction of the second Temple (70 C.E.), when worship and study replaced the Temple rituals, we find that the term *am haaretz* becomes identified with the ignorant man. The Talmud describes an *am haaretz* as one who does not read the *Shema* twice daily, or who does not provide a Jewish education for his children, or who fails to learn the practices of the Oral Law, or refuses to show respect for the rabbis.

From this time on there existed a serious rift between educated and uneducated Jews. The learned strongly discouraged marriages between families of the learned and unlearned. One Sage bluntly stated that an *am haaretz* could not be a pious man. The term not only described the ignorant but was equated with other negative qualities: the boor, the awkward person, the quick-tempered. The great Rabbi Akiba admitted to all these qualities before he became a student of the Torah.

In recent times, especially in eastern Europe, this same class distinction existed between the learned and unlearned Jew. A Jew without learning could not be fully respected by his community, whereas the learned Jew was more highly regarded than the rich, but ignorant, Jew. Wealth in itself did not guarantee a position of respect and leadership, as it does in many circles today.

Perhaps it can be said with justification that the *am haaretz* was the victim of prejudice and bigotry. It is true that in many instances he was the helpless victim of poverty and misery, which did not permit him the opportunity to be educated. Nevertheless, it was this priority that Jews gave to learning that motivated them to seek an education for themselves and their children in spite of serious obstacles. Education became their most sought-after goal in life.

54

GOLEM

גֹּלֶם

Clod (literally: Embryo)

In rabbinic terminology, a *golem* represents an undeveloped mentality. Maimonides observes that the *golem* may possess moral and intellectual virtues, but they are not developed and they do not function properly. Thus, he is in a constant state of confusion and disorganization. That is why he is referred to as a clod; he is like an object beginning to take shape in the hands of the craftsman, but lacking completion.

In the *Ethics of the Fathers,* the *hakham* and the *golem* are classified in complete opposition to one another, since the former possesses well-developed intellectual and moral virtues. The statement implies that the *golem* will be found doing the following: He rushes in to speak; he breaks into his fellow's speech; he speaks in the presence of those who are greater than he; he is in a rush to reply; he asks what is improper and replies irrelevantly; of things that are first, he says that they are last, and of last things, that they are first; he does not acknowledge the truth; he is ashamed to learn and ashamed to say, "I have not heard."

In the eighteenth century, the *golem* became a popular legendary figure associated with the great Talmudist, Rabbi Judah Loew of Prague. After his death, stories circulated about this scholar who labored so hard to protect his people against oppression. Legend had it that the rabbi created a *golem*—a crudely finished robot—to help him in his efforts to save his people against the enemy. The *golem* without a will of its own carried out all the wishes of the rabbi. All the stories deal with feats of superhuman strength, in which some plot against the

117

Jewish community is thwarted. In one legend, the *golem* saves an innocent Jewish girl from forced conversion. In another he discovers that the unleavened bread for Passover has been poisoned, and he helps to bring the culprits to justice. It is always Rabbi Judah who directs him, as he has no mind of his own.

H. Leivick, the well-known Yiddish poet, immortalized some of these legends in his play *The Golem*, which has been produced in this country as well as in Europe and Israel. The French and German cinema have even produced films on these stories.

55

SAMEAH BEHELKO

שָׂמֵחַ בְּחֶלְקוֹ

A Content Person

As a rule, rabbinic Judaism seldom extols poverty as a goal in life. There are, to be sure, exceptions, when, for example, a rabbi urges the student: "A morsel of bread with salt you must eat, and water by measure you must drink; you must sleep upon the ground, and live a life of trouble as you toil in the Torah." This extreme view is rarely expressed in Jewish literature. The majority of the rabbis were realistic enough to appreciate the advantages of prosperity. They were well aware that the man of means was not only free of the shame and embarrassment of depending on others for his basic needs, but he also has the satisfaction of helping those in need.

On the other hand, the Sages discouraged material wealth as a goal in life. They keenly observed what happened around them to men who regarded wealth as the highest goal. They abused their privileges by flaunting their power and exploiting their neighbors; they forgot their humble origin; they denied the Source of their blessings.

If neither poverty nor wealth are desirable goals in themselves, then moderation becomes the ideal. This is what was meant by Ben Zoma, who defines the rich man as one who is content with his portion—*sameah behelko*. Wealth becomes a state of mind. One who is wallowing in luxuries is indeed poor, if he is envious of those who possess more material things than he. However, a man who is content to live within modest means is the truly rich man, for he does not need luxuries to make him happy. He finds his satisfaction in human relationships, in service, and in his life's work.

Material wealth must be understood in relative terms. The poor regard the middle classes as wealthy; the middle classes have their own definitions of wealth, which are not acceptable to the most privileged class, who think in completely different categories. The *sameah behelko* need not compare himself to others to determine his status. His standards of wealth are independent. Only he and no one else can determine his wealth. So long as he is grateful for the things he *does* have and content to find happiness in the many things that money cannot buy, then he has achieved a kind of wealth that can never be taken away from him.

56

GANAV

גַּנָּב

A Thief

The *ganav*, whether he steals from the poor or the rich, defies the eighth commandment of the Decalogue. An ancient commentator exhorts his people to be scrupulous in honoring this commandment: "Sons of Israel, My people, you must not be thieves, nor companions nor accomplices of thieves. There must not be seen in the congregation of Israel a thievish people so that your sons may not arise after you to teach one another to be accomplices of thieves; because of the guilt of theft, famine comes to the world." A stable society is impossible where men seek to receive without earning and to live off the labors of others. Even when the *ganav* claims that he discriminately chooses as his victims the privileged few who live from the labors of others, he may not set himself above the law by deciding who is honest and who is not.

The Torah makes a distinction between robbery and theft. In cases of secret theft, the thief pays as his fine double the amount of the property stolen, whereas in cases of open robbery, the robber simply makes restitution. Theft was considered more serious because the thief fears the punishment of men but not the judgment of God. "He honors the servant more than the Master." The robber, however, who commits his crime openly respects the servant equally with the Master—he respects neither. Therefore, the man who shows greater respect for the authority of man than for the sovereignty of God commits the greater crime and is to be more severely punished.

The Sages concern themselves with more than the problem

of merely restoring stolen property. The offender must also ask forgiveness of the person he has wronged. Only after he has shown genuine repentance will God forgive the thief. Commenting on the verse, "He shall restore that which he took by robbery," the rabbis derived the moral lesson that things taken by force cannot be acquired legally even when full payment of their worth is made to the owner. Only if stolen property is destroyed does the robber return the full value of the object; if it still exists, the object itself must be returned. Furthermore, even after returning the stolen object, the robber must ask forgiveness of his victim, because he has violated a command of the Torah. A personal injury requires personal forgiveness.

57

OHEV YISRAEL

אוֹהֵב יִשְׂרָאֵל

A Friend of the Jewish People

Although the expression *ohev Yisrael* and its opposite, *sonei Yisrael,* usually apply to non-Jews who are either friends or enemies of Israel, they also apply to the attitudes of Jews toward their own people. Just as God loves the people of Israel, so is every Jew bidden to express his love for Israel in prayer and in acts of kindness. He is ever conscious of the bonds that unite him with his fellow Jews throughout the world. He is called upon to make personal sacrifices, if necessary, to assure the survival of his people. To be sure, the *ohev Yisrael* is motivated by humanitarianism. He concerns himself with a fellow Jew not only because he is Jewish, but because he is a human being, a child of God. But *ahavat Yisrael,* love for Israel, gives him added incentive. He is aware that a Jew has an added responsibility to his co-religionist. He cannot rely on the good will of others to care for his fellow Jew, if he does not care himself. He must set the example for others to follow.

The *ohev Yisrael* does not display an interest only in those Jews who share his beliefs. He recognizes all Jews as brothers and worthy of his concern, no matter how strongly he may differ from them in religious, cultural, or social interests.

The Jewish people have also been confronted with the *sonei Yisrael* among their own—Jews who refuse to identify with the problems of their brethren. Until modern times, when Jews lived in closely knit communities, defectors were rare among Jews. Here and there, individual Jews, usually converts from Judaism, would attempt to justify their alienation from Judaism by be-

123

coming informers against Jews or by writing critical tracts against the Hebrew Bible and the Talmud. When Jews were no longer confined to a compulsory Jewish community and were free to live wherever they chose, we find larger numbers of Jews seeking assimilation with the majority. The more they sought acceptance, the more critical they were of Jewish values and institutions. They denied their Jewish origin, they chose different associations, a different address, so that they would not be detected as Jews. They blamed their social problems on the Jew rather than the non-Jew who refused to accept them completely into his society. We are familiar with their tragic end. This was the unhappy fate of large numbers of Jews, especially in Central Europe, who discovered too late that their efforts were futile, that their destiny was the same as those who chose to remain loyal to Judaism.

As mentioned above, *ohev Yisrael* and *sonei Yisrael* usually refer to members of the non-Jewish community. Since the days of the Pharaohs in Egypt, Jews have been the object of scorn and oppression. The Pharaoh in the time of Moses was warned that the Jews were disloyal to the state. They were despised by Haman for their refusal to conform to the majority. The accusation of deicide, however, provided the *sonei Yisrael* with his most lethal weapon against the Jews. To this very day, significant numbers of Christians believe that Jews must continue to suffer for their supposed responsibility in the crucifixion of Jesus.

The Jews, however, were never bereft of friends, even during the bleakest periods of their history. Some were influential enough to save large numbers of Jews from destruction. Others succeeded in hiding Jewish friends in their homes, knowing that their own lives were endangered by their defiance of the law.

In recent years a research organization, The Institute for the Righteous Acts, was formed for the purpose of contacting the thousands of Christians who rescued more than one million Jews from the Nazis during the height of the Hitler terror. The Institute has in its possession numerous accounts of clergymen, peasants, farmers and storekeepers who jeopardized their lives to hide and rescue Jews. Every effort is being made to identify these courageous men and women while they are still able to relate their life-saving experiences during the years of the Holocaust.

The Jewish people cannot forget the *sonei Yisrael,* but they always remember with gratitude the *ohev Yisrael* who has extended sympathy and aid to them.

58

MAH YAFIT

מַה יָפִית

A Subservient Jew
(literally: How Lovely!)

The expression *Mah Yafit* offers a most interesting example of the way in which the meaning of Hebrew words may be completely transformed by virtue of experiences associated with them. Originally *Mah Yafit* was the title of a Sabbath song beginning with the words, "How lovely and delightfully sweet you are, O Sabbath." During the Middle Ages, German and Polish Jewish families chanted the melody around the Sabbath table.

Eventually the *Mah Yafit* became associated with the degradation of Polish Jews, who were commanded to entertain the Polish nobility. *Mah Yafit* was one of the better known songs they would sing and dance to. Cringingly, they would play the clown and poke fun at their own inspirational songs in order to amuse the tyrants. In time, the *Mah Yafit* was no longer sung on the Sabbath because of these unfortunate associations, and the term came to signify a specific character-type–the cringing and submissive Jew who seeks, above all else, the goodwill of the non-Jew.

It is somewhat understandable that a Jew living under the strain of bigotry and discrimination would depend on goodwill to obtain special privileges for himself or his family. But the Jewish community in America has long ago passed the stage of seeking mere tolerance. In spite of our small number we regard ourselves as equal partners entitled to the same privileges and responsibilities as all other groups. Those Jews who continue to seek ways of pleasing non-Jews to win their favor do so at great expense to their people's dignity and betray a woeful lack of confidence in themselves and faith in American democracy.

We should naturally seek the goodwill of others, but not because we are second-class citizens living on sufferance. The best way to achieve goodwill is to show regard for the other man's needs and to respect his individuality, just as we wish to have our own needs and individuality respected. We seek another's goodwill because we are equally involved in creating a more humane society, and not because Jews are expected to please their neighbors.

The *Mah Yafit Yid* performs a disservice to his people, for he continues to cling to *Galut* thinking, namely, that the Jew has no inherent rights in this country and that he should be especially grateful to the non-Jew for extending his generosity. The great strides we have made in this country have come from the efforts of men who were convinced that the American Jew has unalienable rights and who have insisted that these rights be recognized and actualized.

59

NAVI

נָבִיא

A Prophet

There may be disagreement among scholars as to how one becomes a prophet, but it is generally agreed that the prophet was an extraordinary person marked by unusual courage and integrity. He would defy kings, priests, and angry mobs if he felt that they ignored God's moral law.

The greatness of the prophet did not lie in his ability to foretell. True, his brilliant insight permitted him to perceive events that the ordinary person, who was occupied primarily with the present, could not grasp. He knew the consequences of good and evil and how morality could affect an entire people even though they were enjoying prosperity in the present. But he did not claim to be a magician or soothsayer.

He was, above all, a *spokesman* for God, and revealed to his people, whom he loved, what God revealed to him. He was usually reluctant to undertake such an awesome responsibility. He would question his maturity, his fluency of speech, his own moral fitness. But God knew more about him and his capabilities than he knew about himself. Once he embarked on his prophetic career, he became so imbued with God's spirit that he could not compromise with his ideals, his passion for justice and righteousness.

Ahad Ha-am (1912) in his famous essay on *Priest & Prophet* concedes that other nations have at various times had their prophets, "but it is pre-eminently among the ancient Hebrews that prophecy is found. . . . Prophecy is, as it were, the hall-mark of the Hebrew national spirit" (p. 132). From the time of Moses, the greatest of the Hebrew prophets, to Malachi, the Jewish people were reminded of their moral responsibilities to God and their fellow men. Their influence on later generations can never be fully evaluated, for their words continue to this very day to be studied and quoted by most religious groups. Many passages from Isaiah, Amos, and Jeremiah appear as relevant today as in the age in which they were originally uttered.

A *navi* also refers to a scroll written by hand, similar to the Torah scroll; it contains all the prophetic portions read in the synagogue during the year. In most congregations the *Haftarah*, or prophetic portion, is read from the vocalized Bible, for one does not have to memorize the intricate vowels and musical notes. But in some congregations, where there are sufficient men to read from the *navi*, the difficult practice is still retained.

60

SOFER

סוֹפֵר

A Scribe

The title *sofer* (pl. *soferim)* was first given to Ezra and other writer–scholars of his generation, in the fifth century B.C.E., who revised and edited the books of the Bible. Their principal task was to collect the scattered and often corrupt texts of the sacred literature, correct them, and arrange them into an organized anthology.

In addition, they made as many correct copies as possible of the Torah, so that the masses would all learn from a uniform text. They were also entrusted with the task of teaching and inter-preting the biblical texts to the people.

As the sacred literature increased in subsequent years, the *soferim* copied new texts—volumes of the Talmud, the prayer books, the commentaries. They also reproduced copies of the *haggadah*, the *megillah*, marriage contracts, divorce documents, *mezuzot*, etc.

Ever since the time of the *soferim*, rigid rules were set for the scribe who was engaged in the sacred task of copying a Torah scroll. After twenty-three hundred years, these regulations are still in effect. For example, if an error is made in writing God's name, the whole parchment section must be redone since God's name must not be erased. If many errors are found in the scroll, the whole *Sefer Torah* could be considered unfit. At least, the sections of parchment in which the errors occur must be removed and new sections rewritten.

The *sofer* is required to be more than a gifted copyist. He must be generally well versed in Jewish sources, and even more essential, he must demonstrate great reverence for the written word and unusual self-discipline and patience for his painstaking work. The *sofer* is convinced that the more legible and beautiful his handiwork, the greater his contribution to the glory of God. He finds support for his enthusiasm in the following biblical verse and rabbinic comment: " 'This is my God, and I will beautify Him' (Exodus 15:2); Serve Him in a beautiful manner. . . . Prepare a beautiful Scroll of the Torah. Have it written in good ink with a fine quill by an expert *sofer.* "

61

SHOMER SHABBAT

שׁוֹמֵר שַׁבָּת

Sabbath Observer

Literally, the *shomer Shabbat* is a guardian who watches over the Sabbath like one who guards a precious possession. The world *shomer* is used frequently in Jewish terminology in conjunction with other ideals and institutions. The pious Jew is known also as a *shomer mitzvot* (guardian of the commandments); God is referred to in Jewish liturgy as *shomer Yisrael* (Guardian of Israel).

The *shomer Shabbat* is distinguished from the *mehalel Shabbat* (Sabbath violator) in that he recognizes the sanctity of the seventh day and chooses to change his whole weekly routine, if necessary at great personal inconvenience, so that he and his family may experience a spiritual renewal at the end of every week.

The Sabbath observer is not concerned merely with the need for physical rest on the Sabbath. If this were his only purpose, he could choose Sunday or a week day that would serve the same ends. The *shomer Shabbat* knows that the greatest value of Sabbath observance lies in the altogether different atmosphere that the members of the family experience as they put aside their usual problems and cares in order to enjoy each other's company in the spirit of leisure and relaxation.

Sabbath observance implies certain positive requirements—activities to be performed as well as certain prohibitions—activities from which one must refrain. A father who recites *kiddush* on Friday evening and attends the synagogue on *Shabbat* morning will undoubtedly derive more satisfaction than one who ignores the Sabbath completely, but he is not regarded as a *shomer Shabbat* unless he refrains from attending to business matters or working around the house. He takes the prohibitions seriously, because he is aware that routine tasks break the exalted mood of the day and interfere with the time that should be given to spiritual pursuits. The *shomer Shabbat* recognizes that he is out of step with the rest of the American community on this one day, but he is not self-conscious about it. He feels that as he changes his pace every seventh day, his step becomes firmer and more confident during the week; he has more than compensated for the time spent outside of the competitive race.

62

EISHET HAYIL

אֵשֶׁת חַיִל

A Woman of Valor

The Book of Proverbs (31:10–31) praises the virtues of the *Eishet Hayil*, who earns the respect and love of her family as well as of all those who know her. Many years ago, it became customary for the husband to read the passage from Proverbs immediately before he chanted the *kiddush* on Friday evening. The first two words of the poem, *Eishet Hayil*, have appropriately become the name given to the ideal Jewish woman.

The *Eishet Hayil* is by no means depicted here as a passive woman who "knows her place" and is satisfied merely to bring children into the world. She plays many roles, even that of a businesswoman, and she is actively engaged in performing them well:

As wife:

"The heart of her husband does safely trust in her,
And he has no lack of gain.
She does him good and not evil
All the days of her life."

As mother:

"Her children rise up, and call her blessed;
Her husband also, and he praises her."

As homemaker:

"She seeks wool and flax,
And works willingly with her hands . . .
And gives food to her household

And a portion to her maidens . . .
She is unafraid of the snow for her household,
For all her household is clothed with scarlet."

As businesswoman:

"She is like the merchant ships
She brings food from afar . . .
She makes linen garments and sells them
And delivers girdles unto the merchants.
She considers a field and buys it;
With the fruit of her hands she plants a vineyard."

As charity worker:

"She stretches out her hands to the poor;
Yea, she reaches forth her hand to the needy."

Her other virtues:

"Strength and dignity are her clothing,
And she laughs at the time to come.
She opens her mouth with wisdom;
And the law of kindness is on her tongue. . . ."

63

HEVRA KADDISHA

חֶבְרָא קַדִּישָׁא

Sacred Society

One of the most important organizations in the Jewish community is comprised of men and women who care for the deceased and devote themselves to all the necessary details in preparation for the funeral. The *hevra kaddisha* is also helpful in relieving the bereaved family of many painful decisions and problems.

As early as the first century, the interment of the dead was deemed a community responsibility. Josephus writes, "All who pass by when one is buried must accompany the funeral and join in the lamentation." The Babylonian Jews felt even greater responsibility. Every Jew in the community ceased working the moment he was informed of a death, and they all participated in the preparations for the burial.

In the fourth century we hear of societies whose specific purpose was to care for the deceased. It is believed that one of the main reasons for their formation was to relieve the rest of the Jewish community of the burden of attending the funeral. In the Middle Ages, these societies assumed the duties of caring for the sick, providing medicine and clothing, preparing the dead for burial, providing graves and tombstones, arranging for the appropriate rites in the house of mourning, and even helping the mourners financially while away from work. Since these members of the *hevra kaddisha* were fulfilling the highest form of charity, they were usually shown great respect by the members of their community.

In our day many of the responsibilities that were once

undertaken by the *hevra kaddisha* have been assumed by the funeral directors. Suggestions have been made that the *hevra kaddisha*, because it is a voluntary religious association, should once again play a more influential role in the Jewish community to encourage greater uniformity, dignity, and good taste so that these become the standard for all Jewish funerals. In spite of the criticism leveled at the Jewish funeral directors, many of them would probably welcome the efforts of a well-organized association of volunteers provided that they could represent the needs of the majority of the community rather than several societies, each representing a different synagogue with its own practices.

64

MALSHIN

מַלְשִׁין

Informer

The informer was one of the most bitterly resented members of the Jewish community. In fact, the nineteenth blessing of the *Amidah* (Standing Prayer), which was added to the original eighteen, is directed against the *malshinim* (pl.). This additional blessing was originally intended to discourage all Jewish heretics in the generation after the destruction of the Second Temple, because they were responsible for divisiveness among Jews at a very crucial period in their history. But the wording of the original prayer underwent many changes by Jewish and Christian censors, and we do not know exactly how the paragraph read originally.

Eventually, most likely during the Middle Ages, the blessing was directed against Jewish informers. During this period in particular, entire Jewish communities suffered irreparable damage at the hands of traitors who sought personal reward in reporting "subversive" activities among Jews to the church or government authorities.

The best-known informers in the Middle Ages were the apostates, whose testimony was eagerly sought because of their previous background. They were requested to testify that the Talmud or other sacred books were anti-Christian. One incident of informing in Italy (1553) resulted in the burning of thousands of copies of the Talmud and other rabbinic books throughout the country, and in the course of the next generation, the Church instituted a rigid censorship of all Hebrew books, old and new. Because of the work of informers many similar incidents, with even more disastrous results, occurred in other parts of medieval Europe.

The typical informer against a medieval Jewish community was not motivated by loyalty to the ruling power but by revenge or material reward. Even if his information was found to be false, the authorities did not penalize the informer. The act of informing was in itself sufficient to inflame the authorities.

The Jewish courts, which were often empowered to try civil and criminal cases, showed least compassion for the *malshin*. The greatest rabbinical authorities, who ordinarily tempered their decisions with mercy, rigorously sentenced informers to death, primarily as a means of self-defense. They were guided by the talmudic maxim—"If you see a man in the very act of attempting to slay you, and you are left with no choice, you may prevent him, even at the cost of his life."

It is difficult for the average person to understand the motives of the unprincipled informer who is prepared to surrender his own integrity and to endanger the lives of others in order to secure personal advantage. The phenomenon occurred even during the height of the Nazi oppression of Jews. It is clear that its genesis is a sick mind and a distorted personality. But to say this is to give only weak definition to a problem that has plagued the imagination of man for centuries.

65

BATLAN

בַּטְלָן

Man of Leisure, Idler

Though Judaism recognizes that work ennobles man, the *batlan,* who by virtue of age or wealth was not burdened by problems of earning a livelihood, performed a useful function in many communities. The Mishnah defines a city as a place where there are at least ten *batlanim.* They were free to devote time to study and community affairs, and they were relied upon to assure a *minyan* for public worship.

In one of his major addresses, Dr. Solomon Schechter extolled the traditional *batlan:*

> The Talmud, in defining the character of a city in contradistinction to a village, perceives it in the fact that the former can point to ten men of leisure. The talmudical term is *batlan,* but it does not mean lazy or idle people, but, as just indicated, men who are not, by reason of their trade or handicraft, hammering away at the fabric of the world, and can thus afford to devote themselves to the higher spiritual and intellectual interests of the community. Without a sprinkling of such men, the place may boast of millions of inhabitants, but a village it is, and a village it remains. What the Talmud calls a village, would in modern language be called provincial, denoting a state of mind narrow in its horizon, limited in its sympathies. . . . It is just such a society which is redeemed by these men of leisure. They certainly lead also an active—indeed a strenuous life.

In the Middle Ages it was the custom to appoint these men of leisure to act as a permanent congregation. They were frequently paid for this service to the community. The *batlanim* were sometimes regarded as men of great respectability and profound learning. In some communities, as in Baghdad in the twelfth century, they were in charge of community matters, giving decisions on legal questions and deciding disputes between litigants. In later years, however, they lost much of their former respectability, especially because they did not possess the cultural background of their predecessors and were suspected of being too lazy to support themselves and their families in a more dignified manner.

Generally, the term today carries with it a negative connotation, describing a person who imposes on the valuable time of others with useless chatter or with his ambitious plans that never seem to materialize.

The problem of dealing effectively with leisure time will become increasingly important in future years. The shorter work week and earlier retirement will offer the American people many opportunities to develop new interests and skills that would have been impossible for most people years ago. The new *batlan* need not live an unproductive and monotonous life, especially if he will seek ways to serve his community and his congregation. The *batlan* can once again become a symbol of dignity and respectability.

Part VI

THE RESPONSIBILITY TO REMEMBER

66

ZEKHER LITZIAT MITZRAYIM

זֵכֶר לִיצִיאַת מִצְרַיִם

Remembering the Exodus from Egypt

The Jew recalls the Exodus from Egypt not only on Passover, which commemorates the historic event, but on every holiday, every Sabbath, every day of the year. The first commandment of the Decalogue begins with the words: "I am the Lord your God who brought you out of the land of Egypt and out of the house of bondage."

Many commandments of the Torah are based on remembering: "You were strangers in the land of Egypt" and "You shall remember that you were a slave in Egypt."

"You shalt not vex a stranger, nor oppress him . . . for you know the heart of the stranger, seeing you were strangers in the land of Egypt."

Concerning the slave: "You shall furnish him liberally out of your flock, and out of your threshing floor, and out of your winepress . . . and you shall remember that you were a bondsman in the land of Egypt and the Eternal, your God, redeemed you; therefore I command you this thing today."

Concerning the unfortunate: "You shall not pervert the judgment of the stranger, nor of the fatherless, nor take a widow's garment to pledge. But you shall remember that you were a bondsman in Egypt, and the Eternal, your God, redeemed you thence. . . ."

Concerning the Sabbath: "In it you shall not perform any work, you nor your son, nor your daughter, nor your manservant, nor your maid-servant. . . . And remember that you were a bondsman in the land of Egypt, and that the Eternal, your

145

God, brought you out thence by a mighty hand and an outstretched arm. Therefore, the Eternal, your God, commanded
you to keep the Sabbath day."

There is also a group of commandments that refer to the
liberation from Egypt in the form of a condition: "Only on this
condition did I deliver you from the land of Egypt, that you keep
these commandments." They are: maintaining correct scales of
weight; the prohibition against interest; the warning against
pride; the prohibition against eating creeping things; the freeing
of slaves in the Jubilee year, etc.

On Passover, the Jew must not be content merely to remember the Exodus from Egypt. He must regard himself as if he
had personally come forth out of Egypt. He actually relives the
Exodus at the seder table by eating the bread of affliction and by
tasting the bitter herbs and the salt water. He not only remembers the flight from slavery to freedom; he is an active partici-
pant in the drama.

67

YOM HAZIKARON

יוֹם הַזִּכָּרוֹן

The Day of Remembrance

One of the several names of the Jewish New Year is *Yom Hazikaron*, the Day of Memorial or Remembrance. On this day we remember the creation of the world, and God remembers the deeds of His children.

The theme of remembrance is intimately associated with the High Holy Days. Before the first blessing of the *Amidah* is concluded, we insert an appropriate verse during the Ten Days of Penitence: "Remember us unto life, O King Who delights in life. . . ."

The second paragraph of the *Amidah* is also expanded on these days to emphasize further the remembrance theme: "Who may be compared to You, Father of Mercy, Who in love remembers Your creatures unto life?"

The name *Yom Hazikaron* was probably derived from one of the three sections of the Musaf service known as *Zikhronot*, each section culminating in the blowing of the Shofar. These three sections, *Malkhuyot* (Kingship), *Zikhronot* (Remembrance), and *Shofarot* (Revelation), were already referred to in the second century of the Common Era as part of the ritual of the day.

By reciting the *Zikhronot*, the worshiper is heartened with the knowledge that God has never forgotten His people. He remembers the covenant that He made with the Patriarchs concerning the future of the land and people of Israel. The worshiper also recalls that the covenant was not one-sided. God also demanded that Israel fulfill her moral obligations. Otherwise, the covenant was to be dissolved.

The Divine Recorder remembers even those personal events that escape human memory. He has the power to recall every man's deeds and misdeeds, his thoughts and motives. To believe that God has not abandoned the world after creation, thus leaving man to struggle with his fate, can serve as a great source of comfort for the present and confidence for the future.

The sensitive worshiper is painfully aware that in invoking God to remember his past, he is toying with the possibility of having failed to live a moral life. Yet, the willingness to subject himself to investigation is indicative of his humility, his desire to repent.

Commenting on the phrase in the *Mahzor*, "Thou rememberest all forgotten things," a hasidic master explained these words as follows: "Your way, O God, is to remember only what man forgets." When a Jew performs a good deed and then forgets it, God remembers it; if, on the other hand, having performed a *mitzvah*, he continually refers to it, God does not care to remember it. Similarly, those evil deeds that the sinner forgets, God recalls; those evil deeds that he remembers out of remorse, God chooses to forget.

Other names by which Rosh Hashanah is known are: *Yom Hadin*, The Day of Judgment; *Yom Teruah*, The Day of Blowing the Shofar; *Yom Kerav*, The Day of Battle (against the forces of evil).

68

SHABBAT ZAKHOR

שַׁבַּת זָכוֹר

The Sabbath of Remembrance

The Sabbath preceding Purim is distinguished by special features in the service. Two Torah scrolls are read in the synagogue. The *Sidrah* of the week is first read, followed by a special concluding portion taken from Deuteronomy. The opening words of the passage are: "Remember *(Zakhor)* what Amalek did" – hence the special name *Shabbat Zakhor*.

The entire passage reads as follows:

> Remember what Amalek did unto you by the way as you came forth out of Egypt, how he met you by the way, and smote the hindmost of you, all that were enfeebled, in the rear, when you were faint and weary; and he feared not God. Therefore it shall be, when the Lord your God has given you rest from all your enemies round about, in the land which the Lord your God gives you for an inheritance to possess it, that you shall blot out the remembrance of Amalek from under heaven; you shall not forget. [Deut. 25:17–19]

Then the section of the *Haftarah* is read that relates the story of Saul's encounter with Agag, king of the Amalekites. The purpose of this selection on the Sabbath before Purim is to recall Haman, the Agagite, archenemy of the Jews, who was thought to be a descendant of the Amalekite king mentioned in the *Haftarah*. He has been regarded as the later emodiment of the evil spirit of Amalek, whose designs against the Jewish people must never be forgotten.

The Sephardic Jews also insert into the Sabbath morning service a long poem by the beloved poet Judah Halevi. The poem,

149

written during the perilous times of the Crusades, is a para-
phrase of the Book of Esther. It derives from the ancient Persian
story a message of hope for the harassed Jew of his day.

The charge "Remember Amalek" has been reiterated in
many subsequent generations when anti-Semites have sought to
eradicate the Jewish people. This phrase alone was sufficiently
understood by the masses without any need for added commentary. In effect, it served as a battle cry for the Jewish community
to recognize the anti-Semite, to understand his motives, his evil
potential, and to prevent him from fulfilling his evil scheme
before it is too late.

69

YIZKOR

יִזְכּוֹר

Memorial Prayer

Known more formally as *Hazkarat Neshamot*, the memorial prayer is recited in memory of the departed by a son, daughter, or other close relative. It receives its name *Yizkor* from the opening word of the prayer: "May God remember *(Yizkor)* the soul of . . . who has gone to his eternal home."

Originally the memorial prayer was recited only on Yom Kippur, but since the eighteenth century it was included in the service of the three Pilgrimage festivals – on the last day of Pesah, the second day of Shavuot, and the end of Sukkot.

Though the custom of reciting a prayer and contributing to charity on behalf of the deceased is very ancient, the *Yizkor* service as we know it today probably arose during the Middle Ages. After the death of many Jews in the First Crusade (1096 C.E.), the custom arose of reading the names of the victims from the records of the community. It is believed that the *Yizkor* service developed from this public practice.

Jews do not pray to their deceased relatives. They pray to God that He grant the dead everlasting peace and forgiveness for the sins committed during their lifetime. The living and the dead are in need of atonement. Since the dead cannot seek atonement, we offer a prayer on their behalf.

The *Yizkor* prayer is not recited in all synagogues. The Ashkenazic Jews only (not the Sephardic Jews) include these prayers in their service. The *Yizkor* was never intended to be the climax of the service, and yet, many Jews place unwarranted emphasis on this part of the service. Coming to the synagogue

151

merely to recite *Yizkor* gives the worshiper an incomplete and distorted view of the Yom Kippur or Festival liturgy and deprives him of an appreciation for the rich and varied content that the entire service offers. To recite only those prayers associated with death or on behalf of the dying gives the worshiper a false impression about the primary purposes of prayer: to reaffirm eternal truths, to express gratitude to God for the blessings we possess, and to enable us to find proper direction in life.

70

ZEKHER LAHURBAN

זֵכֶר לַחֻרְבָּן

Remembering the Destruction
of the Temple

Ever since the destruction of the Temple by the Romans in the year 70 C.E. every Jew was enjoined to recall this tragic event, marking the loss of Jewish nationhood. Prayers that referred to the sacrificial offerings in the Temple were retained in the liturgy, despite the fact that the sacrifices were discontinued. After the destruction, new prayers were added that contained a vivid description of the sacrificial service on the holidays as it was performed in the Temple. Scholars continued to study the laws of sacrifices with keen interest and enthusiasm. A whole tractate of the Talmud was written about the sacrificial system after the destruction of the Temple.

One would think that the Jews were ignoring reality by their persistence in concentrating on an institution that had vanished. But their motive was very practical. They wanted to create an indelible impression on every future generation of Jews so that by remembering the loss of the Temple in prayer and in study they would some day be witness to its rebuilding. "Those who mourn for Jerusalem will be privileged to see the restoration of her joy." Without memories of the glorious past, however, the initiative to revive it would eventually be lost forever.

The Jews remembered the loss of the Temple without bitterness or thoughts of revenge against their enemies. They were willing to accept full responsibility for its destruction. Their own sinfulness, they asserted in their prayers, was responsible for their tragedy.

To further impress the loss of the Temple on the consciousness of the people, the rabbis ordained that future generations
should adopt certain restraints and restrictions in their daily
lives as a *zekher lahurban*. No person was permitted to indulge in
unrestrained laughter, even when rejoicing in the performance of
a commandment. When entertaining a bride and groom, excessive rejoicing was prohibited. The breaking of the glass by the
groom under the *huppah* was also associated with recalling the
destruction of the Temple in the midst of personal joy. Part of a
new house was to remain unpainted; women were requested to
refrain from adorning themselves with excessive jewelry; a
bride's veil was to contain no silver or gold thread; Jews were
discouraged from living in great luxury even if they could afford
to do so. All these served as memory aids lest the Jew be tempted
to forget a national tragedy in time of personal joy and
prosperity.

Part VII

RESPONSIBILITIES TO THE HOME AND FAMILY

71

HANUKKAT HABAYIT

חֲנֻכַּת הַבַּיִת

Dedication of the Home

One usually associates a dedication ceremony with public buildings, such as the synagogue or community center. There is ancient precedence for this ceremony. King Solomon dedicated the Temple after its completion; so did the Maccabees rededicate the Temple after the Greeks had defiled it. We believe that Psalm 30, entitled "A Song for the Dedication of the House," was composed in celebration of the rededication of the Temple. In fact, the word *Hanukkah* means dedication.

Many people are not aware that a Jewish home is also dedicated soon after a family moves into it. The *hanukkat habayit* is traditionally more than a housewarming or family party. A social event is here elevated to an act of religious significance. The ceremony commences with the fastening of the *mezuzzah* on the door post, accompanied by the benediction: "Blessed are You, O Lord our God, King of the universe, Who has sanctified us with His *mitzvot* and commanded us to fasten the *mezuzzah*." Following an ancient source in the Talmud, the *Sheheheyanu* blessing is also recited. Here, the family expresses gratitude to God for having been permitted to reach a new and eventful stage in their lives.

The dedication ceremony also includes the offering of prayers, one of which reads in part:

> Master of the world, look down from Your holy habitation and accept in mercy and favor the prayer of Your children who are gathered to dedicate this home and to offer their gratitude. . . . Grant that they may live in their home in harmony and friendship.

The ceremony then proceeds with the bringing of bread and salt into the household to symbolize the blessing of prosperity. In some homes a learned person, not necessarily an intimate friend or member of the family, is invited to speak on the religious significance of the *hanukkat habayit.*

The Jew never considered God's presence to reside exclusively in the synagogue. There are more religious ceremonies associated with the home than the synagogue. It is in the home where God's influence can be most keenly felt, for there crucial decisions are made daily, family relationships are built, values are discussed and cultivated. Where, if not in the home, can the spirit of God be more keenly appreciated? It is, therefore, most appropriate that a new home be dedicated with anticipation that God's presence will be experienced by the members of the household.

72

SHELOM BAYIT

שְׁלוֹם בַּיִת

Household Peace

Peace, like charity, begins at home. World or national peace cannot exist unless the small family unit works at creating and maintaining a peaceful atmosphere at home.

Shelom bayit means much more than the absence of strife among the members of the family. Some homes are unusually quiet. There is little communication between brothers and sisters. Mother and father have little to discuss with each other. Sometimes fear of expressing oneself in the presence of a parent keeps the children silent at the dinner table.

On the other hand, some homes may vibrate with heated discussion and debate. Even the young ones are encouraged to express their feelings openly. And yet, *shelom bayit* may permeate the spirit of the family mainly because there is *respect* for one another. Children respect the opinions of parents not merely because they provide clothing, food, and shelter. They realize that their parents have lived through more experiences and gained knowledge and insight that are usually acquired with maturity. In such a home, parents likewise respect their children, though they may disagree with them, primarily because they recognize the need for children to develop independent thinking and to express their opinion in the presence of their elders.

But most essential, in a home where *shelom bayit* prevails, husband and wife must have regard and respect for each other. The Talmud states: "He who loves his wife as much as himself, honors her more than himself, and rears his children in the right

159

manner, that man has peace in his household." Children are usually guided in their own relationships with other members of the family by the attitudes that exist between mother and father.

Our Sages taught that if one brings peace into his household, Scripture gives him credit for bringing peace to all Israel, but if one brings envy and contention into his home, he is blamed for having brought envy and contention to Israel.

73

KIBBUD AV VAEM

כִּבּוּד אָב וָאֵם

Honoring One's Father and Mother

This Jewish value is taken directly from the fifth commandment of the Decalogue, which commands the child to honor both
father and mother. The first half of the Decalogue deals with
commandments between man and God. The second half addresses itself to commandments between man and man. This fifth
command to honor father and mother has been called the link
between the two sections, for in honoring one's parents, a child is
also honoring God.

The biblical commentator Rashi asks why the Decalogue
mentions the father first. Because, he answers, a son may tend to
honor his mother more than his father, since she may win him
over with kind words. To correct this possibility, the father is
here mentioned first. In Leviticus, however, we are commanded
to "revere every man his *mother* and *father*." Here the mother is
mentioned first. Why? Because a son may tend to revere his
father more, since he is the disciplinarian. Therefore, the mother
is here mentioned first to emphasize the reverence that is also
her due.

The rabbis go to great lengths to emphasize respect for
parents even when the parents err. For example: a child sees his
father transgress a law of the Torah. The child must not say to
him, "You have transgressed the words of the Torah." Rather
should he say: "Father, is it not written in the Torah thus and
thus?" This he should do as if he were inquiring rather than
blaming him, and his father would understand and not be put to
shame.

Though respect for parents is equated with respect for God, the Torah does not suggest that a child's obedience should be blind and irrational. If a parent orders a child to profane the Sabbath, the child is not duty-bound to obey. In fact, he is required to follow the higher law, the law of God. Likewise, if a child desires to leave home in order to study Torah because instruction in another place is more adequate, he should leave, even if his father objects. Obviously the duty to study Torah transcends the honor due to parents.

It is abundantly clear from these laws that filial duty does not operate in one direction. Parents should not arbitrarily command children merely to test their loyalty. Nor should they force them to choose between parents and teachers. The Torah regards parents primarily as teachers of their young. When they fail in their responsibility of directing them along moral paths, they abdicate their parental rights and privileges; they invite disagreement and even disobedience.

74

TZAAR GIDDUL BANIM

צַעַר גִּדּוּל בָּנִים

Pain of Raising Children

After Eve ignored God's warning in the Garden of Eden, she was told of her punishment: ". . . In pain you shall bring forth children." According to one rabbinic version, God warned her that she would also suffer the pain of raising children in addition to the pains of labor. The Talmud cites Jacob the Patriarch as a classic example of a father who suffers *tzaar giddul banim* with his ten sons who caused him untold grief.

The Jewish parent has often used the expression *tzaar giddul banim* to describe the problems of raising children to adulthood. There are the physical ailments and diseases that require the parents' constant attention and vigil. There are the "close calls" when children narrowly miss fatal accidents. Then there are the problems involving the education of one's children. There are the social problems of young people, problems of relating to their peers or to the adult world.

The most painful age for many parents is their children's adolescence, when they begin to assert their independence, frequently with outbursts of resentment and hostility. It is at this stage that parents may even begin to question whether it was worthwhile bringing their children into the world, if this is their "reward" for all their years of loving concern and attention.

Yet, this doubtful stage among parents fortunately does not prevail. Just as the young mother conditions herself to forget her birth pangs so that she is willing to undergo the experience again and again, so do most parents learn to accept *tzaar giddul banim* as a necessary aspect of the parental role in the child's maturation process. The wise parent comes to realize that children can never be expected to repay their parents for all the energy and time invested in them, and that it is unrealistic to demand full compensation.

Many centuries ago in Germany, an aged Jewish woman called Glueckel of Hameln (1719) wrote her autobiography in the form of a long letter to her children. She began by telling them by means of a parable what she expected of them:

> A bird once set out to cross a windy sea with its three fledglings. The sea was so wide and the wind so strong, the father bird was forced to carry his young, one by one, in his strong claws. When he was half-way across with the first fledgling, the wind turned to a gale, and he said: "My child, look how I am struggling and risking my life in your behalf. When you are grown up, will you do as much for me and provide for my old age?" The fledgling replied: "Only bring me to safety and when you are old, I shall do everything you ask of me." So the father bird dropped his child into the sea; and it drowned, and he said: "So shall it be done to such a liar as you." Then the father bird returned to shore, set forth with his second fledgling, asked the same question, and received the same answer; he drowned the second child with the cry: "You, too, are a liar." Finally, he set out with the third fledgling and when he asked the same question, he was told: "My dear father, it is true you are struggling mightily and risking your life. I cannot bind myself. This, though, I can promise. When I am grown and have children of my own, I shall do as much for them as you have done for me." Whereupon the father bird said: "Well spoken, my child, and wisely. Your life I will spare, and I will carry you safely to the shore." [pp. 2–3]

75

YIHUS

יִחוּס

Family Status

The desire to have one's child marry into a family with status and position has long been pursued by Jewish parents. Family status, however, was rarely measured by material wealth only. To come from *yihus* generally implied that the family gained prominence for its achievements in philanthropy or in scholarship, preferably both.

Yihus is more than pedigree, since it is not automatically passed on from generation to generation. If a member of the present generation fails to live up to the good name of his ancestors, then his *yihus* diminishes. Moreover, a person may obtain *yihus* for himself and his family even when his parents are unknown *(yihus atzmo)*.

Especially in eastern Europe, the man of learning was acclaimed by the entire community as the most desirable *baal yihus* (man of status).

> . . . Parents dream of marrying their daughter to a learned youth or their son to the daughter of a learned father. The matchmaker, who is a very important institution in the shtetl, has in his notebook a list of all eligible boys and girls within range. Under each name is a detailed account of his *yihus*, in which the most important item is the number of learned men in the family, past and present. The greater the background of learning, the better the match. The sages have said, "A man should sell all he has in order to get for his son a bride who is the daughter of a scholar. [Zborowski and Herzog (1962), pp. 81–82]

165

Every society has its aristocrats, its status symbols, which the "haves" wish to retain and the "have-nots" strive for. All depends on what these symbols of aristocracy are. Who is entitled to be called a *baal yihus?*

We must see to it that we continue the tradition of ascribing *yihus* to our learned men and to those who work for the benefit of the community. We should strive to have our young people aspire to that kind of prestige rather than to the prestige that comes merely with the accumulation of wealth.

Yihus then depends on those values that the group holds in highest esteem. The traditional Jewish view of *yihus*, coupling philanthropy and scholarship as the highest goals, is worthy of imitation.

76

KASHRUT

כַּשְׁרוּת

Dietary Laws (literally: Fitness)

The Torah declares the following foods permissible: (a) all animals that part the hoof and are clovenfooted and chew the cud; (b) all fish with fins and scales; and (c) most domesticated fowl, and by implication, all fruits and vegetables.

Rabbinic law outlines in greater detail the additional steps that must be taken before meat may be eaten. The animal must be ritually slaughtered by a *shohet* (slaughterer) who is especially trained for his work. He must carefully examine the animal after slaughtering to ascertain whether the animal is diseased. Only after the animal is found to be free from serious disease is the meat declared *kasher* or fit.

The meat must then be thoroughly washed within three days. After it is cut, the parts are soaked in water to be cleansed of surface blood. Then it is covered with salt to further draw out the blood. After the salt has been washed off, it is prepared for cooking.

Contrary to popular opinion, the laws of *kashrut* were not promulgated essentially for health reasons. Naturally, our forefathers were concerned with maintaining rigid standards of health, but they were primarily concerned with teaching the Jew a reverence for life. He is not permitted to forget that in eating meat he is responsible for the taking of an animal's life.

The rabbis imply that God would prefer that we abstain from eating meat altogether, but since we are imperfect beings and our desires cannot be thwarted completely, we should at least refrain from consuming all kinds of meat. Even when

167

partaking of permitted animals, we should never forget that they are God's creatures. The Bible clearly says regarding these laws, "You shall be holy for I (the Lord) am holy."

This moral emphasis is very apparent in some of the specific laws of *kashrut:* the animal must be slaughtered in the most painless manner by the *shohet* who pronounces a blessing before taking the life of the animal; blood, the symbol of life, must be removed before eating. (If blood were permitted, one's conscience could eventually become dulled even upon shedding the blood of human beings.)

Maimonides summarized the moral purpose of *kashrut:* it teaches man self-mastery, curbs man's carnal desire, and cleanses him spiritually and physically. Kaufman Kohler elaborated on this opinion: "It cannot be denied that these laws actually disciplined the medieval Jew, so that during centuries of wild dissipation he practiced sobriety and moderation."

Part VIII

Aspects of Faith

77

SHEKHINAH

שְׁכִינָה

God's Nearness

God is known by several expressions, each emphasizing a different quality of His being. Thus *Elohim* is associated with God's justice; *Adonai* with God's love; *Shaddai* with God's power. *Shekhinah* is always associated with God's nearness either to the people of Israel or the individual Jew.

God is never really absent from the world, and yet the rabbis were prepared to accept a contradiction in speaking of the removal of His presence at those times when the individual or the group sinned against Him. They meant, apparently, that the special relationship of loving concern between God and man was removed. God cannot live together in the same environment with sinfulness. The presence of one excludes the presence of the other.

The *Shekhinah* is especially present, we are advised, where men gather for worship, where judges carry out their duties at court, and where even an individual is engaged in the study of Torah. The *Shekhinah* is present with Israel in times of tragedy and even follows the people into exile.

Under what conditions does God remove His presence? When humility gives way to pride and arrogance, the *Shekhinah* removes itself; when a person has no control over his temper, the *Shekhinah* likewise withdraws. Pride and anger both lead to idolatry, say the rabbis, for the proud or violent man sets up a strange god within himself that he worships.

Likewise, the adulterer causes the removal of the *Shekhinah*, for he denies God's knowledge of one's private life. He acts

171

in such a way as if he said to God, "Remove Yourself for a short while, and make room for me." By the same token, the thief causes the removal of God's presence because he too claims that no one is aware of his secret actions. In removing His presence from such men, God's awareness is never absent; only His protectiveness is withdrawn.

Though it is generally agreed that God has no physical form whatsoever, we find in our literature many poetic expressions, especially regarding the *Shekhinah*, that are associated with the physical. The *Shekhinah* "rests" on two persons who study words of Torah. When Israel is worthy, it is gathered "under the wings of the *Shekhinah*." He who commits a sin in secret "is as though he crowds off the feet of the *Shekhinah*." None of these expressions are taken literally; they represent the human craving for understanding of God's influence in their lives.

78

HASHEM

הַשֵׁם

The Name of God

The tradition relates that the name of God – consisting of the four letters *Yod, Hei, Vav, Hei* – was revealed to Moses at the burning bush. Its exact pronunciation was passed on to Aaron and kept as a closely guarded secret among the Priests, lest the masses use God's name irreverently. The only occasion upon which the High Priest uttered the real name of God was on the Day of Atonement, during the confession of sins. When he uttered the holy Name, his voice was lost in the singing of the other Priests, so that the people could not hear the original pronunciation.

Outside the sanctuary, the term *Adonai* was used to connote God's name. Whenever the original four letters are found in the Bible, or when God's name is invoked in prayer, it is pronounced *Adonai*. But even this name of God is confined to sacred purposes only. In conversation, *Hashem*, meaning The Name, is uttered to protect God's name even further from irreverence or blasphemy.

There are several Hebrew expressions signifying faith and trust in God that have been used by religious Jews regardless of the language that they are accustomed to speak. The term *Hashem* comprises part of each of these expressions.

Barukh Hashem – Thank God. When one wishes to show gratitude for his daily blessings from God, he will frequently include this expression of thankfulness. When asked about his health, he may answer simply *"Barukh Hashem,"* as if to say, "I could be much worse. I thank God that I'm holding my own."

173

Beezrat Hashem—with the help of God. The religious Jew plans for the future with the awareness that he needs God's help if his plans are to materialize. He therefore prefaces all plans or resolutions with the expression *Beezrat Hashem*. His correspondence also begins with the Hebrew letters that begin each of these words.

Im Yirtzeh Hashem—If it please God. This expression is also used in connection with plans and hopes. The faithful accompany every promise or wish with either of the last two expressions of faith in God's influence upon their destiny.

79

TORAH MISINAI

תּוֹרָה מִסִינַי

Revelation

Torah Misinai refers to the belief that God dictated the entire Torah, both written and oral, to Moses on Mount Sinai. Although the term is found only once in talmudic literature (in the Ethics of the Fathers) until the latter half of the nineteenth century, almost all Jewish scholarship was predicated on this belief. It expresses the view that Revelation occurred once and for all in the meeting at Sinai, and that therefore the revealed Law is not subject to human alteration.

Moses indicates again and again that he did not author the laws and teachings in the Torah. He is a messenger, transmitting God's word to the people. This surely was one of the primary factors that caused the Torah to be held in such esteem over the centuries, that caused Jews to ponder over every verse, every word. It also explains why the Talmud was studied with such diligence and reverence, for it too represented the Divine Law revealed to Moses at Sinai.

A significant number of Jews continue to understand Revelation in this manner. Others (among them, Jews of the Conservative branch of Judaism) also understand Revelation to be the divinely inspired Word of God. But these Jews do not hold that the Torah (oral and written) was dictated word for word by God on Mount Sinai. They too revere the Torah and Talmud. In addition, they contend that Revelation is a never-ending process, and that those who seek to meet the problems of life *within the spirit of the Torah* are likewise encouraged by God Who regards these students, like their ancestors, as being divinely inspired.

175

The Talmud implies this view in the well-known passage: "God showed Moses the derivations in the Torah and the words of the scholars, and whatever the scholars were to originate in the future."

Dr. Robert Gordis represents this point of view in the following statement about Revelation: "Properly used, both phrases, *Torah min hashamayim* (Torah from Heaven) and *Torah Misinai,* express a fundamental of Judaism, the belief that Jewish law in its entire history and unfoldment bears the same relationship to the Revelation at Sinai as does a spreading oak tree to its original acorn, in which all its own attributes are contained" *(Judaism for the Modern Age,* pp. 160–161).

80

ATTAH VEHARTANU

אַתָּה בְחַרְתָּנוּ

The Election of Israel
(literally: You Have Chosen Us)

Though there is no rabbinic term that is truly equivalent to
the phrase, the "chosenness of Isarel," the phrase *attah vehar-
tanu*, which is taken from our liturgy, is frequently used to
express this idea of Israel's election. Israel's chosenness is one of
the basic teachings of the Torah. In Exodus 19:5, God affirms:
"Now, therefore, if you will hearken to My voice indeed and keep
My covenant, then you shall be My own treasure from among all
peoples; for all the earth is Mine and you shall be unto Me a
kingdom of priests and a holy nation." The prophets also declare
Israel to be selected by God for a special mission.

To affirm that we are God's chosen people never implied
that the Jews were in any way free to exploit other peoples or to
consider themselves as God's spoiled darlings, assured of His
protection regardless of their behavior. The belief in election
carried with it serious responsibility and commitments to uphold
and to teach the moral law to the rest of humanity. Failure to live
up to what God required of His people would count more heavily
against them than against those who were not elected. The
eighth-century (B.C.E.) prophet Amos dispelled any notions of
God's favored treatment toward His people when he declared:
"You only have I known of all the families of the earth; therefore
will I visit upon you all your iniquities."

The Jewish people is not portrayed merely as the chosen
people. It is also the "choosing people" who among all the nations
accepted God, agreed to submit to His will and to study and

177

follow His commandments. They were prepared to bind themselves to God's covenant, as told in Exodus: "And all the people answered together, and said, 'All that the Lord has spoken we will do.'"

Some Jews contend that the idea of the chosen people should no longer be taken seriously, because it draws a contrast between Israel and the other nations. Furthermore, they say, this contrast is no longer factually defensible, since the modern Jews are no more religiously dedicated than are other groups.

There is no question but that the present generation of Jews has lost much of the religious fervor and dedication experienced by Jews in the past. In fact, modern studies indicate that Jews are less religiously motivated than other groups in our country. Many Jews, alas, choose to ignore their unique religious role; they prefer to deny that their responsibilities to God and the world exceed those of other people. Such denial by a segment of the Jewish people, however, does not automatically eliminate the responsibility. One may deny his parental duties, but mere nonacceptance does not morally absolve him from his responsibilities. So, likewise, Jews cannot be absolved from a responsibility which has been a motivating concept in the life of the Jews since the days of the Bible.

81

BEHIRAH HOFSHIT

בְּחִירָה חָפְשִׁית

Freedom of Will

The term *behirah hofshit* is used for the first time by the medieval Jewish philosophers, but the question of free will vs. determinism occupied the minds of Jewish scholars and Sages centuries before the Middle Ages. The Torah leaves no doubt that man has freedom of will: "I have set before you life and death, the blessing and the curse; choose life, then, that you and your descendants may live" (Deut. 30:19).

The Sages, however, are aware of the problem of accepting the contradictions of this notion. If God knows everything that is going to happen, how can man be considered free to choose between good or evil? His choice appears to be predetermined. One opinion given by the Sages is that God knows and determines everything in life—excepting man's moral choice. God permits man to determine whether he wants to choose good or evil.

It is understandable why this question perplexed our ancestors. If man is not a free agent, then how can he be responsible for his sins? The concept of sin must be based on man's own failure to make a wise choice. Without *behirah hofshit* man is no more than a puppet and cannot be held accountable for this actions.

Religious skeptics have frequently pointed to the question of Pharaoh's refusal to free the Israelites as a denial of free will. Did God not harden the Pharaoh's heart after each plague? How then could he undergo a change of heart even if he so desired? Maimonides explains Pharaoh's action in this way: He sinned, first of his own free will, until he forfeited the opportunity to repent. By this, the philosopher implied that at the outset man is free to choose any path of action he desires. He is given equal opportunity to do good or evil. But as soon as he has made his first choice, then the opportunities facing him are no longer so evenly balanced. The more he persists in the first path of his choosing—the evil path—the harder it becomes for him to revert to the good path, even though his essential freedom of choice is not affected. God has not hampered his freedom. He has by his own choice and persistence placed obstacles in his own way.

Erich Fromm (1967) offers the following illustration from the game of chess to emphasize this very thought:

> Assuming that two equally skilled players begin a game, both have the same chance of winning; in other words, each has the same freedom to win. After, say, five moves, the picture is already different. Both still *can* win, but A, who has made a better move, already has a greater chance of winning. He has, as it were, more freedom to win than his opponent, B. Yet B is still free to win. After some more moves, A, having continued to make correct moves that were not effectively countered by B, is almost sure to win, but only *almost*. B *can* still win. After some further moves the game is decided. B, provided he is a skilled player, recognizes that he has no longer the freedom to win; he sees that he has already lost before he is actually checkmated. . . . [p. 135]

82

MAZAL TOV

מַזָּל טוֹב

Good Fortune; Congratulations

There are several expressions in Hebrew that are still used extensively, though their original meaning has lost its significance. In the Bible and Talmud, *mazal* was a constellation of the Zodiac or a planet. Many ancient people—the Egyptians, the Babylonians, the Jews—believed that the position of the stars had special powers over man and could influence his destiny. Hence, the word *mazal* assumed the meaning of fortune or fate to which mortals were subjected.

During the Middle Ages, enlightened Jews warned their brethren not to place their confidence in astrology. Maimonides, quoting from Leviticus, strenuously opposes any dependence on omens derived from the stars: "Do not practice divination or soothsaying." He urges the Jews to pay no heed to the view held by the ignorant masses that God decrees at a man's birth whether than man shall be wicked or righteous. He equates astrology with idolatry.

Despite their growing disbelief in astrology, the Jews continued to employ the expression *mazal* to signify a fortunate occurrence or good luck. Especially on joyful family occasions, the expression *mazal tov* was extended to the celebrants by well-wishers, even though all traces of its origin were forgotten. At Jewish weddings, immediately after the groom breaks the glass, the entire assembly of guests frequently shouts, "*mazal tov*," in unison. Among Sephardic Jews, the expression *siman tov*, also meaning a good omen, is frequently extended to the celebrants. The Yiddish vernacular adopted several expressions

derived from the term *mazal: mazeldig,* lucky; *shlimmazel,* a
luckless fellow; *shlimmazeldig,* unlucky.

It is essential to understand why fatalism runs contrary to
mature religion. Belief in fate precludes the belief in free will.
Without the freedom to choose between two paths of action, man
is deprived of his most essential human quality. Man could never
be held accountable for his decisions were God to determine
beforehand what the results would be. Admittedly, man frequently inherits certain physical, mental, or social conditions that
may strongly influence his decisions; they may help or hinder him
in his thought and action, but his future is seldom sealed even by
the severest handicaps or the most fortunate assets handed to
him at birth. True, we have no say as to the cards handed to us,
but we may choose which way we shall play them.

83

YETZER HARA

יֵצֶר הָרָע

Evil Impulse

In opposition to the *yetzer tov* (good impulse), the *yetzer hara*, probably an earlier expression, is responsible for man's destructive drive. Though the term *yetzer* stands alone in the Torah, it is followed by the adjective *ra* — *"the impulse of man is evil."* The Sages formed the two words into a concept that has played an essential role in rabbinic thinking.

This evil inclination, which is deeply rooted in man's nature, is constantly warring with man's better self. Thus when the good *yetzer* prompts a man to give charity, the evil *yetzer* in him says, "Why should you do a *mitzvah* and diminish your property? Rather than give to strangers, give to your children." Sometimes it appeals to his vanity, telling him not to pay a condolence call because he is too important.

The evil *yetzer* is described as seductive and tempting. It appears first as a modest traveler, then as a welcome guest, finally requiring obedience as the master of the house. Only a strong desire to make the good *yetzer* victorious will keep the evil *yetzer* subdued. The struggle is constant; vigilance must be maintained as long as man lives.

By the interplay of these two opposing factions within man, Judaism wisely avoids the extreme of describing man as either a brute or an angel. True, he is sinful, but he is not hopelessly bound by a sinful nature. He is capable of goodness if he remains alert to the temptations that constantly befall him.

Unlike the ancient Persians who believed in a god of good and a god of evil, Jewish thought emphasizes that one God created both impulses. The evil *yetzer* can serve a most constructive purpose if properly channeled. Sexual desire, for example, can lead men to immorality and the destruction of the family. Yet the rabbis were aware that this natural desire, though described as the *yetzer hara,* also was responsible for the foundation of the family. "Were it not for the sex impulse, no man would build a house or marry a woman or engage in an occupation." The rabbis interpret the well-known passage from the *Shema* as follows: "You shall love the Lord your God with all your heart—with both your drives, the evil drive and the good drive."

84

SAKHAR VAONESH

שָׂכָר וָעֹנֶשׁ

Reward and Punishment

One of the basic concepts of Judaism similarly expressed in most religions is the belief in *sakhar vaonesh,* reward for the righteous and punishment for the wicked.

The Torah emphasizes this idea, especially in the Book of Deuteronomy, where the blessing or the curse is left entirely in the hands of man. The prophets too dwell on this theme, contending that there is a direct correlation between goodness and reward, evil and punishment. Individual and national catastrophe are both traced to man's sinfulness. Talmudic ethics stresses a similar pattern—even though we are exhorted to live the good life for its own sake and without expectation of reward, nevertheless it is implicitly understood that reward is in store for those who follow the correct path.

And yet, we are confused when we see the wicked rewarded and the righteous condemned. Even our attempts to explain this paradox leave us dissatisfied. We may rationalize that the wicked must live with their guilty consciences and the righteous have the satisfaction of knowing that their hands are clean. But do the wicked really feel guilt equal to their sin? Does the satisfaction of the righteous compensate for their pain and torture?

The tradition should be properly understood. It has never claimed that people who are afflicted are necessarily wicked and that the prosperous are all worthy. Goodness, however, usually leads to rewards that can enable a person to withstand pain because he is blessed with the respect of family, the loving concern of well-wishing friends. A noble and charitable man may suffer physically, but he will not suffer alone. Others will share his suffering, which is in a sense dearer than any other reward.

By the same token, a parent who bequeaths high moral standards and values to children will most likely be rewarded in seeing his sons and daughters inculcating the same values in their children. Such concern does not insure parents against poverty and pain, but most parents would probably consider *nahat* from their children as a most ample reward for their efforts.

On the other hand, miserliness and selfishness usually breed loneliness, for which prosperity or sound health can never compensate. Pain or pleasure, poverty or wealth are not always indicative of punishment or reward.

More significant, man often interferes with God's plan to reward the righteous and punish the wicked. We should not look upon God as an Oriental potentate whose will cannot be interfered with. Man can undermine God's plan if he chooses to contribute to the success of dishonest people by patronizing them. When we honor the worthy in the community—men who will not buy honor—we are furthering God's plan of *sakhar vaonesh*. When we help further the success of honest, not necessarily aggressive businessmen, we are again cooperating with God's law of reward and punishment. This is how men can help "perfect the world under the Kingship of the Almighty."

85

NESHAMAH

נְשָׁמָה

Soul

In biblical times, no clear distinction is found between body and soul. Like the word *nefesh*, *neshamah* is taken to mean breath of life. The soul gives life and vitality to the body. When it leaves the body in death the bodily functions cease.

In rabbinic times, however, the *neshamah* begins to take on a more distinctive meaning. The body and soul become separate entities. Unlike the body, the soul is purely spiritual and immortal. It is the divine aspect of man. According to one talmudic view, God created all individual souls when He created the world, and at the time of birth they join the bodies to which they have been assigned. The rabbis were undoubtedly influenced somewhat by Greek thinkers who treated body and soul as two hostile elements, the former material and corrupt, the latter totally spiritual and perfect.

However, with the exception of a few extreme views, the rabbis do not treat body and soul as opposites. The pure soul is by no means imprisoned within the impure body. On the contrary, the body is God's handiwork and none of its natural functions are inherently evil, if properly controlled. When man sins, the whole being, body and soul, are responsible. A charming story in the Talmud highlights this mutual responsibility of body and soul:

Two beggars, one blind and the other lame, are walking outside the king's garden. They are eager to taste his delicious fruit. Since the blind man cannot see and the lame one cannot walk, the former carries the latter to the tree and together they manage to obtain the fruit. When they are arrested by the king, each man protests innocence, pointing to his physical disability as proof. Not to be deceived, the king commands the blind man to put the lame man on his shoulders, and sentences them as one criminal to atone for their sin. Similarly, says the Talmud, neither the soul nor the body can claim innocence when a man sins. The whole man must assume responsibility.

In traditional Jewish thought, resurrection of the body and immortality of the soul are frequently coupled. However, today, even many Jews who reject the theory of resurrection still cling to the belief in the soul's immortality. They do not profess to know anything about its function or state of consciousness after life, other than its return to its original and eternal source, to God.

86

GAN EDEN

גַּן עֵדֶן

Paradise, Heaven
(literally: Garden of Eden)

The Hebrew term for the home assigned to righteous souls
is *Gan Eden*. Clearly the term is borrowed from the place on
earth where Adam and Eve blissfully lived before committing
their sin of disobedience. It is strange that the rich Hebrew
language must borrow a term from an earthly place to express
the concept of Paradise or Heaven. But evidently this concept
was not an original Jewish thought. It was adopted by the Jews
during a period of close contact with the Persians.

Though belief in Heaven as a home for the righteous souls
was never elevated to a dogma or essential doctrine in Judaism,
nevertheless it gave great comfort to the suffering and moral
incentive to live the righteous life. The deprivations and discom-
forts of this world would not last forever. Eventually the righteous would be released from the cares of this world and would
lead a life of eternal bliss.

Naturally, this craving for Heaven led many people to think
of it as an actual place, though there was no agreement as to its
location or size. The more educated, however, were not concerned with the geography of *Gan Eden*. To them it was more a
state of being, the satisfaction of being near God and in communion with Him, and at the same time free of material cares and
physical desires.

The Talmud describes *Gan Eden* in this way: "In the world
to come there is no eating nor drinking, no begetting of children,
no commerce, no envy, no hatred, no competition—there is only

this, that the righteous sit with crowns on their heads and take delight in God's splendor." This was the Talmud's way of saying that the living cannot experience or understand the meaning of Heaven. It cannot be compared in any way to the limited happiness of this world.

Contemporary Jews are not as preoccupied with thoughts of Heaven or Hell as their ancestors. Their thoughts are more centered on achieving the blessings that God offers in this world. *The crucial question is not where the ideal place is but what the ideal is.* An ideal is worthy of being called *Gan Eden* even if we may never attain it in our lifetime. If man's picture of the ideal existence is one in which spiritual values predominate, where cooperation is more important than competition, where creativity is more important than destructiveness, then he believes in *Gan Eden* no less than the man who believes that he will inherit Paradise after the completion of his life on earth.

87

GEHINOM

גֵּיהִנֹּם

Hell (literally: Valley of Hinom)

Like the term *Gan Eden*, meaning Heaven, *Gehinom* is also a term borrowed from an actual place on earth. *Gei-Ben Hinom* can be located south of Jerusalem, in a valley where the wicked once sacrificed their children to false gods. Thus when the Jew learned about the concept of Hell from his neighbors, he used this appropriate name to signify the home of the wicked beyond the grave.

The Talmud, which in some ways is similar to an encyclopedia of Jewish thought, includes various viewpoints about Hell—viewpoints that range from the most simple to the most sophisticated. One Midrash expresses the view that Hell is so hot that it is sixty times more intense than an earthly fire. On the other hand, we have the view that regards the whole subject as if Hell were nothing more than a figure of speech: "Hell awaits one who uses unseemly speech or who instructs an unworthy student." Despite the extreme differences in opinion about the meaning of Hell, it is nowhere considered to be a dogma or doctrine of faith that Jews are required to profess. Even those Sages who delighted in describing the torments of Hell were usually aware that they were permitting their imagination to roam freely.

During the Middle Ages when Jews were susceptible to the folklore and myths of their neighbors, belief in *Gehinom* was most evident. The Jewish scholars, however, sought to discourage belief in physical torture and punishment after life. They interpreted reward and punishment in the hereafter in a spiritual

191

way. To Judah Loew of Prague the hereafter was a purely spiritual state; neither its rewards nor its punishments were physical. Its "joys" consisted of union with God; its "tortures" consisted of alienation from God. To another thinker, Heaven was the satisfaction of life well lived; Hell was the pain or remorse for having failed to live the good life.

88

GEULAH

גְּאֻלָּה

Redemption

The Jewish concept of redemption differs from the Christian in that it does not generally refer to redemption from sin, nor does it apply to the individual, but to the group. *Geulah* connotes either freedom from bondage in Egypt or the future redemption from oppression that will take place in the Messianic era. The references to redemption in the *Shema* section of the prayerbook refer in the main to the Exodus, and in the *Amidah* that follows, the redemption from future bondage is implied.

The rabbis claim that the redemption of the past and future are closely associated. Rabbi Nathan says that the festival of the departure from Egypt also commemorates a festival of the freedom of the world. Rabbi Abraham Isaac Kook expresses the same view when he writes that "Redemption is continuous. The redemption from Egypt and the Final Redemption are part of the same process . . . Moses and Elijah belong to the same redemptive act; one represents its beginning and the other its culmination, so that together they fulfill its purpose. . . ." (Hertzberg, 1971, p. 425).

The redemption of the future applies not only to the Jewish people; all the nations will be redeemed along with Israel. The redemption will arrive when Israel and the nations undergo a moral transformation. Israel must seek forgiveness for her sins, and the nations must turn from pursuit of power and seek a new world order based on a common acceptance of one God. When the prophet Isaiah envisioned an age in which the wolf and the lamb would dwell together, he expressed the hope that some day the stronger nations would put aside their agggressiveness and choose to live by a new code based on mutual respect.

The rabbis felt, however, that the redemption of mankind, marking the end to conflict, did not entirely depend on human effort. God would steer man toward His inevitable goal. Man could hasten or retard the *geulah* but not prevent it indefinitely, for the Divine Will must eventually be fulfilled.

The Jew fervently believed that the beginning of universal redemption *(athalta digeulah)* would be marked by the return of the Jewish people to Israel. The freedom of the land from foreign domination was a prerequisite for the advent of the new society. This conviction gave great impetus to some of the fathers of modern Zionism who settled in Palestine. *Eretz Yisrael* would become a pilot plan for the ideal society, which in turn would shed its moral influence on the other nations, thus hastening the greater redemption of mankind.

89

MASHIAH

מָשִׁיחַ

Messiah (literally: Anointed One)

The word *mashiah* originally refers to the ancient ceremony of anointing a king with oil, highlighting the importance of his new position of leadership. The Bible frequently uses the term *mashiah* when referring to kings: Saul, David, Zedekiah; even the pagan King Cyrus of Persia is designated as *mashiah*.

Later, however, *mashiah* is identified primarily with King David, who represents the ideal ruler. From this developed the belief than an unusual person endowed with unique gifts of spirituality and wisdom would spring forth from the House of David. He would execute justice in the land, and Israel would be blessed with peace through his efforts. Not only would Israel be affected by the influence of this spiritual leader, the Messiah would usher in an era of freedom and peace for the whole world.

The role of the Messianic king as a universal leader is most beautifully expressed by the eighth-century B.C.E. prophets Isaiah and Micah who foresaw a Messianic Age.

And it shall come to pass in the end of days that the mountain of the Lord's house shall be established as the top of the mountains, and it shall be exalted above the hills; and all people shall flow upon it. And many nations shall go and say, "Come ye, and let us go up to the mountain of the Lord and to the house of the God of Jacob; and He will teach us of His ways, and we will walk in His paths." For out of Zion shall go forth the law, and the word of the Lord from Jerusalem. And He shall judge between many peoples, and shall decide concerning mighty nations afar off; and they shall beat their

swords into plowshares and their spears into pruning hooks;
nation shall not lift up sword against nation, neither shall
they learn war anymore. [Micah 4:1-3, Isaiah 2:1-4]

Later in Jewish history, especially during the darkest periods, we find imaginative minds ascribing supernatural powers to
the Messiah. He will, by virtue of his superhuman gifts, bring
about a new order completely different from man's present
experience and beyond his ability to picture or comprehend.

People began to calculate the time of the Messiah's arrival
and plan accordingly. It is essential, however, to remember the
more sober and realistic views that, like Isaiah and Micah, put
less emphasis on the man and more on the age.

Maimonides gives his impression of what the Messianic Age
will be like: "There will not be in these days any famine, war,
jealousy, or quarrel, because the good things will be in plenty,
and even luxuries will be found everywhere; all will concern
themselves with trying to know the Lord."

In a way, all good men who are striving and working for a
better world are Messiahs, there being no need to transfer the
responsibility to another who may come at a future date. Only
when men everywhere will be morally prepared to create the
Messianic Age will it ultimately arrive.

90

TEHIYYAT HAMETIM

תְּחִיַּת הַמֵּתִים

Resurrection

The belief in resurrection was so important to the rabbis that the Mishnah lists among those excluded from the world to come, the person "who denies resurrection of the dead." The second blessing of the *Amidah*, recited three times daily, deals with God's power to resurrect the dead.

Though traditionalists have differed as to the duration of the resurrection, supposed by some to be eternal and by others to be limited, nevertheless the belief in the revival of the body and soul was almost universally held at one time. The bodies will arise from their graves, the souls will be summoned from their resting place, and both will once again be united to stand before God.

The ancients, accepting the belief in resurrection as having been revealed at Sinai, were nevertheless conscious of the difficulty in comprehending the mystery of the afterlife. This has perhaps contributed to their vagueness in describing the concept of immortality. And yet, they could more readily conceive of a bodily resurrection than understand how a disembodied soul could come to life. It is altogether possible that they insisted on bodily resurrection for another reason: they were protesting against those who belittled the flesh, who denied their bodies earthly pleasure, since the soul alone was deemed to be important. The rabbis insisted that the soul and the body were of divine origin and were together responsible for man's goodness.

Even in ancient times, however, there were scholars, especially among the philosophers, who interpreted *tehiyyat hametim* figuratively. Philo of Alexandria, the earliest of Jewish philosophers, was among those who preferred to think in terms of survival of the soul. Maimonides, too, rejected bodily survival, assigning the afterlife exclusively to the soul. He was aware that denial of bodily resurrection would disappoint the faithful, but he exhorted them to believe in the "great bliss which the soul is to enjoy in the world to come . . . and cannot bear comparison with the happiness of this world except in a figurative manner."

91

MIDDAT HARAHAMIM

מִדַּת הָרַחֲמִים

God's Love

Though the concept *middat harahamim* (lit. quality of love) does not contain God's name, it is clearly understood to mean "God's love." *Middat harahamim* stands in contrast to *middat hadin* (God's justice) throughout rabbinic literature. When God created the world, He combined both qualities of justice and mercy, for the world could not be sustained without these two vital elements. God alone knows how to administer justice and love simultaneously. Only He can penalize man for his transgressions and feel great compassion for him at the same moment.

Though justice is an essential quality of God, His love is more dominant than His justice. It is for this reason that prayer and atonement are required of the Jew. Man can always appeal to the compassionate and merciful qualities of God, no matter how undeserving man may be. When the rabbis ask us to emulate God's ways they have in mind *middat harahamim* – His mercy, compassion, and patience. They speak time and again of God's forgiving quality, of His willingness to receive the atoning sinner, and of the ways that His compassion moderates His justice. His reward is always in greater measure than His punishment. Even the biblical verse asserting that God visits the sins of the fathers on the children unto the third and fourth generation is followed immediately by the verse, "And showing mercy unto the thousandth generation of them that love Me and keep My commandments" (Exodus 20:5–6).

The claim that the Old Testament God of justice stands in contrast to the New Testament God of love represents a gross distortion of both books. Every objective biblical scholar, Christian and Jewish alike, knows that the Hebrew Bible conceived of God in terms of both love and justice, just as the New Testament God manifested Himself in justice as well as love. The authors of both books rightfully understood that a God exclusively just could not inspire men to love Him; a God exclusively loving could not elicit reverence from His children.

92

SHELOSH ESREI MIDDOT

שְׁלֹשׁ עֶשְׂרֵה מִדּוֹת

Thirteen Attributes of God

Although it is impossible to describe God's essence, an attempt was made by the rabbis to list thirteen moral qualities by which He may be known to man. They derive these divine qualities from two verses in Exodus (34:6–7) by analyzing the implications of each phrase: "The Lord! a God compassionate and gracious, slow to anger, rich in kindness and truth extending kindness to the thousandth generation, forgiving iniquity, transgression and sin; yet He will by no means clear the guilty."

The first two attributes are derived from the repetition of the Lord's name *(Adonai)*.

1. God is merciful before a man commits a sin.
2. He is the same merciful God after a man has sinned. The only change that may occur must come from the heart of the sinner, and not in the nature of God.
3. The name for God *(El)* here implies His might and power as supreme Ruler of nature and man. Within His power is the ability to carry out His will.
4. God is compassionate *(rahum);* He is in sympathy with the sufferings and miseries of man.
5. God is gracious *(hannun)*. He assists the afflicted and raises up the oppressed.
6. He is slow to anger *(erekh appayim)*. God does not hasten to punish the transgressor; He offers him the opportunity to alter his evil course.
7. He is rich in steadfast kindness *(rav hesed)*. God grants greater blessings to man than he deserves.

8. God is truthful *(veemet)*. He is faithful in fulfilling His promises to mankind.

9. God extends kindness to the thousandth generation *(notzer hesed laalafim)*. He rewards the descendants of the righteous.

10. He forgives iniquity *(nosei avon)*. He is even ready to receive those whose intentions are malicious and crooked, helping them return to their innocence once again.

11. God pardons transgressions *(pesha)* of the most serious kind — rebellion against Him.

12. He will certainly forgive those sins *(het)* committed in error or through carelessness and misdirection.

13. God acquits *(venakkeh)* the sincere penitent.

The thirteenth attribute is not a true rendition of the biblical passage that assures that God "will by no means clear the guilty." However, the rabbis who developed these attributes of God wanted to underscore God's quality of mercy *(middat rahamim)* over that of strict justice *(middat hadin)*. Hence, they took the first word of the phrase — *venakkeh* — and omitted the other two words, *lo yenakkeh*, to conform with their theme of God's compassion. These attributes were to become the ideal toward which man should strive.

These verses comprising the *Shelosh Esrei Middot* are recited before the open ark on all holidays except when the holiday falls on a Sabbath. The recitation of the attributes at this point in the service originated in the Middle Ages under the influence of the mystic Isaac Luria.

93

ZEKHUT AVOT

זְכוּת אָבוֹת

Merit of the Fathers

The phrase, "God of Abraham, God of Isaac, and God of Jacob," is well known to worshipers because it is recited three times daily at the beginning of the *Amidah*. The reference to the three patriarchs gave rise to the belief that God remembers their goodness and continues to show kindness to their descendants because of the merit of these founding fathers *(zekhut avot)*.

The concept of *zekhut avot* is not fully developed in the Torah, even though it frequently implies that a righteous individual may sustain other individuals or even an entire group. Thus, Lot is saved from annihilation when God destroys Sodom and Gomorrah, not because of his own righteousness, but through the merit of Abraham. When Israel was about to be destroyed after worshipping the golden calf, the intercession of Moses saved the people. The Torah thus implies that the individual is of supreme importance, and that from his actions may flow beneficial consequences for all society.

The rabbinic concept of *zekhut avot* played an important role in Jewish thinking. It gave the Jew confidence that the righteous few not only shed influence on their own generation, but on all generations to come. Thus, God judges us not as isolated individuals but rather as members of a historic family that commenced with the righteous patriarchs.

Zekhut avot never implied, however, that later generations of Jews were to be absolved of moral responsibility because of the righteousness of former generations. "Let not a man say, 'My father was a pious man; I shall be saved for his sake.'" Dr.

Solomon Schechter (1909) in his brilliant essay on *zekhut avot* clarifies its meaning: "What this *zekhut* served mostly to establish was the consciousness of the historic continuity, and to increase the reverence for the past which has become both foundation and inspiration" (pp. 183–184).

The term *avot* is understood to include not only the original patriarchs, but also one's more immediate ancestors who exerted their influence on succeeding generations. The patterns that they set have helped considerably to determine the lives that their children and grandchildren choose to live.

Moreover, the present generation will eventually become ancestors *(avot)*. Future generations will be largely guided by the standards that this generation decides to uphold and by the institutions that shall have been established for them. Rather than an excuse for inaction, then, *zekhut avot* is a call to each generation of potential ancestors to assume moral responsibility for those who will follow them.

94

KABBALAH

קַבָּלָה

Mystical Lore (literally: Tradition)

The term *Kabbalah* derives from the Hebrew word "tradition" or "receiving," and represents a special branch of Jewish tradition based on a mystical understanding of God and the universe. Unlike the Jewish rationalists like Maimonides and Saadya, who were influenced by Greek philosophy and science to arrive at an understanding of God, the Kabbalists rebelled against any attempt to reduce religion to a philosophy. They were more concerned with *feeling* God's nearness through experience rather than with analyzing His relationship to man.

The *Kabbalah* took hundreds of years to develop into a mature mystical teaching. Its origin can be traced to the inner life of the Essenes, a mystic brotherhood of about 4,000 souls, who flourished in the time of the Second Temple. They were ascetics who lived together and adhered to a strict code of discipline. They preferred silence, wore white clothes, ate and prayed together. They despised fame and riches and practiced benevolence and a high degree of morality. Kabbalistic ideas can be seen in the visions of the prophet Ezekiel. Glimpses of *Kabbalah* mysticism can be found also in talmudic and midrashic literature. Beginning with the thirteenth century, interest in the *Kabbalah* became widespread and reached a climax in Spain in the following two centuries. Then after an interval of a century it reappeared in Safed, Palestine, where it again reached a heightened pitch.

Although the different schools of *Kabbalah* differed in emphasis, they had much in common. They all relied heavily on the earliest document in the literature of *Kabbalah*, *The Book of Creation*, which appeared between the third and sixth centuries. They all regarded each part of the Torah–every dot, letter, or word–to be filled with profound symbolic meaning. Further, they all considered each of the twenty-two letters of the Hebrew alphabet to be endowed with similar symbolic content. Numbers and names also played an essential role in their understanding of creation.

One of the most important doctrines of the *Kabbalah* is that of the *Sefirot* or "emanations"; this was an attempt to explain the contradiction between the infinite God who is beyond involvement, desire, and change, and the God who actively participates in the drama of life. If God is infinite–the doctrine read–how can He be responsible for creation or the redemption of man? The Kabbalists assumed that there are two levels of being in God. On the one hand, God is *En Sof*, the Boundless and Infinite One, Who is beyond human understanding. But then God also abandons His self-contained position; He enters creation by manifesting Himself in *Sefirot*, ten emanations from God that enable man to see His influence around and in him. These emanations are ten rays of light that are responsible for the creation. They are not something apart from the Creator; they emanate from Him like the relationship of a flame to a burning coal.

Each emanation of God has a name and is responsible for a different part of Man. From the Crown is derived the head; from Wisdom and Intelligence are derived the two sides of the brain; from Mercy and Power come the two hands, etc. All the divine *Sefirot* are combined to develop the concept of Man, primordial man, from which Adam was later created. Thus, while God has no shape or form, He possesses within Himself an image transmitted to Man. Man becomes the crown of creation, created in God's image.

The Kabbalists were reticent about publicly teaching such mystical doctrines. Despite their elaborate explanations they still could not completely remove the paradox of an infinite God participating in the world of the finite. Their ideas were too subtle, their interpretations too daring for the average man to grasp. That is why they believed that those who wanted to study the *Kabbalah* had to be selected to make certain that they would not distort their learning. They were convinced that only the chosen in each generation were worthy of receiving the wisdom of the *Kabbalah*.

Part IX

THOSE WHO PRAY AND THE LANGUAGE OF PRAYER

95

BAAL TEFILLAH

בַּעַל תְּפִלָּה

Leader of the Service
(literally: Master of Prayer)

Until the sixteenth century, when the professional *hazzan* became the leader of prayers in the synagogue, the religious service was always led by a *baal tefillah,* known also as the *sheliah tzibbur,* or emissary of the congregation. Although the *hazzan* is a professional and his services to the congregation are varied, he is still regarded primarily as a *baal tefillah* or *sheliah tzibbur.* Regardless of his cantorial skill or musical ability, he is not a performer separated from the congregation, but one who prays with and on behalf of the worshipers, even as he leads them in prayer.

The Talmud was very much concerned about the character and piety of the *baal tefillah.* He was expected to be conscious of his responsibilities as congregational representative in prayer. When asked to lead the prayers, he was advised to declare that he was unworthy of the honor and to proceed to the reading desk only if asked three times. Other requirements set down by the Talmud for the leader of the service are that his conduct during his youth be blameless; he should be a hard-working man with a sizeable family and a modest income. Such a man would more likely pray with sincerity for himself and the congregation. Naturally, he was required to have a pleasing voice and expert knowledge of the liturgy and the readings from Scriptures for every occasion.

To impress further upon the *baal tefillah* the need for humility in prayer, ancient synagogues would set the lectern below the level of the floor where the congregation worshiped. When called upon to lead the congregation in prayer, the *baal tefillah* was addressed by the words: "Descend before the lectern." In this lowered position, he fulfilled the verse from the Psalms: "Out of the depths have I called upon You."

As emissary of the congregation, the *baal tefillah* does not pray in their stead. Very few prayers are recited solely by the leader. One of the few exceptions is the repetition of the Silent Devotion or *Amidah*, a tradition that developed out of necessity before prayer books were used by the congregation. Since most congregants did not know the liturgy and the order of the blessings in the *Amidah*, the leader repeated it aloud, thus permitting the worshipers to hear the blessings and respond "Amen" after each blessing.

Even though most larger synagogues engage the services of a *hazzan* for Sabbaths and holidays, the simple *baal tefillah* has not disappeared. Many Orthodox synagogues continue to request one of their worshipers to lead the prayer service on Sabbaths and holidays. During the week, all congregations that hold daily services choose a layman to lead the congregation in worship. Preferably a mourner who has lost a member of the family is called upon to serve as *baal tefillah*, as prescribed by Jewish tradition.

96

MINYAN

מִנְיָן

Quorum of Ten Men
(literally: Number)

A *minyan*, ten men of the Jewish faith, constitute a synagogue and are permitted to conduct a full service wherever they
choose to congregate. Though public prayer is deemed more
desirable than private prayer, each individual may recite almost
a complete service at home.

The synagogue, unlike the home, is not meant primarily for
private meditation; it is the place for community worship where
God's greatness may be demonstrated publicly (*Kiddush
Hashem*). God's holiness can only be asserted in the presence of
witnesses and, therefore, through prayers in which the community participates—a minimum of ten men. Hence the prayers of
Kaddish and *Kedushah*, forms of *Kiddush Hashem* that publicly
proclaim the sacredness of God's name, are said only as part of
congregational services. An individual may hallow God's name by
moral acts in private, but God's name can be hallowed by words of
mouth, by prayer, only in the presence and with the participation
of a congregation of witnesses.

Why does a minimum of ten men constitute a congregation,
a religious community? The rabbis derive the decision from that
part of the Bible that deals with Abraham's pleading with God to
save the righteous of Sodom. God finally conceded to save the
sinful city if at least ten righteous men could be found there. The
rabbis then conclude that ten men were a minimum to form a
congregation, a religious community. They also cite the spy
incident in the Book of Numbers where the ten spies (excluding

213

Joshua and Caleb) return to Moses with their discouraging report on the inadvisability of the Israelites to attempt conquering the land of Canaan. God then exclaims: "How long shall I bear with this evil congregation (*edah*)?" Here, too, "congregation" is equated with the number ten.

Children are not counted as part of a *minyan* primarily because they cannot yet fully appreciate the meaning of prayer. It is essential that when ten people gather in a synagogue to recite their prayers in unison that they give God the respect that is due Him by concentrating on the liturgy and responding to the need for prayer in their lives. Such devotion requires the maturity of an adult.

At some Jewish ceremonies a *minyan* is highly desirable but not required, if ten men are unavailable. Examples of these are the *brit milah* and the wedding ceremony.

97

AVODAH

עֲבוֹדָה

Service, Work

We have had occasion throughout these pages to note that many Hebrew terms have assumed varying meanings in the changing historical contexts from which they grew. *Avodah* is such a term.

Until the destruction of the Temple in Jerusalem in the year 70 C.E., *Avodah* was the name given to the Temple service conducted by the Priests. Basically, this service consisted in the offering of animal sacrifices. Simon the Just, who was himself a High Priest, referred to the Temple Service – *Avodah* – as one of the three pillars on which the world stands. (We refer to the portion of the Yom Kippur service, which recalls the ancient ritual conducted by the Priests on that day, as the *Avodah.)*

When the Temple was destroyed, animal sacrifices were discontinued. The Temple service was replaced by public worship, known as *avodah shebalev*, the service of the heart. God was to be served differently, but in a way no less effective than was the previous way. In fact, all Israelites, not only the priests, were now granted the privilege of participating in this new *Avodah*.

In the latter half of the nineteenth century, the old word, *avodah*, meaning work or servitude, became the slogan with which Jewish writers in eastern Europe sought to kindle an interest in manual labor – especially in agriculture – which had long been neglected by Russian Jews. *Avodah* would enable Jews to live with dignity, since they would depend on the labor of their own hands, instead of the non-Jew to produce for them. One of the best-known poets of the *Haskalah* (Enlightenment), J. L. Gordon, admonished his fellow Jews:

Every reasonable man should try to win knowledge;
Let others learn all sorts of arts and crafts,
Those who are brave should serve in the army;
Farmers should buy fields and ploughs.

Another writer, Aaron David Gordon, did more than write about labor as a Jewish ideal. In 1904, at the age of 48, he left a desk job in Russia and journeyed to Palestine where he became one of the founders of Degania, the first *kibbutz*. He plowed and planted the land, drained marshes, and built roads. For Gordon, working with one's hands was a religious experience that he called *Dat Haavodah*, "The Religion of Labor." He taught by precept and example that physical labor was the only means by which Jews could reclaim *Eretz Yisrael* and at the same time liberate themselves from their long experience as small merchants and tradesmen.

Gordon (1938) sums up his philosophy in an essay entitled "People and Labor":

> In Palestine we must do with our own hands all the things that make up the sum total of life. We must ourselves do all the work, from the least strenuous, cleanest, and most sophisticated, to the dirtiest and most difficult. In our own way, we must feel what a worker feels and think what a worker thinks – then, and only then, shall we have a culture of our own, for then we shall have a life of our own.

98

BERAKHAH

בְּרָכָה

Benediction:
Prayer of Gratitude or Praise

Tradition requires the Jew to recite a hundred *berakhot* daily. Every time he has occasion to recite the well-known formula *"Barukh Atah Adonai . . ."* he is pronouncing a *berakhah* in which he praises or thanks God for some spiritual or material blessing.

People who think of a *berakhah* as "blessing God" are in error. Man cannot bless God; only God can confer blessing. He has the power to sanctify us by our fulfilling His commandments. The second part of the *berakhah* formula says just that: *"Asher kidshanu bemitzvotav,* Who has sanctified us by His commandments."

Though the formula of every *berakhah* begins in the same way, the functions of the benedictions are varied: for example, we recite an appropriate *berakhah* before partaking of regular pleasurable acts such as eating or drinking. In so doing, one is moved to sense God's kindness continually even as he receives the usual benefits of life that are so often ignored or taken for granted.

Then there are *berakhot* that are recited as one witnesses an awesome or wonderful occurrence, for example, those recited upon hearing thunder, seeing lightning, or coming in contact with an unusually wise person.

In the *Siddur,* most of the *berakhot* are found at the end of a paragraph. The *berakhah* usually summarizes the entire paragraph. This function of the *berakhah* is especially apparent in the Eighteen Benedictions of the *Amidah.*

217

The Jew recites a *berakhah* praising God not merely when his heart is brimming with joy. Even in the presence of death the survivor stands as his garment is cut, and he glorifies God with the *berakhah:* "Praised be Thou, O Lord our God, King of the Universe, who is the true Judge."

99

BERAKHAH LEVATALAH

בְּרָכָה לְבַטָּלָה

A Blessing Made in Vain

Though spontaneous prayer is consistently encouraged in Judaism, care must be taken not to compose one's own blessings. The *berakhot (commencing with the words, Barukh Atah Adonai)* were set by the rabbis centuries ago, and any attempt to add one's own *berakhot* or to recite them without following through with an appropriate act is interpreted as taking God's name in vain.

Examples of blessings made in vain are: reciting the blessing over wine followed by drinking water, which requires a different blessing; reciting the comprehensive blessing over bread at the beginning of the meal followed by blessings over specific foods eaten at the same meal; reciting the same *berakhah* over wine on Saturday morning that should have been recited at the Friday evening *Kiddush*, i.e., *mekadesh haShabbat*. The most common *berakhah levatalah* is committed when one fails to partake of the food or drink after having recited the *berakhah*.

Teachers of the young, however, were assured that they were not trespassing the law if they merely recited a *berakhah* in the process of teaching.

The Sages were so careful to avoid the *berakhah levatalah* that they introduced new customs to comply with the law. For example, the custom of gazing at the finger nails after the blessing over the *havdalah* candle was introduced to accompany that blessing with a tangible act. Likewise, the custom of eating a new fruit on the second night of Rosh Hashanah was instituted to relieve any doubt that the blessing of *Sheheheyanu* ("Who has

219

kept us in life") may be said on the second evening as well as the first.

The *berakhah* is not to be understood as a magical formula that, if recited incorrectly or without an accompanying act, incurs God's wrath. Concern for such detail was stressed to encourage an attitude of reverence for God and the utterance of His name. In a popular sense, a *berakhah levatalah* is applied to any task that has little chance of turning out successfully—all the effort put into it will be expended in vain.

100

KAVVANAH

כַּוָּנָה

Concentration, Devotion

Like so many other Hebraic terms, *kavvanah* cannot be translated exactly into English. It implies concentration, inner devotion, single-mindedness. The rabbis discuss at great length whether a commandment requires concentration during its performance, and they finally conclude that a *mitzvah* does require *kavvanah*. One does not fulfill his obligations merely by routine performance.

Especially in discussing prayer does the question of *kavvanah* arise. Despite the fact that concentration is not always possible when one recites the conventional prayers regularly, *kavvanah* is nevertheless emphasized as a goal that the worshiper aspires to. Without concentration we cheapen the value of prayer, we reduce it to a magical formula, hoping that the mere mouthing of proper words will force a reaction from God. "Prayer without *kavvanah* is like a body without a soul."

It is not generally known that the Jewish tradition encourages spontaneous prayer in addition to the set prayers. To recite only the prescribed prayers is regarded as *tefillat keva*—routine prayer. Individual prayers composed by the worshiper help him to experience more devotion, since he must search for the proper word and articulate what he feels inside rather than glibly repeat what he may have committed to memory. Individual prayers may either be included in the *Amidah* (Silent Devotion) or completely new prayers may be recited, as was the practice throughout Jewish history. The *Selihot*, penitential prayers that we recite on the High Holy Days, were individually composed and eventually incorporated into the liturgy because of their profound religious fervor.

The only restriction set by the Sages is that a spontaneous prayer should not be recited in the form of a *berakhah*. New prayers should be kept distinct from permanent or "official" prayers that all Jews recite together, such as the *berakhot* found in the *Amidah*.

101

HITLAHAVUT

הִתְלַהֲבוּת

Enthusiasm

Derived from the verb meaning "to kindle," the expression *hitlahavut* was coined by the followers of the Baal Shem Tov, the founder of the Hasidic movement in the eighteenth century. The Hasidim considered enthusiasm in prayer or in performance of any religious act as a great virtue. *Hitlahavut* is more active than the rabbinic expression *kavvanah*, inner devotion, though both expressions are intended to discourage the mechanical and life-less performance of a religious duty. *Hitlahavut* is responsible for the spontaneous chant, the vigorous swaying in prayer that has been so characteristic of Hasidic Jews. Almost unmindful of the world around him when engaged in religious activity, the enthusiast musters all his energies to concentrate on the *mitzvah* before him.

His religious enthusiasm springs primarily from love of God. Fear of God does not produce the same enthusiasm, the same intense desire to rush toward the performance of a religious act. Nor is he motivated by hope of reward for the act that he is performing. His reward has already been given to him—the opportunity and privilege of fulfilling the *mitzvah* that he does not take for granted. Said the Baal Shem Tov: "The first time a thing occurs in nature, it is called a miracle; later it becomes natural, and no attention is paid to it. Let your worship and your service be a fresh miracle every day to you. Only such worship, performed from the heart with enthusiasm, is acceptable."

One does not have to understand all the principles of Ha-sidism to appreciate the value of religious enthusiasm. To approach prayer in the spirit of anticipating a new insight and a new message can generate *hitlahavut.* True, the liturgy is the same, but the worshiper has changed each time he recites the service anew.

Abraham Heschel (1954) describes with unusual sensitivity this lack of anticipation and excitement in the modern synagogue:

> Services are conducted with dignity and precision. The rendition of the liturgy is smooth. Everything is present: decorum, voice, ceremony. But one thing is missing: *Life.* One knows in advance what will ensue. There will be no surprise, no adventure of the soul; there will be no sudden outburst of devotion. Nothing is going to happen to the soul. Nothing unpredictable must happen to the person who prays. He will attain no insight into the words he reads; he will attain no new perspective for the life he lives. Our motto is monotony. The fire has gone out of worship. It is cold, stiff, dead. . . . [p. 49]

102

ALIYAH

עֲלִיָּה

Going Up

The privilege of being called to recite the blessings before and after the Torah reading is known as an *aliyah,* because the worshiper ascends from the congregation to the reader's desk. He also experiences a spiritual ascent as he draws near to the Torah scroll.

One may be honored with an *aliyah* any time that the Torah is read. There needn't be any special occasion in order to be "called up." However, there are times when the Jew regards it a duty to request an *aliyah.* These occasions are:

1. The Sabbath before one's marriage.
2. The Sabbath after the birth of a girl at which time she is given a Hebrew name. (The boy is named at the *brit milah* ceremony on the eighth day.)
3. On the Sabbath of a *Bar Mitzvah;* both son and father are given an *aliyah.*
4. During the illness of a dear one.
5. On recovering from serious illness.
6. On the *Yahrzeit* (anniversary of death) of a close relative.
7. On returning from a long trip, usually overseas.

None of these occasions require an *aliyah* on the Sabbath. It may be offered to the worshiper any time that the Torah is read, such as a Monday or Thursday morning.

In the Torah the Hebrew migration from Egypt in the south

to Canaan was described as "going up." In more modern times
aliyah is used to denote immigration to Israel from any part of
the world regardless of geographical location. It is the spiritually
uplifting effect of voluntary immigration in particular that gives
special cogency to the term *aliyah*.

103

SIDDUR

סִדּוּר

Prayer Book

The *Siddur*, meaning order of prayers, contains the liturgy for daily, Sabbath, and holiday worship. It is arranged according to the frequency with which the prayers are recited–the daily service appearing at the beginning of the book followed by the Sabbath, Festival, and High Holy Day prayers.

The *Siddur* we use contains prayers that are as ancient as the Bible. The *Shema* and the Psalms, for example, are taken from the Bible. Other prayers, such as the *Lekha Dodi* recited on Friday evening, are of much more recent date, having been composed during the many centuries in which the Jews were in exile. Through those centuries many changes occurred in the prayer book. Some material was eliminated, and because of changing needs, new material was added.

The first complete *Siddur* known to us was drawn up in the ninth century by Rabbi Amram, the rector of the great Academy of Sura in Babylonia. He set down the texts of the required prayers for every occasion and laid down the rules of synagogue and home worship. His text won acceptance among the Sephardic Jews who resided in Spain, North Africa, and Egypt. The Ashkenazic liturgy for most Jews living in England, France, North America and South America was set down by Simha ben Samuel of Vitry, France, in the twelfth century.

The *Siddur* has been more familiar to the average Jew than the Holy Scriptures. It has been the daily companion of the Jew who would use it not merely at the synagogue services, but also in the home. More than any other book, the *Siddur* reflects the basic ideas of Judaism; it mirrors more completely the various moods of the Jewish people, ranging from depression and fear to the dazzling heights of ecstasy and joy.

The *Siddur* is frequently studied as a book of instruction demonstrating how our ancestors composed their prayers when they were moved by the Presence of God. The text also serves to teach us how to capture their prayerful mood. Thus, as we recite these set prayers we are motivated to interpret them in the light of our own religious experiences and needs.

104

KERIAT SHEMA

קְרִיאַת שְׁמַע

The Reading of the Shema Section

The *Shema* sometimes refers to the single verse (Hear O Israel . . .), but more often it includes the three sections following the *Shema Yisrael*. Whenever the *Shema* is recited in the synagogue, one senses that he has reached a climax in the service.

First, the familiarity with the *Shema* permits all the worshipers to participate especially in this prayer. It is the first prayer that a child is taught in the home long before he attends religious school.

Second, the *Shema* is given added prestige because it is possibly the oldest prayer in the *Siddur*. The first paragraph is found in the sixth chapter of Deuteronomy. The following two sections are from the Bible (Deuteronomy 11 and Numbers 15). Third, the contents of the *Shema* deal with some of the most essential principles of Judaism:

The uniqueness of God. God is not only One but unique in every way; no human being is comparable to God in capacity or degree of perfection. The modern translation of the Torah published by the Jewish Publication Society translates *ehad* as "alone" to emphasize God's uniqueness.

Accepting God's majesty. In the second verse immediately after the *Shema Yisrael* we recite in an undertone (except on Yom Kippur) the phrase: "Blessed be His sovereign glory for ever and ever." Though this verse is not found in the Bible, its meaning has assumed major importance in Jewish thought. The Jew is prepared to affirm *Malkhut Shamayim*, the Kingship of God, over the entire world. With these words every Jew expresses his acceptance of a world ruled by God.

229

The love of God. "You shall love the Lord your God with all your heart, with all your soul, and with all your might." This verse affirms that *Ahavat Hashem,* love for God, is one of the first principles of Judaism. If it is true that many religions originated in fear of the unknown, Judaism, at a very early stage in its development, saw the greater good in loving God.

Study of Torah. We express our love for God through continuous study of the Torah from early morning to late evening, and no matter where we may be, at home or abroad. *Talmud Torah* is not only the requirement to study but to teach our children what we have learned.

Reward and Punishment. In the second paragraph of the *Shema,* we affirm that there is a direct relationship between goodness and prosperity, evil conduct and deprivation. We assert that despite the apparent contradictions, justice does operate in God's world.

Mitzvah. Three ritual commandments, *mezuzzah, tefillin, tzitzit,* are here required to be observed to remind us through visual aids of our moral responsibilities.

105

AMIDAH

עֲמִידָה

The Standing Prayer

Each of the three daily services is highlighted by the silent *Amidah*, so called because the worshiper remains standing throughout its recitation. It is also called *Shemoneh Esrei*, the Eighteen, because it originally contained eighteen benedictions, and though a nineteenth was eventually added, the old title has been retained. The *Amidah* is also known by the name *Hatefillah*, *The Prayer*, because of its importance in the service.

The *Amidah* was originally formulated by The Men of the Great Assembly in the early period of the Second Temple but was given final form after its destruction when the nineteenth blessing, directed against heretics, was added.

The structure of the *Amidah* is based on the principle that praise of God must precede prayers of request. Thus the first three blessings *(berakhot)* contain praises of God followed by requests for knowledge, forgiveness, health, etc. The last three blessings contain a request for the restoration of Zion, an expression of gratitude for our daily existence, and a prayer for peace.

In the morning and afternoon service, the *Amidah* is repeated by the leader, originally for the sake of those who could not read the *Amidah* themselves. The repetition of the Amidah contains a few additions: the *Kedushah* (Holiness Prayer), which is recited by the leader and congregation, and the Priestly Blessing. On special occasions such as *Rosh Hodesh* (new month), Hanukkah, Purim, and fast days, other prayers are added by the worshiper and then repeated aloud by the leader.

On Sabbath and Festivals, the *Amidah* consists of only

seven blessings. The first and last three are similar to those
recited in the daily *Amidah*, but in place of the thirteen middle
blessings of petition, only one blessing is inserted that recalls the
special sanctity of that Sabbath or Festival *(Kedushat Hayom)*.

106

BIRKAT KOHANIM

בִּרְכַּת כֹּהֲנִים

The Priestly Blessing

In the Book of Numbers, God charges Moses to teach Aaron and his sons the Priestly Blessing:

The Lord bless you and keep you;
The Lord make His face to shine upon you and be gracious
    unto you;
The Lord lift up His countenance upon you and grant you
    peace.

The *Kohanim* recited this ancient formula not in their own names but in the name of God. The blessing cannot be bestowed by man but only by God, the source of all blessing. The Priests could merely invoke God and call upon Him to bless the people of Israel.

The *Birkat Kohanim* was an impressive feature of the ancient Temple service. It was recited twice daily – in the morning and afternoon. The Levites who ministered to the needs of the Temple cleansed the Priests before they delivered the blessing. The Priests would then ascend a special platform called *Dukhan* with heads covered, arms outstretched, and fingers spread as they chanted the blessing.

After the destruction of the Temple, the descendants of the priests continued to recite the blessing as part of the daily synagogue service. In time, however, the custom was dropped everywhere except in Israel, where, to this day, the *Kohanim* still deliver the *Birkat Kohanim* every day. In the Diaspora, the leader of the service merely reads this blessing when repeating the *Amidah*. On festivals, however, the *Kohanim* continue in

233

many synagogues outside Israel to chant the Priestly Blessing in the same manner as their ancient ancestors.

The *Birkat Kohanim* is comprised of fifteen words in the Hebrew text. The first phrase contains three words; the second, five words; the third, seven words. It ascends by gradual stages from a petition for material blessings, to seeking divine favor in the form of a spiritual blessing, and climaxes in a petition for God's most consummate gift, *shalom*, meaning peace.

The *Birkat Kohanim* gave rise to a few very interesting customs:

The *Dukhan* or platform upon which the ancient priests stood developed into the word *Dukhanin*, which is a popular expression for *Birkat Kohanim*.

Rabbinic custom forbade the layman from gazing upon the *Kohanim* as they pronounced their blessings. This has given rise to the widespread practice among Jews and non-Jews to stand with bowed heads whenever a benediction is recited by a rabbi or minister.

The *Birkat Kohanim* is the best-known benediction in the Bible. On Sabbath eve fathers have invoked God's blessing on their children with these words for many generations. The blessing is frequently recited at the conclusion of a service, at *Bar Mitzvahs*, and weddings. It has also been adopted by Catholics and Protestants throughout the world.

107

BIRKAT HAMAZON

בִּרְכַּת הַמָּזוֹן

Grace after Meals

Just as the Jew is bidden to recite a blessing before partaking of food, so is he required to praise God after he has been
satisfied. In fact, it is more praiseworthy to remember God's
goodness after a meal when he is more prone to forget the source
of his nourishment.

The *mitzvah* of reciting the Grace after Meals is cited from
the Torah, though the present form of the prayer was formulated
throughout many centuries. The Mishnah derives the requirement to say Grace from the verse in Deuteronomy that reads,
"When you have eaten and are satisfied, you shall *bless* the Lord
your God . . ." (Deut. 8:10).

We believe that the four *berakhot* in the Grace after Meals
were added in crucial eras of Jewish history. The first blessing of
gratitude for food was instituted by Moses. When the land was
conquered under Joshua, the second blessing for the land was
inserted. In the days of King David mention was made of Jerusalem and the Temple, and after the destruction of the Temple
the third blessing for the rebuilding of Zion was added.

A fourth benediction was included after the rebellion of Bar
Kochba was suppressed by the Romans in 137 c.e. Though hope
for an independent state was finally destroyed, the fourth
blessing was introduced to affirm faith in God's kindness and love
in spite of Israel's final defeat at the hands of the Romans.

Besides the more recent additions to the Grace there are
other prayers that are inserted on special occasions: The *Al
Hanissim* on Hanukkah and Purim; the *Yaale Veyavo* at the

235

beginning of the new month and on Festivals, the *Retzeh* on the Sabbath, etc.

An ancient introduction to the Grace is recited only if there are three or more males present at the table. Usually, ten persons comprise a congregation, but at the table three is a sufficient number to be transformed into a small congregation. The host or an appointed guest calls upon the other participants to join him in the Grace; the others respond by asking that God's name be blessed forever.

108

ALENU

עָלֵינוּ

Concluding Prayer

The *Alenu*, with which each service is concluded, was orig-inally recited exclusively on Rosh Hashanah; by the fourteenth century it was added to the end of every daily, Sabbath, and holiday service. The famous third-century talmudist, Rav, is credited with the authorship of this prayer, which proclaims God as King over Israel and Supreme Ruler of the whole universe.

The *Alenu* was often attacked as an anti-Christian prayer. One sentence in particular was subjected to slanderous accusa-tion: "For they bow down to vanity and emptiness and pray to a God that does not save." In 1703 the Prussian government issued an edict forbidding the recitation of this passage, and ordered that the *Alenu* be recited aloud so that special officers who were commissioned to visit the synagogue would see that the edict was observed. To this day the controversial verse is deleted from the *Alenu*. Actually it is highly doubtful that Rav was directing these words against Christianity since he lived most of his life in Babylonia where there were almost no Christians. Furthermore, Rav chose his words from the prophet Isaiah who lived long before the birth of Christianity.

The *Alenu* was described by Solomon Schechter as the "Marseillaise" of the Jewish people. Like the *Shema*, it became a declaration of faith in the one God. Martyrs in the Middle Ages recited the *Alenu* as they willingly prepared to give up their lives for *Kiddush Hashem*, sanctification of God's name.

On Rosh Hashanah and Yom Kippur when the *hazzan* recites the *Alenu* in the *Musaf* service, he kneels to the floor as he sings, "We bend the knee and prostrate ourselves before the King of Kings." In the very traditional synagogues some of the worshipers also fall to the floor at this point of the service. At all other times when the *Alenu* is recited, the *hazzan* and congregation merely bend the knee and bow before the ark, since kneeling was generally abolished among Jews after it became a Christian practice.

The two paragraphs of the *Alenu* appear to be contradictory at first sight. In the first section, the worshiper praises God for having made the Jews unlike the other people of the earth. The second section expresses the hope that the world will be perfected under God and all men will recognize His kingship. Actually, both ideals – the national and universal – are found together in Jewish thought. The prophets were in love with their people, and yet believed in the one God of all mankind.

Some people find it difficult to accept both ideals simultaneously. They will either express loyalty to a particular group and ignore the needs of mankind, or they declare themselves citizens of the world and ignore the needs of their particular group.

The *Alenu* teaches that love for humanity commences with loving concern for one's own people. Otherwise, our love for mankind becomes an abstraction, confusing and meaningless.

109

KADDISH

קַדִּישׁ

A Prayer in Which God's Name Is Sanctified

One of the best-known but least understood prayers is the *Kaddish*, which is always recited in the presence of a congregation *(minyan)*. Like most other acts of *Kiddush Hashem* that are demonstrated publicly, the *Kaddish* is another way, namely through prayer, to proclaim His presence and His influence in the world.

The language of the *Kaddish* is Aramaic, which was spoken extensively by Jews throughout the Middle East in rabbinic times. After a study session it was customary for the lecturer to complete his discourse with the *Kaddish*, in the same language as he conducted the class.

Eventually the end of the synagogue service was also marked by the recitation of the *Kaddish*, slightly different from the Scholar's *Kaddish* marking the end of the lecture. In the course of time, a short *Kaddish* prayer was added at the close of each section of the liturgy and came to be known as half-*Kaddish*.

The recitation of *Kaddish* by the mourner developed at a relatively late date, most probably during the Middle Ages. We do not know exactly how this association came about, but it has been suggested that the son would attend the House of Study after his father's death to honor his memory by taking an active part in the discussion. After the discussion he would be privileged to recite the closing Scholar's *Kaddish*. In the course of time this custom of studying Torah in honor of the deceased was practiced with less regularity and only the *Kaddish* was retained as a mark of respect for the dead. A shortened form of the original Scholar's *Kaddish* came to be known as the Mourner's *Kaddish*, though no mention of death is to be found in it.

The congregational response during the *Kaddish (yehei shemei rabbah mevorakh . . .)* constitutes the oldest part of the *Kaddish*. During the days of the First Temple the congregation would respond with a similar formula in Hebrew when they would hear the priests pronounce the Name of God. The congregation was in effect reaffirming their faith in God's greatness when they heard His name pronounced.

These are the various forms of *Kaddish* that are still recited today: (1) *Kaddish di-Rabbanan*, Scholar's *Kaddish*, recited upon completion of a study session; (2) *Kaddish Shalem*, full *Kaddish*, recited at the close of a major part of the service; (3) Half *Kaddish*, short *Kaddish*, separating one service from another; (4) Burial *Kaddish*, recited by the mourners at the cemetery, immediately after the coffin has been lowered to the grave; (5) Mourner's *Kaddish*, recited by the mourners, during the first eleven months, and at every Yahrzeit.

110

YIGDAL

יִגְדַּל

"May He Be Magnified"–Opening or Closing Hymn

Although it is customary to chant the *Yigdal* at the end of the service, it appears in the beginning of the prayer book with the *Adon Olam*. Originally the *Yigdal* was recited only at the commencement of the service, but it gradually became a popular closing hymn. Scholars attribute the authorship of this medieval poem to an Italian Jew, Daniel ben Judah Dayyan of the fourteenth century.

The author adapted to poetry the Thirteen Principles of Faith, known popularly as *Ani Maamin* (I Believe), which were formulated by Moses Maimonides in his commentary to the *Mishnah Sanhedrin*. Each of the principles begins with the words, "I believe with a perfect faith . . ." These principles can be summarized as follows:

1. God is the Creator and guides all creation.
2. God is one and unique. He alone is our God.
3. God is incorporeal. He has no form whatsoever.
4. God is the first and the last.
5. God only and no one else is worthy of our prayers.
6. All the words of His prophets are true.
7. Moses was the greatest of the prophets.
8. Our Torah is the same given to Moses.
9. The Torah will not be changed nor will another Torah be given by God.
10. God is aware of all human deeds and thoughts.

11. God rewards the righteous and punishes those who trans-
    gress His commandments.
12. The Messiah, although he may tarry, will eventually arrive.
13. The dead will be resurrected when God wills it.

It is questionable whether Maimonides ever intended to
make dogmas of these articles of faith. Otherwise he would have
given them a more prominent place in his writings or, at least,
would have referred to them a second time. He never referred to
them again after they were originally written in the commentary
to the Mishnah.

Nevertheless, he was criticized by his contemporaries and
successors even for attempting to require acceptance of these
thirteen articles of faith. It was felt that Maimonides was imitating the non-Jewish scholars in formulating a creed.

We should, however, understand the historical circumstances that impelled Maimonides to develop this creed for Jews.
It was the twelfth century, a critical era for Jews and Judaism.
Moslems were appealing to Jews to join their ranks. Christians
were seeking Jewish converts. Both religions were claiming that
they proclaimed the "truth." The more fanatical Moslems and
Christians did not seek to entice the Jews by persuasion. They
offered them limited alternatives—exile, conversion, or the
sword. Jews were confused. They were curious to know precisely
and clearly what Judaism stood for and what doctrines a Jew
must be required to follow. The *Ani Maamin* was a precise
answer to their crucial question: He who earnestly believes these
thirteen principles is an Israelite. The people then knew that
they had an understandable and specific doctrine to believe and
follow.

111

ADON OLAM

אֲדוֹן עוֹלָם

"Lord of the Universe" – Hymn

Like the *Yigdal, Adon Olam* is found at the very beginning of the morning service, but it gradually became a well-known closing hymn. It is customary among the pious to recite the *Adon Olam* before retiring, since the closing words allude to the sleep of the faithful:

My soul I give unto His care,
Asleep, awake, for He is near,
And with my soul, my body, too;
God is with me, I have no fear.

Time and again Jewish liturgy refers to God's remoteness and His nearness. God is King and Father. God is exalted and yet near. He is unapproachable and yet intimately involved in the lives of men. The *Adon Olam* deals with this very theme of God's immanence and His transcendence.

The first two stanzas describe God's timelessness, His eternity. Before the creation of the world, before time itself was created, God existed. After the world will cease to exist, the Timeless One will continue to live on. The prophet Isaiah (55:6) also referred to God's eternity:

I am the first, and I am the last,
And beside Me there is no God.

The third stanza refers to another attribute of God, His uniqueness:

Incomparable, unique is He
No other can His Oneness share.

The medieval Jewish philosophers emphasize this attribute of God above all others. Maimonides asserts that the uniqueness of God, His incomparability to anything or anybody, is *the* essential quality of God. God's uniqueness makes it possible for us to speak of His timelessness, His eternity. Otherwise, we would measure God by human standards and since no living thing is eternal, we would conclude that God is also limited to a beginning and end. But since God is unique, He alone is eternal, independent of time.

The anonymous author of the hymn then switches in the fourth stanza from the philosophical God to the intimate God. He is *my* living God, *my* Rock, *my* Banner, *my* Refuge, *my* bounteous Portion. Although He is eternal and transcendent, He is near to man to protect and deliver him in time of trouble. Though He is impersonal, He is also concerned with the needs of His creatures and is moved by their faith and prayers. Judaism has long realized that these two descriptions of God as personal and impersonal represent a paradox. Yet, an effective religion requires both elements: an appeal to our emotions *and* our reason, so beautifully synthesized in the *Adon Olam*.

112

MAHZOR

מַחֲזוֹר

High Holy Day Prayer Book
(literally: Cycle)

It is not generally known that the traditional *Siddur* contains the basic prayers for the High Holy Days, excepting only the liturgical poems *(piyyutim)*. Nor do we usually speak of the *Mahzor* in connection with the three major festivals. But in reality, each of the five holidays mentioned in the Bible (Pesah, Shavuot, Sukkot, Rosh Hashanah, and Yom Kippur) has its individual *Mahzor* containing all the basic prayers, Torah readings, and liturgical poems that are recited on those days. The most widely known and most elaborate are the *Mahzorim* for Rosh Hashanah and Yom Kippur, frequently found in one volume.

The basic structure of the *Mahzor* is similar to the *Siddur*, but with more elaboration. The four services recited every Sabbath—*Maariv, Shaharit, Musaf,* and *Minhah*—are also recited on the High Holy Days. The only additional service found in the *Mahzor* is the *Neilah*, which is recited at the conclusion of Yom Kippur.

The difference between the *Siddur* and *Mahzor* lies primarily in the many liturgical poems included in the latter, some of which were created in the early centuries of the Common Era in Palestine. Most of these *piyyutim*, however, were composed and introduced during the Medieval Age by Jews residing in Spain, Italy, France, Germany, and eastern Europe. They often reflect the conditions of Jewish life at the time of their composition. In fact, they yield a great deal of historical data that would otherwise have remained unknown to us.

So humble were the composers of these religious poems that to this very day scholars have not been able to determine who wrote many of them. In some cases, however, the letters of the author's name have been artistically woven into the poem. Sometimes the style of the poet reveals his identity. Prior to the composition of these hundreds of poems, it is well known that the two men mainly responsible for the development of the *Mahzor* were the third-century scholars, Rav and Samuel. Rav is credited with having composed the three sections of the *Musaf* recited on Rosh Hashanah and Yom Kippur, called *Malkhuyot, Zikhronot,* and *Shofarot*—including the well-known *Alenu* prayer. Samuel is known to have composed the confessional prayers that are repeated at each of the five services on Yom Kippur.

113

KOL NIDRE

כָּל נִדְרֵי

All Vows

A central feature of the Yom Kippur service is the recitation of *Kol Nidre*, which curiously is not part of the service, nor even a prayer. Technically it is a legal document recited in Aramaic, consisting of a declaration that all vows, promises, and oaths made by any member of the congregation during the next year shall be made null and void if they are not fulfilled.

The *hazzan* and two men who hold the Torah scrolls during the chanting of *Kol Nidre* recall the ancient court consisting of three men before whom one would appear if he sought to have his vows annulled. The *Kol Nidre* is recited three times since this was the practice with all legal formulae. The recitation takes place immediately before Yom Kippur commences, since the court procedure could not be conducted on a holiday.

The Torah is very explicit about the importance of keeping one's vows. "If a man makes a vow unto the Lord or swears an oath to bind his soul with a bond, he shall not break his word. He shall do according to all that proceeds out of his mouth." However, the tradition is conscious of the frailty of human nature, which often prompts a man to make a promise or swear in haste without premeditation. He was therefore granted the privilege of absolving his vows under special circumstances set forth in the Talmud.

Some Jewish scholars strongly objected to the *Kol Nidre*, since they feared that people would take their vows lightly, knowing that they could be annulled on Yom Kippur. Nevertheless, by the end of the tenth century the practice took hold in many European communities. Its prevalence was due to the persecutions and discriminations that frequently impelled people to take vows under stress. The *Kol Nidre* held special meaning for Jews who were compelled to vow loyalty to Christianity during the Spanish Inquisition (1391–1492). They came secretly to the synagogue on Yom Kippur to ask that their vows taken under duress be absolved, or to ask God's forgiveness for not yet returning to the Jewish faith despite their vows to do so.

It is understood that on Yom Kippur annulment is valid primarily in cases of vows made between man and God, such as the resolution to undergo a form of self-discipline. No annulment can be made for vows made to another person, or to a court, or to the government. Similarly, vows involving a pledge to the community cannot be annulled.

The content of the *Kol Nidre* does not hold the same appeal that it did during the Middle Ages, but the melody in which it is chanted continues to fill the worshiper with a feeling of solemnity and awe. The traditional melody, which is traced to the sixteenth century, absorbed into it the anguish of Jewish suffering and martyrdom. The *Kol Nidre* is first sung in a low and soft voice, and the volume is increased with each repetition.

114

VIDDUI

וִדּוּי

Confessional

Confessing one's sins is erroneously associated exclusively with Yom Kippur, but the Talmud records the opinion of Rav, who asserted that on weekdays, too, one may recite personal petitions after the *Amidah* even if they are as long as the order of the *Viddui* of Yom Kippur. Maimonides, in the *Mishnah Torah*, cites other occasions when confession is required: "He who bodily injured his neighbor or hurt him in money matters, though he made restitution for what he owed him, has not atoned until he confessed and determined never to repeat the offense."

The Confession of the Dying is prescribed in the Code of Jewish Law. The dying Jew deems it a solemn duty to recite the Yom Kippur Confessional in the singular if he possesses the consciousness and strength to do so. He concludes his confession with the *Shema Yisrael*.

The Confessional is recited in the *Amidah* at each of the five services on Yom Kippur and is repeated a second time by the *hazzan* and congregation at each of these services. The first part of the Confessional, *Ashamnu* ("We have trespassed"), deals with twenty-five general types of transgressions for which people are morally responsible: We lie, we provoke, we rebel, we counsel evil, etc. The second section, *Al Het* ("For the sin we have committed before Thee"), deals with more specific sins between man and man: "For the sin we have committed before Thee by bribery." "For the sin we have committed before Thee in commerce." "For the sin we have committed before Thee by idle gossip."

249

We note certain distinguishing features about the Yom Kippur Confessional. First, each transgression is recited in the first person plural. Even where the worshiper may not have committed a specific sin mentioned in the Confessional, nevertheless, he is prepared to assume responsibility for the moral state of the community. The sins of omission are often as grave as the sins of commission. Secondly, the Confessional does not deal with violations of ritual. The desecration of Sabbaths and Festivals are categorized by the Talmud as "sins between man and God." Only the sins between man and man are here detailed. It is more difficult to break with moral infractions against God. Arrogance and pride militate against confessing moral wrongs. Man can find many reasons to justify immoral behavior against his neighbor. It takes years to break with unwholesome habits we are conditioned to accept as normal behavior. Perhaps God has greater patience with those who have failed to appreciate the beauty of ritual than those who brazenly ignore the laws of morality. The recognition of moral failing is urgent. The need for repentance through confession is immediate.

115

NEILAH

נְעִילָה

Concluding Service on Yom Kippur
(literally: Closing)

The final dramatic service on Yom Kippur is called *Neilah*, either to recall the Temple gates that were usually closed at the end of the day or the Gates of Heaven, said to be closing, thus reminding the worshipers to seek God's forgiveness while there was yet time. One of the most moving prayers of the *Neilah* service refers to this allegorical interpretation of the closing of the gates:

> *Open for us the gate*
> *At the time of the gate's closing.*
> *The day is done,*
> *The sun is setting, soon to be gone,*
> *Let us enter Your gates.*

There are several distinguishing features about the last service that help to create an aura of special urgency and solemnity. In many synagogues the ark remains open and the worshipers stand during the entire service; the *Kaddish* introducing the Silent Devotion is especially moving and is frequently intoned by congregation and Cantor; the congregation requests for the first time that they be *sealed* in the Book of Life instead of the usual petition during the High Holy Days to be *inscribed* in the Book of Life. At the conclusion of the service the Cantor and congregation chant the Three Professions of Faith—the *Shema* (once), the phrase, "Blessed be the Name of His Kingdom forever and ever" (three times), and "The Lord, He is God" (seven times).

251

Finally, the *shofar* is blown reminding the worshipers that the Day of Atonement is concluded and that they may return to their homes and break their fast.

The *Neilah* service has inspired many creative men to write about its transforming effect upon them. Aimé Pallière, a French Catholic theological student, visited a synagogue for the first time during *Neilah*. His impressions of the service and congregation in prayer were so indelible that he was motivated to study Judaism, eventually leading to his conversion. His reflections are vividly described in *The Unknown Sanctuary* (1928).

Israel Zangwill (1892) describes the effect of the *Neilah* upon his heroine Esther:

> Suddenly there fell a vast silence. . . . It was as if all creation paused to hear a pregnant word.
>
> 'Hear, O Israel, the Lord our God, the Lord is One!" said the cantor frenziedly.
>
> And all the ghostly congregation answered with a great cry, 'Hear, O Israel, the Lord our God, the Lord is One!'
>
> They seemed like a great army of sheeted dead risen to testify to the Unity. The magnetic tremor that ran through the synagogue thrilled the lonely girl to the core, and from her lips came in rapturous surrender to an over-mastering impulse the half-hysterical protestation:
>
> 'Hear, O Israel, the Lord our God, the Lord is One!'
>
> . . . The roar (of the congregation) dwindled to a solemn silence. Then the ram's horn shrilled—a stern long-drawn-out note, that rose at last into a mighty peal of sacred jubilation. The Atonement was complete. [p. 542–546]

Part X

SABBATH AND FESTIVALS

116

LUAH

לוּחַ

Jewish Calendar (literally: Tablet)

The Jewish calendar, which has not been altered since the fourth century when it was written down, is a product of great genius. Unlike the civil calendar, which is based on the revolution of the earth around the sun, the Jewish calendar is based on a lunar year, the months corresponding with the time it takes the moon to make a complete revolution around the earth. Since it takes 365¼ days for the earth to travel around the sun, the twelve civil months consist of thirty or thirty–one days, totaling one entire revolution of the earth. Since it takes the moon about twenty-nine and a half days to revolve around the earth, each Hebrew month consists of twenty-nine or thirty days, totaling 354 days.

Obviously something had to be done to compensate for those extra days of the solar year; otherwise the Jewish holidays would be observed out of season. Passover, for example, would slip back about eleven days. After ten years it would slip back one hundred and ten days and would take place in January. It is most important that Passover arrive in the spring, for the Bible requires that it be celebrated at that time. In order to solve this problem, an additional month, called second Adar, was added to the Jewish calendar seven times in nineteen years.

The *luah* that is displayed in many synagogues contains much more information than the dates on which holidays and other significant events occur. One may find in detail all the prayers that are recited or omitted in the synagogue throughout the year; the ritual observances connected with the Sabbath and

255

holidays are described; the Torah readings are given for every occasion.

The following table lists the Jewish holidays, their Hebrew dates, and the months in which they occur on the civil calendar:

Hebrew month and day	Holiday	Month in civil calendar
Tishri		
1–2	Rosh Hashanah	September or October
3	Fast of Gedaliah	September or October
10	Yom Kippur	September or October
15–16	Sukkot (first days)	October
22–23	Shemini Atzeret Simhat Torah	October
Kislev		
25	Hanukkah (first day)	December
Tevet		
2	Hanukkah (last day)	December
10	Asarah Betevet (fast)	December or January
Shevat		
15	Tu Bishevat	January or February
Adar (AdarII)		
14	Purim	February or March
Nisan		
15–22	Pesah	March or April
Iyyar		
18	Lag Baomer	May
Sivan		
6–7	Shavuot	May or June
Tammuz		
17	Shivah Asar Betammuz (fast)	July
Av		
9	Tishah B'av (fast)	July orAugust

117

SHABBAT KODESH

שַׁבָּת קֹדֶשׁ

Holy Sabbath

All the major Jewish festivals are regarded as holy days, but holiness is most frequently associated with the Sabbath day. The biblical account of creation sets the official tone for this association: "And on the seventh day, God had finished His work which He had done and He rested on the seventh day from all the work He had done. And God blessed the seventh day and *made it holy* ..." (Genesis 2:2–3). In the fourth commandment man is bidden to hallow the Sabbath day by observing it. Both God and man hallow the Sabbath. This intimate association of the Sabbath with holiness prevails throughout Jewish literature and is implicit even when the two concepts are not mentioned together.

There are many reasons why holiness is ascribed especially to the Sabbath. Among them are: the uniqueness of the day, despite its frequency of occurrence, and the unusual spiritual opportunities that the Sabbath provides to those who choose to honor it.

As to its uniqueness, no holiday with the exception of Yom Kippur (the holiest day of the year) is filled with so many prohibitions. On the Festival of Sukkot, for example, cooking is permitted, but on the Sabbath this, too, is prohibited. And yet, with all the restrictions associated with the Sabbath, it is by no means a solemn day as is Yom Kippur. Voluntary fasting and demonstrations of grief are prohibited. The *shivah* period of mourning is interrupted by the Sabbath. The Eighteen Benedictions containing prayers of confession, repentance, and petition are omitted since the spirit of joy and inner peace must not be

257

curtailed on the Sabbath. Thus, it is the "otherness" of the day, set apart from the rest of the week and the festivals of the year, that invests it with holiness.

Of further significance are the unusual opportunities the Sabbath gives to the individual to experience holiness in his personal life. The Jew is required to live and think in an altogether different dimension this one day of the week. He puts aside his mundane problems and dedicates himself to strengthening his relationships with his God, his family, and his fellow man. By altering his pace of living on the seventh day he permits himself to dine more leisurely and converse more casually with his family. In prayer and song he shows greater awareness of the many blessings—material and spiritual—with which God has favored him.

The rabbis regarded the Sabbath symbolically as a foretaste of the ideal world to come. Just as the Sabbath emphasizes cooperation between man and man, and harmony between man and nature—even a flower or blade of grass may not be uprooted—so in the ideal future a similar spirit of harmony will prevail every day of the week.

118

NESHAMAH YETERAH

נְשָׁמָה יְתֵרָה

Additional Soul

Legend has it that on the Sabbath every Jew is given an additional and more exalted soul that remains with him throughout the day of rest. This higher soul enables the Jew to forget his problems and woes so that he may concentrate on the joy and happiness of the Sabbath.

The legend is probably based on the statement of Simeon ben Lakish in the Talmud: "On Sabbath eve the Holy One, blessed be He, gives man an extra soul. At the conclusion of the Sabbath, this extra soul is taken away from him, as is written in the Scriptures concerning the Sabbath day, *'Shavat Vayinafash':* i.e., as soon as He completed the Sabbath, it is woeful because the soul is gone."

In later centuries this idea was expanded in the mystical writings, such as the *Zohar,* which claims that four angels accompany each individual Sabbath soul into the world. The well-known song *Shalom Aleikhem* employs this theme in which the Jew welcomes the ministering angels at the onset of the Sabbath.

Whether the Jew of the past accepted literally the belief in an oversoul is not really significant. What is significant, however, is that he felt the transformation that overcame him with the advent of the seventh day. His thoughts took on a new dimension. He felt relief from the tensions of the week. He was at one with himself, with his fellow man, and with God. Because he knew from experience how vital this feeling was for his sense of well-being, he began to anticipate it again as soon as the Sabbath was over, and he built up enthusiasm as the week progressed.

The Jew could not visualize the world to come, but he felt instinctively that it was somewhat similar to the inner feeling of serenity that he sensed on the Sabbath day. The Sabbath was a foretaste of the future world, and the soul that possessed him on that day would eventually become a permanent possession.

One symbolic interpretation offered for the smelling of spices at the end of the Sabbath is that in so doing the soul, which has been saddened because of the Sabbath's departure, is cheered and revived with their fragrance.

119

ONEG SHABBAT

עֹנֶג שַׁבָּת

Sabbath Delight

The *Oneg Shabbat* is a gathering, usually in the home or synagogue, in which the participants create a Sabbath atmosphere with song, study, or informal discussion.

The phrase is not a recent addition to the Hebrew language. It is found in the Bible, where the prophet Isaiah urged his fellow Jews to "call the Sabbath a delight." He referred to the joy and cheer pervading the Sabbath and to the unique spiritual or cultural activities of the day.

The *Oneg Shabbat* as an institution, however, is relatively new, coming from twentieth-century Palestine. In fact, it was the first visible spiritual influence to emanate from Palestine and reach a large segment of the American Jewish community before Israel became an independent State. In Palestine working men would gather in their community halls on Saturday afternoon to discuss current problems. These Sabbath assemblies were the secular counterparts of the gatherings of east European Jews in the synagogue to hear a sermon or to study the Bible and Talmud.

The poet Hayyim Nahman Bialik conceived of the idea of the *Oneg Shabbat* as a permanent institution in Palestine. Convinced that tradition had to be strengthened in Palestine, and that the Sabbath was the cornerstone of Judaism, Bialik would convene a group of his readers and admirers in the assembly hall every *Shabbat* afternoon, where he or his invited guests would lead discussions on topics of religious, literary, or sociological interest. After the discussion, the participants would sing appropriate

Sabbath melodies, Hasidic tunes, and modern Hebrew songs. Toward the end of the Sabbath, the group would hear the *havdalah* chanted by a cantor. As the words "The Jews had light and joy, gladness and honor" were intoned, all the lights were suddenly kindled. They then greeted the new week with song.

Many American Jewish tourists attended these *Onegei Shabbat* and found them warm and meaningful. They spoke of their impressions to fellow Jews in America. Eventually, American Jews adopted this new experiment in their respective communities, based on the custom practiced in Tel Aviv.

The *Oneg Shabbat* in America aims at informality and relaxation, stressing group participation, especially in the singing. Appropriate discussions and refreshments enhance the Sabbath atmosphere. Many American synagogues conduct an *Oneg Shabbat* after the service on Friday evening with community singing and a lecture or discussion on a Jewish theme.

120

ZEMIROT

זְמִירוֹת

Sabbath Table Melodies

We assume that the general custom of singing songs around the table dates back to the days of the Second Temple. After the destruction of the Temple, Jews were prohibited from singing aloud or from playing instrumental music, as a sign of national mourning. The Sabbath, however, was an exception. Israel was permitted to welcome the day with joy and song. In the darkest periods of Jewish history, some of the most joyous Sabbath songs were written, in order to lift the morale of a downtrodden people.

In the Middle Ages, when Hebrew poetry began to flourish, poets would compose religious poems and set them to popular secular melodies that the masses loved to sing and hear. Some of these sacred songs were introduced into the home and sung around the table on the Sabbath.

Many of the *zemirot* sung today were composed by Jewish mystics, particularly in the sixteenth century. These mystics deeply felt the power of song in prayer. The heavy-hearted could not feel the same closeness of God in their silence as those who poured out their feelings in song. The very act of singing helped to transform the mood of worshipers from sadness to joy, enabling them to be more receptive to the presence of God. Isaac Luria and his disciples were among the foremost mystics who composed joyous and rhythmic *zemirot* for each of the three Sabbath meals.

The *zemirot* sung around the Sabbath table seldom follow a uniform pattern. Some are in Hebrew; others, such as the *Yah Ribbon*, are in Aramaic. Many melodies, especially those from

Hasidic sources, are songs without words. Guests at the table are encouraged to introduce new *zemirot,* or at least new melodies to old poems that they have learned in their travels. Songs from modern-day Israel are frequently included in the repertoire. Songs are frequently introduced between the courses; others are reserved until after the meal, the selection usually depending on the father of the household.

As a rule different *zemirot* are chosen for Friday evening, Sabbath midday, and the *Shalosh Seudot* (the third Sabbath meal at the end of the day). The selection for each meal has its distinctive character. For the first two meals lively melodies are generally chosen; but for the outgoing of the Sabbath, mystical and solemn melodies are sung in keeping with the spirit of nostalgia for the Sabbath that is about to depart.

One of the best known *zemirot, Tsur Mishelo,* is paraphrased as follows:

OUR ROCK

> *Rock from whose store we have eaten—*
> *Bless Him, my faithful companions.*
> *Eaten have we and left over—*
>   *This was the word of the Lord.*
> *Feeding His world like a shepherd—*
> *Father whose bread we have eaten,*
> *Father whose wine we have drunk,*
> *Now to His name we are singing,*
> *Praising Him loud with our voices,*
> *Saying and singing forever:*
>   *Holy is none like the Lord.*

121

HAVDALAH

הַבְדָּלָה

Ceremony Distinguishing the Sabbath from the Weekday

At the Sabbath's end the observing Jew differentiates between the day of rest and the working days to come by reciting the *havdalah* in the synagogue and at home. He may then resume his business affairs or any other form of work prohibited on the Sabbath.

Three blessings are recited at the *havdalah* ceremony: for wine, for spices, and for light. Then the following blessing, which stresses the *havdalah* theme, is intoned: "Blessed are You, O Lord, our God, King of the Universe, who makes a distinction between holy and profane, between light and darkness, between Israel and the other peoples, between the seventh day and the six days of labor. Blessed are You, O Lord, who distinguishes between the holy and profane."

The use of wine at *havdalah* developed from the usual custom of drinking wine before and after meals. And since the third Sabbath meal was completed immediately before the end of the Sabbath, the custom was incorporated into the special religious ceremony.

Similarly, the use of spices grew from an ordinary custom in ancient times of cleansing the hands after a meal by passing them over heated spices. On the Sabbath this custom was suspended, but since the third meal was completed at the end of the Sabbath, the spices were once again used. Thus, the spices like the wine eventually became associated with the *havdalah* ceremony. The function of spices was also explained symbolically – to cheer the soul that was saddened by the departure of the Sabbath.

The use of candle light in a religious ceremony developed from the custom of bringing light into the room at the end of the Sabbath, since darkness had already set in. Again, an ordinary act was elevated to a religious performance. Others gave a religious explanation for the use of candle light, and say that it reminds us to commemorate the light that God brought into the world at the beginning of the week.

The candlestick is usually made of several combined wicks. The participants gaze at their finger tips as they recite the blessing over light to signify that they are making some use of the light. Not to use the light for a purpose would constitute a *berakhah levatalah* – a useless blessing.

122

MELAVEH MALKAH

מְלַוֶּה מַלְכָּה

Farewell to the Sabbath Queen

The Sabbath has been alternately symbolized as bride and queen, both being objects of love and respect. When the Sabbath departs, the Jew reluctantly bids farewell to the Sabbath Queen by remaining with her as long as possible before she takes leave for another week.

Many traditional Jews hold a Saturday night meal, which is called *Melaveh Malkah*. This custom is not new. It is mentioned in the Talmud, which describes in detail the importance of the special meal. One talmudic Sage states that everyone should have his table set for a Saturday night repast even though little food is eaten. Another source claims that if one cannot eat a regular meal, he should at least eat cake to honor the departing Queen Sabbath.

It is customary to recite at the *Melaveh Malkah*, "This is the meal of King David." According to legend, David was told by God that he would die on the Sabbath. At the conclusion of every Sabbath he would celebrate his having been spared from death. All the people of Israel would participate in the feast of their beloved king. Thus, a link between the *Melaveh Malkah* and King David's feast of gratitude is created.

Many of the songs that are sung on Saturday evening make reference to Elijah the Prophet. In the Jewish tradition, Elijah will announce the coming of the Messiah. Hence, a prayer is intoned on Saturday evening that God send Elijah to announce the redemption of Israel and Messiah's arrival. It is especially appropriate that the song dedicated to Elijah be sung at the close of the Sabbath because of the popular belief that if the Jews throughout the world were to observe only one Sabbath properly, then the Messianic Age would arrive.

In some synagogues the *Melaveh Malkah* has become a public observance with appropriate programs and refreshments, songs and dances that help to revitalize the traditional atmosphere once experienced by the great majority of Jews on Saturday evening.

123

SHABBAT NAHAMU

שַׁבָּת נַחֲמוּ

Sabbath of Comfort

Just as the Sabbath preceding Tishah B'av is known by the opening word of the *Haftarah*, taken from the first chapter of Isaiah—*Hazon*, meaning vision—so the Sabbath following the fast is called by the opening words from the fortieth chapter of Isaiah: "Comfort you, comfort you, My people, says your God; bid Jerusalem take courage." It is thus referred to as *Shabbat Nahamu*, the Sabbath of Comfort. The prophecy from Isaiah prepares the Jewish people for the coming fast by cautioning them of the consequences of forgetting God's moral law. The reading for *Shabbat Nahamu* sounds a note of consolation and encouragement in the bleakest hour of Jewish history, when the Temple was destroyed and Jewish independence lost.

The prophetic reading for *Shabbat Nahamu* is the first of seven consecutive *Haftarot*, all taken from the book of Isaiah, that deal with the theme of consolation. In these prophecies, Isaiah assures his dejected people that all is not lost, their exile is only temporary. Eventually God will restore them to their homeland where they will again experience the joy of national and spiritual redemption.

Although it is generally agreed that Chapters 1 and 40 were produced by different men, it is not at all rare to find a single prophet expressing extremes of anger and compassion, bitterness and love for his people. This was the prophetic approach: to afflict the comfortable and comfort the afflicted. Isaiah was convinced that God would not permit the complete destruction of Israel. God was too intimately involved in their destiny. God was

269

"afflicted in their affliction." Therefore the separation between God and His people is only temporary, but God's love of Israel is eternal.

The Jews never regarded Isaiah merely as a historical personality who spoke to his generation alone. They related his prophecies to themselves and their own predicament. Whatever the tragedies they were enduring, they were, nevertheless, able to gather hope and comfort for the future. The prophet was speaking to them as intimately as to the generation in which he lived. They were certain that the day would arrive when "every valley shall be lifted up, and every mountain and hill shall be made low; and the rugged shall be made level, and the rough places a plain; and the glory of the Lord shall be revealed, and all flesh shall see it together; For the mouth of the Lord has spoken it" (Is. 40:4–5).

124

ROSH HODESH

רֹאשׁ חֹדֶשׁ

New Moon
(literally: Beginning of the Month)

From earliest times, the beginning of the month had special significance for Jews. Before the exile, all work and trade were suspended on *Rosh Hodesh*, as on the Sabbath. The prophets would refer to the Sabbath and the new moon in the same context. The eighth-century B.C.E. prophet Amos quotes the hardened businessmen of his day: "When will the New Moon be over, that we may sell again? And the Sabbath that we may offer corn?"

In time, the New Moon assumed less importance than the Sabbath, and the prohibition against work and commerce was lifted. Although special sacrifices were still offered on *Rosh Hodesh*, it was nevertheless reduced to the rank of a half-holiday. In spite of its secondary importance as a holiday, it had to be accurately fixed so that the festival days occurring during the month could be exactly determined.

During the existence of the Second Temple, the calendar was regulated by the testimony of witnesses. The Sanhedrin, the supreme court in Jerusalem, consisting of seventy-one members, sent witnesses for the specific purpose of observing the first appearance of the new moon. After the witnesses were examined, and their testimony accepted by the court, the judges would hold a special ceremony of announcing the new month. The president of the court would say: "The new month is proclaimed," and all present would repeat, "Proclaimed, proclaimed!"

On that evening, fires were kindled on the highest peak near

Jerusalem to signal nearby villages that *Rosh Hodesh* was officially proclaimed. Then other fires would be set near these villages to notify those in more distant settlements. Thus the news was carried to all the residents of Palestine. Even the Jews of Babylonia were informed by relays of torches and bonfires. The following day was celebrated as *Rosh Hodesh*, the beginning of the month.

Commencing in the middle of the fourth century C.E., scientific rules for the computation of the calendar were published by Hillel II. From that era on, it was possible to determine the exact time of *Rosh Hodesh* and all the other holidays without the testimony of witnesses and proclamation of the court. However, there is still a reminiscence of the ancient proclamation of the New Moon in our synagogue service on the Sabbath preceding *Rosh Hodesh*. A prayer is recited by the congregation requesting God's blessing for the coming month followed by a public announcement notifying the worshipers when *Rosh Hodesh* will take place.

Rosh Hodesh consists of either one or two days. If the previous month consists of twenty-nine days, only one day of *Rosh Hodesh* is observed. However, when the previous month has thirty days, two days of *Rosh Hodesh* are observed—the thirtieth day of the old month and the first day of the new month. Very traditional Jews consider the day before *Rosh Hodesh* as *Yom Kippur Kattan*, a minor day of atonement; they fast as they beseech God for atonement.

Special prayers are recited in the synagogue on *Rosh Hodesh*. The *Hallel* is recited, consisting of selected Psalms; an appropriate passage from the Torah is read, at which time four persons are called up; an additional *Musaf Amidah* is also included in the service.

125

YAMIM NORAIM

יָמִים נוֹרָאִים

Days of Awe

Though there is no biblical connection between Rosh Hashanah and Yom Kippur, the two solemn holidays are traditionally referred together as *Yamim Noraim*, Days of Awe. In fact, the High Holy Day season consisting of ten days is also represented by the same name or by the more precise term, *Aseret Yemei Teshuvah*, Ten Days of Repentance. During this period, the Jew is bidden to examine his thoughts and deeds of the past year and to dedicate himself to moral and spiritual improvement.

Actually, a mood of solemnity commences a month before Rosh Hashanah. Every morning during the month of *Elul*, the *Shofar* is blown to stir the people to repent. Maimonides interprets the purpose of blowing the *Shofar* with this admonition to worshipers:

Awake, ye sleepers from your slumber, and rouse you from your lethargy. Scrutinize your deeds and return in repentance. Remember your Creator, you who forget eternal truth in the trifles of the hour, and go astray all your years after vain illusions which can neither profit or deliver. Look well into your souls and view your ways and your actions; let each one of you forsake his evil path and his unworthy purpose, and return to God, so that He may have compassion upon you. [Mishneh Torah]

Because the Jew is conscious that he is being judged by God during these ten days, his entire demeanor undergoes a change. He is more humble and introspective; he seeks out others whom

273

he has hurt during the year, asking that he be forgiven for wrongs committed wittingly or unwittingly. Knowing that on the Day of Atonement sins committed against God are forgiven only after he has sought reconciliation with his fellow man, he realizes that time does not permit him to harbor a grudge against another.

It is not primarily the fear of divine punishment that is responsible for the feeling of awe on these days, but rather the awareness of individual responsibility. It is as if the whole world depends on the individual whose moral commitment is decisive in determining the future of mankind.

> Everyone throughout the year should regard himself as half innocent and half guilty, and should regard the whole of mankind as half innocent and half guilty. If then he commits one more transgression, he presses down the scale of guilt against himself and the whole world and is responsible for its destruction. If he fullfills one commandment, he turns the scale of merit in his favor and in that of the whole world; he brings salvation and deliverance to all his fellow men and to himself, as it is said, "The righteous man is the foundation of the world" (Proverbs 10:25). [*Kiddushin* 40b]

In this dramatic statement, the rabbis sought to present a vivid picture to the individual Jew of his awesome moral responsibility as a member of society. Whether he accepted the literal interpretation of the passage was not their concern, as long as he recognized the crucial role of the individual and his single acts, which could determine the future of the world. For this reason the rabbis encouraged every Jew to increase his charities and other good deeds from New Year to the Day of Atonement, and engage in performing *mitzvot* at this period to a larger extent than during the rest of the year.

126

SHALOSH REGALIM

שָׁלֹשׁ רְגָלִים

Three Pilgrim Festivals

The festivals of Pesah, Shavuot, and Sukkot, vividly described in the Torah, are commonly known as the "Three Pilgrim Festivals." Each holiday was a joyous occasion on which the Israelites would journey to the Holy City from their towns and villages to offer their sacrifices and express their thanksgiving to God. Especially while the Temple existed, the *Shalosh Regalim* were periods of great joy. The anticipation of visiting the center of Israel's spiritual life three times annually and of participating in colorful religious celebrations, each marking a new season of the year, undoubtedly heartened the participants.

The *Shalosh Regalim* have many aspects in common. Each originated as a nature festival even before its historical significance became evident. Passover originally marked the beginning of the barley harvest in ancient Palestine; Shavuot is described in Scripture primarily in connection with the wheat harvest; Sukkot commemorated the coming of autumn and the late harvests. Since most people lived close to the soil and were dependent on the success of their crops, it was entirely appropriate to express their gratitude to God, the provider of man's needs. In time the three festivals became even more important; they were invested with national and historical significance. Pesah commemorated the Exodus from Egypt; Shavuot became associated primarily with the Revelation on Mount Sinai; Sukkot recalled God's protection during the period when Israel dwelt in the wilderness. Though the seasonal aspect of each of these festivals is still evident in some of the prayers and rituals, their role as

275

commemorators of historical events in Israel's life has far over-
shadowed the earlier agricultural celebration.

The format of the service for each of the *Shalosh Regalim* is
strikingly similar. The *Hallel,* consisting of Psalms of praise, is
recited on each of the holidays; the additional service *(Musaf)* is
similar for each holiday, the only difference being the references
made to the particular holiday that is being celebrated; each
Festival is associated with a public reading from a *Megillah*
(scroll): Pesah—the Song of Songs; Shavuot—the Book of Ruth;
Sukkot—Ecclesiastes. The *Hazzan* also intones the same melodies on each of these three Festivals. All the laws concerning
forbidden and permissible forms of work apply equally to these
three major holidays.

127

ARBAAH MINIM (SUKKOT)

אַרְבָּעָה מִינִים

Four Species of Plants

The Festival of Sukkot is celebrated in the autumn before the long winter season sets in. Prayers of thanksgiving for the blessings already received and petition for productiveness for the coming season are associated with Sukkot. The Torah clearly emphasizes the thanksgiving aspect of the festival in the verse:

And you shall take on the first day the fruit of goodly trees, branches of palm trees, and the boughs of thick trees, and willows of the brook, and you shall rejoice before the Lord, your God, for seven days. [Leviticus 23:40]

The wording of the Torah is not easily understood, for the first part of the verse speaks of the observance of the ceremony for the first day only. One is not sure whether the rejoicing for seven days also includes the use of the four plants. In Temple times, the *Tannaim* explained the biblical law to mean that on the first day all Jews were to observe the ceremony with the four plants, while in the Temple it was to continue for the seven days of the festival.

After the destruction of the Temple, a new regulation was enacted ordering the ceremony to be observed everywhere for the seven days of Sukkot. This has been the universal practice since the destruction of the Temple.

Another difficulty arose from the biblical verse. Only two of the four species are specifically mentioned in Leviticus – the palm branch and willow. It was decided long ago that "fruit of the goodly trees" was to be the *etrog* (citron), for it was the most precious citrus fruit of the country. The *hadas* (myrtle) was closest to the biblical description, "the branch of the thickly grown tree." The rabbis further delineated how and when the four species were to be used on the holiday. The *etrog* is held in the left hand, and the *lulav* (palm branch), myrtle, and willows, which are tied together, are held with the right hand.

Before the service or immediately before *Hallel*, a *berakhah* over the *lulav* is pronounced by each worshiper as the *arbaah minim* are taken in hand. When the Hallel service is recited, the four plants are held by the leader of the service as well as by all congregants who possess their own.

Many fascinating interpretations of the four species have been offered by the Sages. One compares each of the species with an organ of the human body. The palm branch suggests the spine; the myrtle represents the eye; the shape of the willow is like that of the mouth; and the citron is like the heart. Just as all the four species must be held together during prayer, so the worshiper should dedicate his whole being to serving God.

128

HATAN TORAH
(SIMHAT TORAH)

חֲתַן תּוֹרָה

Groom of the Torah

The privilege of being the last person called to the Torah before its completion is usually offered to a learned and pious Jew. He is given the title, *Hatan Torah*. This is but one of several traditions associated with the most joyous day of the year, Simhat Torah. Immediately after the reading of the last book of the Torah is completed, one reads the first part of Genesis, indicating in this way that the study of Torah is never completed. The man called to the reading of that portion is given the name *Hatan Bereshit*, Groom of the First Portion.

Before the men are called by name, a prayer is publicly recited on their behalf. For the *Hatan Torah*, the prayer concludes with these words:

> Thus may it be acceptable before the Almighty to grant life and grace, and to crown with virtue (the name is inserted), who has been chosen to complete the reading of the Torah.
>
> Stand forth, stand forth, stand forth (name), *Hatan Ha-Torah*.
>
> By the merit of this deed, may you be deemed worthy by the God we revere, to behold children and children's children delighting in the Torah.

It has been suggested that the service on Simhat Torah is really an imitation of a wedding service and symbolizes the marriage of Israel to the Law. Theodor Gaster (1952) observes that the bridegrooms are attended by "bridesmen," counterparts of the "best man," who stand beside them. He also links the tradition of marching around the synagogue with the scrolls on

Simhat Torah *(Hakafot)* with the once widespread custom of walking around the bridal couple seven (or three) times. Moreover, the custom in some localities for the worshipers to throw nuts during the march is also reminiscent of the wedding ceremony, at which guests would similarly shower the bride and groom.

The origin of Simhat Torah deserves special consideration, for it is the youngest of our festivals, having come into being during the Middle Ages. In the talmudic period it was merely the second day of Shemini Atzeret, which was observed on the eighth and ninth days of the Sukkot season. In fact, it is still called Shemini Atzeret in the prayer book. On this second day of Shemini Atzeret the closing section of Deuteronomy was read. Eventually, the second day of the holiday developed into Simhat Torah, a joyous holiday celebrating the completion of the Torah reading. The custom of reading the opening section of Genesis, began in the fourteenth century so that the Jews would never be accused of having finished the Torah without the desire to study it any longer. The origin of Simhat Torah illustrates once again the capacity of the Jewish people to create new religious forms and institutions even in the darkest periods of history.

129

HAGGADAH (PESAH)

הַגָּדָה

Text Used at the Passover Table

The Torah emphasizes that it is the duty of every Israelite to relate the history of the Exodus from Egypt and the significance of the Pesah celebration to his children. The book that contains this story is known as the *Haggadah* (lit., telling).

The *Haggadah* is really an anthology containing passages and quotations from the Bible, the Talmud, and Midrash, in addition to prayers, songs, anecdotes—all appropriately woven together into the Passover theme. The narrative, however, does not start with events immediately before the Exodus. It touches on the beginnings of the Jewish people, when they were still idolators, and leads up to the story of the Exodus.

Several pedagogic devices are used in the *Haggadah*, obviously meant to sustain the interest of the younger people so that their impressions of the Passover ceremony would linger throughout the year. The four questions, the four sons, the recitation of the ten plagues, each song with its repetition of words and phrases holds its fascination for young and old alike. The *Haggadah* also lends itself to further questioning by the participants, thus providing the father with the opportunity to teach the more profound meaning of the holiday. What is meant by the phrase, "This year we are slaves, next year we will be free"? Why is the name of Moses conspicuously absent from the *Haggadah?* Why are the four questions not answered outright in the *Haggadah?* Is the *Had Gadya* nothing more than a simple little ditty or does it have deeper significance for us?

Since the *Haggadah* is long, it is divided into two parts,

281

separated by the festive meal. Some contend that this intermission was arranged to enable the younger children to retire if necessary after the first part has been recited. Since the *Hallel* (Hymns of praise) is interrupted to serve the meal, some observe that this is done specifically to impress upon us that eating, like praying, is an act of holiness. Therefore, the meal is not regarded as an interruption; it is rather one continuous act of praise to God.

A climax in the reading of the *Haggadah* is reached with the verse: "In every generation one ought to regard himself as if he personally had gone out of Egypt. . . . Not our ancestors alone did the Holy One, blessed is He, redeem, but also us has He redeemed with them. . . ." The whole purpose of the *Seder* and the reading of the *Haggadah* can be found in these few words. It is to view the redemption from Egypt not merely as a remote event in history but as a contemporary event that affects every Jew up to the present day. The struggle for freedom must be rewon in every generation.

130

ZEMAN MATTAN TORATENU (SHAVUOT)

זְמַן מַתַּן תּוֹרָתֵנוּ

The Season of Giving Our Torah

The festival of Shavuot is known by more names than any other holiday. In addition to The Feast of Weeks *(Hag Hashavuot)*, it is called The Feast of Harvest, the Day of the First Fruits, and the Concluding Festival *(Atzeret)* because it concludes a period of seven weeks commencing with Passover. All of these names, however, are associated exclusively with the agricultural aspects of the holiday. It was on this holiday that the first fruits of the wheat harvest were offered in gratitude to God.

Shavuot retained its character as a nature festival longer than Sukkot and Passover. Eventually it also assumed historical and national significance and became known as *Zeman Mattan Toratenu*, the Season of Giving Our Torah. The rabbis cited a number of passages in the Scriptures to prove that the giving of the Torah on Mount Sinai took place on the sixth day of *Sivan*, which is the first day of Shavuot. The Torah reading in the synagogue for Shavuot consists of those passages leading up to the Revelation followed by the reading of the Ten Commandments.

Our teachers have indicated that there are important parallels between the agricultural and historical aspects of Shavuot. Just as the ingathering of crops is necessary for material prosperity in each ensuing year, so the acceptance of the Torah is the necessary condition of Israel's existence as a people. Moreover, as the harvest is renewed from year to year, so too is the acceptance of the Torah by the Jewish people. Our Sages have repeatedly reminded us that all the future generations of Israel were released from Egypt and were present at Mount Sinai. God's revelation and covenant with Israel are continuous and are no more confined to a single event at Sinai than is the process of nature to a single harvest.

In the nineteenth century Reform Jews originated a custom of using the holiday of Shavuot as a day of confirmation, in which boys and girls who reached their thirteenth birthday declared their faith in their heritage. In more recent years, this custom was also adopted by many Orthodox and Conservative congregations. The ceremony varies, however, according to the congregation. In some synagogues only girls are confirmed since they do not celebrate the *Bat Mitzvah;* in others, boys and girls are confirmed from ages ranging from fourteen to seventeen years. In all congregations where the ceremony is held, it is intimately connected with the spiritual significance of the holiday, namely, the centrality of Torah in the life of the Jew.

131

AL HANISSIM
(HANUKKAH)

עַל הַנִּסִּים

For the Miracles

On the two minor holidays of Purim and Hanukkah, a brief history of each is inserted in the *Amidah* (Silent Devotion) and *Birkat Hamazon* (Grace after Meals). Both narratives are introduced by a single prayer of gratitude to God: the *Al Hanissim*.

> We thank You for the miracles, for the redemption, for the mighty deeds and saving acts wrought by You, as well as for the battles which You did wage for our fathers in days of old, at this season.

Since the *Al Hanissim* is not a petitional prayer, it is appropriately inserted in that section of the *Amidah* reserved for expressions of gratitude and thanksgiving to God.

One would expect to read about the miracle of oil so popularly associated with Hanukkah. But it is conspicuously absent in the narrative. The author mentions lights without a single reference to the miracle. They are kindled, he says, because at the time when the Jews cleansed the Temple and restored the service, they kindled lights in the courts of the sanctuary. The military exploits of the Maccabees are also minimized in the *Al Hanissim* for Hanukkah. It concludes with the reconquest of the Temple and passes over the military conquests of the Jews in the many years of warfare that followed, suggesting that they do not constitute the lasting importance of the holiday.

What then is the real miracle of Hanukkah? "You delivered the strong into the hands of the weak, the many into the hands of the few, the impure into the hands of the pure, the wicked into the hands of the righteous, and the arrogant into the hands of those that occupied themselves with Your Torah." It is the victory of spiritual power over numerical strength or physical force that constitutes the miracle celebrated on Hanukkah.

Although the Bible and Talmud record many supernatural miracles, Judaism, unlike Christianity, does not depend on the acceptance or rejection of such miracles. Maimonides, the greatest Jewish mind of the Middle Ages, reinterpreted some of the miracle stories in Scripture. He was even brazen enough to offer an interpretation of the miracle of resurrection that was consistent with his scientific background. Moreover, he taught that the people of Israel did not believe in Moses because of the miracles he performed, but because of what occurred at Mount Sinai, which was not based on a suspension of nature's laws.

Rabbi Milton Steinberg called miracle "the achievement by spirit of what by every law of logic and common sense seems impossible. . . . When the immovable is moved, when the insuperable is conquered, when the impossible is achieved what else is that but a miracle?" It is this invincible power of the spirit over any obstacle that gives meaning to the miracle of Hanukkah.

132

SEFIRAT HAOMER

סְפִירַת הָעֹמֶר

Counting the Omer

Passover, like the other two pilgrimage festivals, was originally observed as an agricultural holiday marking "the season of
the month of ripeness," when the barley sown in the winter had
become ripe. To emphasize this important season in the nation's
economy, the Torah required the Israelites to bring an *Omer*–a
sheaf of new barley–to the Temple on the second day of Passover. The flour was then offered as a meal offering in the Temple.
Only after the sheaf had been offered in the Temple was the
produce of the new harvest permitted for general use. Starting
with this day the Jew was to begin counting for forty-nine
consecutive days until Shavuot, The Feast of the Wheat Harvest.

After the Temple was destroyed, the *Omer* could no longer
be brought to the Priest, but the tradition of *Sefirat Haomer*,
counting the days between Pesah and Shavuot, continued to be
observed throughout the centuries. The counting takes place at
nightfall, when the new day begins in the Hebrew calendar.

The order of *Sefirah* (as this is called) begins with the
recitation of a Psalm. The *berakhah* on counting the Omer is then
recited, and finally, the number of days since the counting began
is named. For example, "This day completes twenty days, which
are two weeks and six days of the *Omer.*"

After years of exile, the days between Pesah and Shavuot
were associated with tragedies in Jewish history. When the Jews
rebelled against the Romans in the second century, a severe
plague raged among the disciples of Rabbi Akiba during this
period of the year. During the Middle Ages, many Jews were

destroyed by the Crusaders at this season. In recent times the revolt of the ghetto took place in the month of Nisan during the *Sefirah* period.

Hence, the several weeks of *Sefirah* have been observed by traditional Jews as a period of mourning in which no weddings are celebrated, the exception being the thirty-third day of the *Omer*. It was on Lag Baomer (the thirty-third day) that the plague among Akiba's disciples had suddenly ceased. For this reason, Lag Baomer was also known as "The Scholar's Festival." Jewish schools throughout the world hold special celebrations to mark the occasion.

A more recent exception in the *Sefirah* period is Israel Independence Day, which was established on the fifth day of the month of *Iyar*. In spite of its coincidence with *Sefirah,* celebrations are permitted on this youngest of Jewish holidays.

133

TAANIT

תַּעֲנִית

A Fast

The various fast days throughout the Jewish year were instituted for different purposes—to express repentance for one's sins, to seek special requests, or to mourn a tragic event. Some fasts fall into more than one classification.

The Jewish people were reminded that the mere abstention from food and drink would not automatically influence God on their behalf. The prophet Isaiah severely criticizes those who adhere strictly to form without change of moral behavior. "Is such the fast that I have chosen? The day for a man to afflict his soul? . . . Is not this the fast that I have chosen? To loose the fetters of wickedness, to undo the bands of the yoke? . . . Then shall you call and the Lord will answer, then you shall cry and He will speak."

Thus, fasting was a means of effecting a more sober and compassionate mood and was never considered an end in itself. One should never expect to force the hand of God to act on one's behalf by performing the ritual act of fasting.

Some of the widely known fast days in the Jewish calendar are:

1. *Yom Kippur,* occurring on the tenth day of the month of *Tishri.* It is the only holiday of this kind that is mentioned in the Torah. Even in Leviticus the requirement to fast is not specific. However, the words, "and you shall afflict your souls" (Lev. 16:31), have been understood as a command to fast this day.

2. *Tisha B'av*, The Ninth Day of *Av*, the most solemn day of the calendar, commemorates the destruction of the First Temple by the Babylonians in 586 B.C.E. and the Second Temple by the Romans in 70 C.E. The Talmud includes three other tragic events that took place on this day.

3. *Asarah Betevet*, The Tenth Day of *Tevet*, when the siege of Jerusalem leading up to the destruction of the First Temple began.

4. *Taanit Esther*, The Fast of Esther, occurring on the day before Purim. It was on this day that the Queen fasted before going to King Ahasueros to plead for her people.

5. *The Fast of the Bridal Couple*. Just as all Jews fast on Yom Kippur as they repent and resolve to improve their behavior, so on their wedding day do bride and groom fast before the wedding ceremony to repent and resolve to assume major spiritual obligations in their new life together.

Part XI

LIFE CYCLE OF THE JEW

134

BRIT MILAH

בְּרִית מִילָה

Circumcision

No *mitzvah* is more universally observed among Jews than the rite of circumcision. From the days of the Patriarch Abraham to the present, the vast majority of parents have accepted this covenant with God as a solemn responsibility.

The Jews are not the only people who practice circumcision. Muslims also attach religious significance to it. Many Christian children are circumcised today for hygienic reasons. No people, however, place the same priority on the rite of circumcision as the Jews. The *Brit Milah* is observed on the eighth day, even if the eighth day is the Sabbath or Yom Kippur. It may be postponed only on reliable medical advice, or if it is impossible to obtain the services of a *mohel* (circumcisor).

Anti-Jewish rulers had little success in trying to abolish circumcision. King Antiochus proclaimed its practice punishable by death, hoping that Jews would assimilate with the Hellenistic majority; the Jews, however, could not accept the prohibition even if it resulted in their annihilation by the enemy. After the destruction of the Second Temple, several Roman rulers decreed the prohibition of circumcision. Again Jews risked their lives for the right to continue their ritual. In the fifth century, the Spanish King Sisibut ordered Jews to accept baptism in place of circumcision, thus assuring them equal rights. Their answer was unequivocal: "The law of circumcision is the root of our religion . . . . Hasten our death for we will not surrender a single law, especially one so important."

The main participants in the ceremony in addition to the

father and *mohel* are the *sandek* and godparents. The *sandek* who holds the infant during the ceremony is usually the oldest or most respected member of the family, frequently the baby's grandfather. It is customary to prepare an ornate chair to serve as the "Chair of Elijah," since the prophet is referred to in the Bible as "the angel of the covenant" and in folklore as the protector of children.

Many people assume that the mere performance of the operation on the child fulfills the religious requirement, and will therefore seek the services of a non-Jewish physician instead of a *mohel*. Jewish law requires, however, that a Jew, preferably a *mohel*, perform the operation so that he may recite the appropriate blessing before the circumcision. A visiting rabbi may confer the Hebrew name upon the child at the ceremony but he may not recite the blessing over the *milah*.

135

PIDYON HABEN

פִּדְיוֹן הַבֵּן

Redemption of the First-born Son

In very ancient times some peoples offered their first-born male children as sacrifices to their gods. The Hebrews too accepted the biblical injunction that all the first born belonged to God. They willingly offered the first produce of the land and their first cattle to God; the latter were offered as sacrifices in the Holy Temple. But the Torah rejected the sacrifice of children – as is so clearly indicated in the story of Abraham and Isaac on Mount Moriah. So in earliest Jewish history the first-born males were dedicated to God's service, acting as servants in the Temple.

This practice must have proven a hardship in most families, since parents were reluctant to part with their oldest child. Thus, the tribe of Levi was appointed to act as servants in the Temple, and did away in this manner with the requirement of service for the first-born. We read in the Book of Numbers: "And I have taken the Levites instead of every first-born; and the Levites shall be Mine." In return for the assumption of this duty by the Levites, every first-born Israelite was required to be redeemed by a payment of five shekels to a member of the tribe of Levi.

Despite the destruction of the Temple, this ancient redemption ceremony continued to take place and is still widely observed today. On the thirty-first day after the birth of the first son, a ceremony, to which relatives and friends are invited, is arranged in the home. Among the guests is a *Kohen*, descendant of the tribe of Levi. The father places the child before the *Kohen* and says: "My wife, like myself an Israelite (and not a *Kohen* or *Levi*), has given birth to this first-born son and I hereby present him to

295

you." The *Kohen* replies: "What do you prefer, your first-born or the five *shekalim* you are obliged to give me in order to redeem him?"

The father says: "I prefer my first-born son, and here is the money for redeeming him as I am required to give."

The *Kohen* usually returns the money to the parents, who contribute it to a worthy cause. The ceremony is then followed by a reception to express public thanksgiving for the privilege of redemption.

Two very important lessons should be gained by the parents from this ceremony. First, they should learn that the child is not an absolute possession, but rather a sacred charge entrusted into their care. Second, the *Kohen* who asks the father whether he wishes to part with the money or the child emphasizes in the spirit of his question that the value of children is incomparable to money. Moreover, the father must promise that he will provide the child with spiritual training requiring the greatest financial sacrifices, if necessary, to obtain the best education for the child.

136

BAR MITZVAH

בַּר מִצְוָה

Man of Duty
(literally: Son of a Commandment)

Among many ancient people the thirteenth year, marking the beginning of puberty, was celebrated with tribal initiation ceremonies. Only after proving his ability to endure an ordeal of pain was the thirteen year old accepted as a member of the adult community.

Sometime during the period of the Second Temple, this tribal ceremony of initiation took on a spiritual meaning among Jews commemorating a religious transformation in the life of the Jewish male. As early as the first century the Mishnah refers to the thirteenth year as the age when a son becomes responsible to observe the 613 commandments on his own. R. Eleazar says, "Until the thirteenth year it is the father's duty to raise his son, after which he should say, 'Blessed be He Who has relieved me of responsibility for this boy.'"

It is this assumption of religious duties and privileges that is the essential meaning of *Bar Mitzvah*. He is required to wear *tefillin* (phylacteries) at morning prayer; he is permitted to be counted among the ten men *(minyan)* required for public prayer. Most significantly, he may be called to recite the blessings over the Torah.

Those who speak of *Bar Mitzvah* as a single event in the lifetime of the Jew are in error. The male becomes a *Bar Mitzvah* for the first time at thirteen but retains this same status as a "man of duty" for the remainder of his lifetime. One of the reasons why many Jews fail to continue their religious commitments after thirteen is due to this misconception about *Bar Mitzvah*. The ceremony should be regarded merely as a reminder of a transitional stage in which the boy begins to accept full status as a responsible Jew in the home and synagogue.

Although women are not obligated to observe the many *mitzvot* that are required of men, the recent innovation of *Bat Mitvah* as a solemn reminder of new religious responsibilities has served an essential purpose in Jewish life. The *Bat Mitzvah* is assured that she has a vital role to play in a religion that is basically home-centered and that her well-rounded Jewish education is as vital as that of the *Bar Mitzvah*. Abraham Segal, the prominent Jewish educator, writes: "Intelligent informed women are just as vital to community welfare in Jewish religious life as intelligent informed men. A girl should certainly be welcomed into our community as warmly as a boy."

137

KIDDUSHIN

קִדּוּשִׁין

Consecration; Holy Matrimony

Another expression related to the term *kadosh*, "holy," is *kiddushin*, which belongs to the same family of words as *kiddush, kaddish, kedushah, kiddush Hashem*. The marriage ceremony is frequently referred to as *kiddushin* or *huppah* and *kiddushin*, the latter phrase taken from a blessing recited at the outset of the wedding ceremony: "Blessed are You, O Lord, who hallows His people Israel by rite of *huppah* and *kiddushin*." The most essential point of the ceremony takes place when the groom places the ring on the bride and recites these words: "Behold, you are consecrated unto me *(mekudeshet li)* with this ring, according to the law of Moses and Israel."

From its very beginning, Judaism regarded the union of man and wife as a sacred venture, blessed by God. Unlike some of the early Church doctrines that looked upon marriage as a compromise with the devil or barely better than illicit love, the Jewish view is clearly stated in Genesis: "And the Lord God said, 'It is not good that man should be alone, I will make a help meet for him.'" To marry and rear a family is the first command addressed by God to man: "Be fruitful and multiply."

The rabbis of the Talmud continue to refer to marriage as a fulfillment of God's command, a sacred bond. "One who does not marry dwells without joy, without blessing, without good." "God awaits impatiently for man to marry." The groom and attendants are freed from observing all other ritual commandments, "for one who is occupied with the performance of a divine command *(mitzvah)* is free from all others." The High Priest was not permitted to perform the atonement rites on Yom Kippur unless he was married.

These references to the institution of marriage are not to be understood merely as perfunctory praises. The implications are far-reaching. The marriage ceremony is elevated to a religious sacrament, and is not merely a legal contract entered into by two parties signing a business transaction. More essential is the religious emphasis affirming that God becomes the third partner in a marriage. His relationship to husband and wife takes on a new dimension now that they are prepared to live their lives more completely in union with one another. Still another implication of associating *kiddushin* with marriage is the sanctification of sex in marriage. The satisfaction of our drives is a duty, provided that these drives are properly directed. The sexual aspect of marriage is not something obscene, sinful, or shameful, but a desirable goal—the culmination of a loving relationship in which man and wife have an equal share and find mutual satisfaction.

138

KETUBAH

כְּתֻבָּה

Marriage Document

The *Ketubah*, which is filled out by the rabbi before the wedding and then read during the ceremony, is an ancient document intended to protect the wife should she become widowed or divorced. It assigns to her a fixed sum that remains a prior claim on the man's estate. The document testifies that on the date of marriage the bridegroom said to his bride: "Be my wife according to the law of Moses and Israel. I will work for you; I will honor you; I will support and maintain you, even as it becomes a Jewish husband to do, who works for his wife, honors, supports and maintains her in faithfulness." The *Ketubah* then reads, "And the bride plighted her troth unto him, and consented to become his wife." It is signed just before the ceremony by the bride, the groom, and two competent witnesses – adult males, not related either to bride or groom.

It is apparent that the basic aim of this document is to affirm the dignity of the wife by conferring special rights and privileges upon her. It serves to deter the husband from arbitrarily severing the marriage without consideration of the wife's needs. When the present form of the *Ketubah* was introduced in rabbinic times, most neighboring people regarded their wives as objects of possession; they were considered merely as servants of their husbands. The overwhelming acceptance of this innovation left no doubt about the opinion of the rabbis on the importance of the woman in marriage.

The wording of the *Ketubah* was never rigidly fixed; it varied in different periods of Jewish history, not only according

301

to the countries where Jews lived, but also among the different groups or sects into which Jews were divided. For example, most Jewish communities wrote the document in Aramaic, but the text of the Samaritan *Ketubah* was in Hebrew. The Sephardic Jews, who were not bound by the Ashkenazic law against polygamy, would insert a special clause in the contract to the effect that the husband cannot marry a second wife without the first wife's permission. The Sephardim also included in their *Ketubah* a clause forbidding the husband to see his wife's possessions or to take a voyage by water unless, before embarking, he give his wife a conditional divorce and sufficient means for her sustenance. The most recent change in the language of the *Ketubah* was introduced by the authorities of the Jewish Theological Seminary requiring both bride and groom to submit to arbitration before a *Bet Din* (rabbinic council) should either party request it.

139

HUPPAH

חֻפָּה

Marriage Canopy

The Psalmist compares the rising sun to the "bridegroom coming forth from his *huppah*," thus suggesting the most ancient meaning of the term: a wedding tent or chamber belonging to the groom. Upon entering the *huppah* of the groom, the bride passed from her father's domain to that of her husband.

In the talmudic era, the *huppah* was often elaborately decorated by friends of the groom. Fruits and delicacies were suspended from it. In some instances the *huppah* was especially built out of lumber from trees planted upon the birth of bride and groom.

In the Middle Ages, the former purpose of the *huppah* no longer obtained among Jews in western countries, since it was the custom for the groom to go from his father's home to the home of the bride's father. Nevertheless, the *huppah* persisted in a different form. In one region, the veil covering the bride was called *huppah*. In another, the heads of the bride and groom were covered by a single kerchief which was called *huppah*. In another country, *huppah* referred to the custom of wrapping the couple in a *tallit* (prayer shawl).

In sixteenth-century Poland, which served as the center of Jewish life in that period, the portable canopy was used in marriage. The *huppah* was a combination of a curtain and tent suspended above the bridal couple. This type of *huppah* became almost universally accepted among European Jews. Now bride and groom were led not into the *huppah* as in ancient times, but under the *huppah*, which was placed either in the courtyard or inside the synagogue.

303

The usual *huppah* used today consists of four poles that hold up a covering, giving it the appearance of a tent and symbolizing the new home about to be established by the bride and groom.

Israeli scholar Eliyahu Kitov (1963) offers a thought provoking suggestion when he observes that the tradition of reciting the seven benedictions under the *huppah* was repeated in the couple's home during the following week. He suggests that bride and groom should celebrate the week after their marriage in their own home, indicating that here their future joy will be found. The custom of traveling on a honeymoon, he claims, is not praiseworthy; it is a tiring and unsettling affair. "Perhaps the point of the honeymoon is to distract the bride and groom from a very difficult period of transition, until the adjustment is made. But Jews find holiness and sublimity in marriage and have no need of such a distraction. A Jewish bride and groom can do no better than to rejoice in their own home, in rest and tranquility and in genuine happiness" (p. 36).

140

SHEVA BERAKHOT

שֶׁבַע בְּרָכוֹת

Seven Blessings

After the wedding ceremony, a repast is served in honor of the celebrants. Before the *Birkat Hamazon* (Grace after Meals) is said, seven benedictions, the *sheva berakhot*, are publicly recited with the wine cup upheld. These are the same benedictions (*birkhot nesuin*) that were recited during the wedding ceremony by the officiating rabbi. The *sheva berakhot* may also be recited for seven days following the wedding where ten men are present at the meal, and at least one of the participants is a new guest.

Each of the seven blessings recited during the ceremony and repeated before the Grace has special significance for bride and groom.

The first blessing is recited over wine, for "there is no rejoicing without wine."

The second blessing recalls the creation of the universe. For bride and groom, marriage is like the renewal of the world.

The third blessing refers to the creation of man signifying that on this day the bridal couple is reborn, as it were.

The fourth blessing recognizes God's influence in uniting the bridal couple in marriage.

The fifth blessing expresses faith in the restoration of Zion. The hope of a restored homeland takes precedence over individual joy. It is for this reason that the glass is broken at the end of the ceremony, for in spite of the happiness of the occasion, the Jew cannot forget the tragedy that befell an entire people, when their Temple and homeland were destroyed.

The sixth blessing expresses the hope that the happiness of bride and bridegroom be comparable to that of Adam and Eve in Eden.

The final blessing is a culmination of the expression of happiness in the other six blessings. It praises God for having enriched all of human life through the happiness granted to bride and groom, and for having bestowed on mankind the capacity for love and brotherhood, friendship and peace.

Thus, with the recitation of these seven blessings, both bride and groom identify themselves with the story of Creation, with the history of Israel, and with its hopes and aspirations.

141

AVELUT

אֲבֵלוּת

Mourning

Avelut is divided into five periods:

1. *Aninut:* from the moment of death until the burial the mourner is known as an *onain.* He is exempt from fulfilling the religious commandments, including prayer.
2. The first three days after the burial. During this period even the poorest mourner who lives on charity is forbidden to engage in work.
3. *Shivah:* the seven days of intense mourning in which the family of the deceased is required to remain at home. Only under special circumstances is the *avel* (mourner) permitted to leave the home during *shivah.* For example, a physician may attend to his patients or a teacher may instruct his pupils in Torah after the third day.
4. *Sheloshim:* the first thirty days of mourning. The Bible relates that the children of Israel mourned the death of Moses for thirty days. During this first month, the mourner abstains from attending parties or receptions. It is customary not to wear new clothes or to engage in pleasurable pursuits during this period.
5. The first year of mourning: the year's mourning period applies only to children of the deceased. The restrictions that are applied to other mourners for the thirty day period are observed by sons and daughters for an entire year. The sons are required to attend the synagogue daily and to recite the Mourner's *Kaddish* for eleven months and on the anniversary of the parent's death *(Yahrzeit).*

The laws of *avelut* pertain mostly to the *shivah* period, during which the mourners are required to remain within the home, there to deliberate on their loss and to receive the condolences of friends *(nihum avelim)*.

Some of the laws of *avelut* during the *shivah* week are: Mourners are expected to sit on low stools. They should wear nonleather shoes as a symbol of their mourning. The mourners abstain from cutting their hair. The more traditional do not shave during this seven-day period. Cooking and other household chores may be done by the mourners solely for their own use. Tradition requires that friends and neighbors prepare the first meal for mourners returning from the cemetery. This is known as *seudat havraah*. During the *shivah*, a candle is kept burning in memory of the departed soul.

It is customary to have all mirrors covered for the seven days.This wide-spread custom, which is not based upon a specific Jewish law, has been invested with symbolic meaning: The mourners should reflect less upon their own personal needs during this period and more on the deceased and the more profound meaning of life and death.

Whenever possible, morning and evening services should be held in the home during the week of *shivah*. Mourners should, however, attend the synagogue on the Sabbath since the customs of mourning in the home are suspended on the Sabbath and Festivals.

142

KERIAH

קְרִיעָה

Rending the Garment

The custom of rending one's garment after the death of a close relative dates back at least as long ago as the days of King David. We read in the Book of Kings upon hearing of his son Absalom's sudden death: "Then the king arose, and rent his garments, and lay on the earth. . . ."

The mourners are asked to rise before the funeral service and recite the blessing, "Blessed are You O Lord our God King of the Universe, who is the righteous Judge." The blessing implies an acceptance of the reality of death precisely at the time when the family of the deceased would be inclined to question God's justice.

Upon the death of a mother or father the cut is made on the left side of the garment near the heart. Upon the death of other blood relatives it is made on the right side. Many mourners, instead of cutting their garment, wear a black ribbon that is cut.

The *keriah* is performed even if news of a parent's death has not reached the children for months or years. However, if news of the passing of other relatives has been delayed over thirty days, the *keriah* is not performed.

Rabbi Joseph H. Hertz (1935), who was Chief Rabbi of Great Britain, interpreted the *keriah* in this way:

According to ancient Jewish custom the ceremony of cutting our garments, when our nearest and dearest on earth is lying dead before us, is to be performed while standing upright. The future may be dark, veiled from the eye of mortals, but not the manner in which we are to meet the future. To rail at

309

life, to rebel against a destiny that has cast our lives in unpleasant places, is of little avail. We cannot lay down terms to life. Life must be accepted on its own terms. But hard as life's terms are, life (it has been finely said) never dictates unrighteousness, unholiness, dishonor. [p. 297]

The *keriah* serves another wholesome purpose. The rent garment is a vivid reminder of the tragedy that the family has sustained, thus giving the mourners another realistic picture of the anguish that death brings. Judaism wisely does not attempt to shield the bereaved of reminders that their loss is real rather than imaginary. We should not be afraid of admitting our grief to ourselves or to others, if that is what we genuinely feel.

Part XII

SACRED PLACES

143

BET HAMIKDASH

בֵּית הַמִּקְדָּשׁ

Holy Temple

Until the reign of King Solomon, God's Presence was said to reside in the tabernacle, a portable tent. King David wanted to construct a permanent Temple, and had prepared the material for it. However, this privilege was given to his son, Solomon, who with the help of King Hiram of Tyre, constructed the First Temple in Jerusalem.

The *Bet Hamikdash* (as it was called) contained a palace section in the front, known as "Holy," which was distinct from the inner shrine, the "Holy of Holies," containing the Ark of the Covenant and other sacred objects. This inner room was used only once a year, on Yom Kippur, when the High Priest entered it.

After four hundred years of existence, the First Temple was destroyed by the Babylonian King Nebuchadnezzar, and the Judeans were exiled to Babylonia. Upon their return, the first exiles were content to build an altar on the Temple mount. However, the prophets Haggai and Zechariah pressed for the rebuilding of the Temple, and thus the foundations were laid in 520 B.C.E. It was completed in four years, but was not nearly as magnificent as the First Temple. In the Second Temple the Holy of Holies was empty, since the original Ark disappeared.

This Temple was desecrated by King Antiochus in the second century, but after three years it was rededicated by the Maccabees and new vessels were made for it. After Pompey stormed the Temple it was not considered ample enough for the luxury-loving King Herod the Great, so he planned to build a magnificent new structure, which, however, was never completed.

In the year 70 C.E. the Temple was burned to the ground by the Romans. It was never to be rebuilt. Only the western wall with its giant hewn stones continued to stand. This wall was not part of the Temple proper, but was part of an enclosure that once surrounded the Temple area.

The Jews never permitted themselves to forget the glory of their Temple. They remembered it in their prayers, eagerly seeking the day when it would be rebuilt and the land on which it stood restored to the people of Israel. The Temple meant more to them than a great structure in which the sacrifices were offered. It was rather a symbol of their lost national independence and religious unity.

To this very day the traditional prayerbook still contains prayers petitioning God that the Temple worship be restored. Other prayerbooks recall the glory of the ancient Temple and its sacrifices in the past, but do not seek their restoration, since they feel that synagogue prayer is a more appropriate form of worship for our day than are Temple sacrifices.

144

BET HATEFILLAH

בֵּית הַתְּפִלָּה

House of Prayer

The main purpose of the synagogue is to serve as a house of public worship. Services are held three times daily throughout the year. Here the worshiper comes to express prayers of gratitude and petition; here he reaffirms his loyalty to God and people through prayer; here he recites a liturgy, part of which possibly dates back to the days of the First Temple.

We cannot be certain when congregational prayer had its beginning in Jewish history. Some scholars are of the opinion that even before the destruction of the First Temple (586 B.C.E.) those Jews who lived a long distance from the Temple in Jerusalem would gather in their homes on the Sabbath to read from the Torah scroll and the prophets, followed by several prayers, those same Psalms that were part of the Temple service in Jerusalem.

Most scholars assume that the synagogue originated after the destruction of the First Temple, when those exiled to Babylonia would gather together for mutual strength and consolation. Levites in exile probably recited the same prayers and chanted the same melodies that they once intoned when the Temple was standing. The learned probably read from scrolls that contained moral and ritual laws, prophecies, and historical records. Eventually these assemblies were held with regularity, and a definite form was given to them.

When the exiles returned from Babylonia and the Temple was rebuilt, the synagogue continued to exist in addition to the Temple, serving as a modest house of prayer and instruction

315

wherever Jews chose to congregate. Synagogues arose in towns and villages. Unlike the Temple, the building that housed these congregations was not important to the vitality of the synagogue. It was solely the congregation of men and their religious dedication that were vital. Services were modeled after the Temple service and were recited regularly morning and evening, at the same time that the Temple sacrifices were offered. Much of the service as we now recite it was developed during those centuries after the return from Babylonia.

When the Second Temple was destroyed by the Romans (70 C.E.), the synagogue service, which once existed alongside the Temple service, became the only method of worship. The "service of the heart," i.e., prayer, replaced the Temple Service as the appropriate means of communication with God. New prayers were introduced into the synagogue liturgy, giving expression to the hopes of Israel's restoration and the rebuilding of the Temple.

The synagogue became the "portable homeland" of the Jews accompanying them wherever they settled, providing them with rich memories of their glorious past and with strength to endure the present and aspire to a brighter future.

145

ARON HAKODESH

אֲרוֹן הַקֹּדֶשׁ

The Holy Ark

The Ark in which the Torah scrolls are kept is the most conspicuous and ornate object in the synagogue. It is traditionally placed at the eastern wall of the synagogue in the direction of Zion where worshipers face in prayer. The Ark is always elevated above the floor on which the worshipers stand to accentuate its importance as the home of the sacred scrolls. Whenever the *Aron Hakodesh* is opened, the congregation rises as a gesture of respect for the Torah scrolls that are in view.

In most synagogues some kind of tablet containing the first words of each of the Ten Commandments is affixed above the Ark, and the *Ner Tamid*, Eternal Light, is suspended over it. A *parokhet*, a curtain of costly material and meaningful design, usually covers the front of the Ark.

The *Aron Hakodesh* in the synagogue serves as a reminder of the first Ark of the covenant that God commanded Moses to build for the tablets of the Law. In their travels from Sinai, the Ark always preceded the Israelites and was a signal for their advance. The room that housed the Ark of the covenant was the most sacred section of the tabernacle—the Holy of Holies. Even Aaron, the High Priest, was forbidden to enter the room except on the Day of Atonement.

The Talmud abounds with fascinating legends and folklore about the miraculous powers of the Ark. Legend relates that the priests who were delegated to carry the Ark over the River Jordan were in turn carried by the Ark. The Ark leveled the hills before the Israelites in their travels. It also protected the Isra-

317

elites against their enemies. The Ark sent off sparks that killed dangerous serpents and scorpions and burned the thorns; the smoke sent a sweet fragrance throughout the world, causing the nations of the world to take note and admire the miracle.

The Talmud also discusses the ultimate fate of the original Ark when the Temple was destroyed. Some speculate that it was brought into Babylonia where the Judeans were exiled. Another view was that it remained in Jerusalem and was hidden away in a special compartment of the Temple. Still another view is that King Josiah hid the Ark and other sacred vessels before the siege of Jerusalem for fear that if they were brought to Babylonia, they would never be returned.

What is more amazing than the many legends about the fate of the original Ark is the fact that every synagogue throughout the world contains a symbolic representation of the original Ark. The consciousness of our ancient past commencing with biblical times will remain with us so long as the synagogue survives.

146

BET HAMIDRASH

בֵּית הַמִּדְרָשׁ

House of Study

We can easily understand why the German word for "school" (Schule) became the Yiddish word for synagogue (Shul). One of the basic functions of the synagogue is to provide the congregants with opportunities to study, since learning is the highest form of worship.

Ever since the day when Ezra returned with the exiles from Babylonia, study became an integral part of the synagogue. One of his first acts was to gather the people together to hear a reading from the Torah scroll. Interpreters explained what was read to the masses. This public reading of the Torah symbolized the regiving of the Torah to the people of Israel. It set the pattern for the synagogue service for all times, which would henceforth include the reading of the Torah before the entire congregation, and thus offered the opportunity for all people, even the humblest, to learn regularly.

For many years a translator stood beside the reader and translated each verse into Aramaic, the language that the masses spoke and understood. The sermon too served the purpose of further explaining the Bible so that the congregation could be instructed in the laws of the Torah and other biblical books that were not read at the service. Eventually, the reading of a prophetic book (*haftarah*) was incorporated into the service, as a means of offering added opportunity for instruction.

Throughout Jewish history, the synagogue provided classes for adults and children, as it does in modern times. In eastern Europe the young men who were unable to continue their studies

319

in a higher academy would study alongside the adults before and after the services. Some would study individually and others with the group led by one of the learned men in the community.

Almost every male member of the community participated in at least one study group either in Bible, Talmud, or some other text. Among the students were men who interrupted their Yeshiva studies because of marriage, but were still relatively free to devote several hours a day to study. Businessmen, too, assembled in the *Bet Hamidrash* after they had completed their day's work. The unemployed and the aged spent a major part of the day in the synagogues, combining their study hours with worship and relaxation.

Of the three terms used for the synagogue, the masses of eastern Europe most frequently used the term *Bet Hamidrash*, indicating that the role of study was to them a vital element of the experience of worship.

Today in America most religious schools for the young are conducted by the synagogue. Great effort is being made to revitalize study groups for adults. Though much of the interest and motivation is lacking for Torah study among the adult Jewish community, synagogues are becoming increasingly aware of their historic role as houses of study for all ages.

147

BET HAKNESSET

בֵּית הַכְּנֶסֶת

House of Assembly

The synagogue is known by three terms in Hebrew, each describing one of its functions. In addition to a house of study and prayer, the synagogue has traditionally served as a meeting place where Jews of the community would gather to celebrate important events in the life of the family. They would also meet there to seek each other's counsel in times of crisis. Each person knew that he could gain strength in meeting with his fellow Jew, especially when he needed sympathy and concern.

Especially in eastern Europe, the "house of assembly" was frequently the town hall where community business was conducted. In the small towns all important announcements were made in the synagogue—from new decrees of the government to announcements of marriages, births, or deaths of members. It was in the synagogue that officers and delegates of the Jewish community were elected.

The *Bet Haknesset* was also used to express complaints or grievances against the leaders of the community or, for that matter, against any Jew who had allegedly wronged another. Before the Torah reading, a person wishing to air a complaint would stand up and seek the attention of the congregation. Even strike meetings were known to have been held in the synagogues of eastern Europe. The workers would express their demands for better working conditions and higher pay in the presence of their employers and the other members of the congregation.

The Jew saw no conflict between the religious and secular activities held in the synagogue. Judaism was not held to be solely a religion but embraced all of life. In what more appropriate place could demands for justice be made than in the synagogue, where the Torah and prophets were read, where God's presence was most closely felt?

Most American synagogues also serve as a "house of assembly," serving as meeting places for adults and children, for Jewish organizations and other special-interest groups.

148

BET OLAM

בֵּית עוֹלָם

Cemetery (literally: Eternal Home)

The Jewish cemetery is known by several names: *Bet Hay-yim*, House of Life; *Bet Hakevarot*, the House of Graves; *Bet Olam*, Eternal Home. It was also called Garden of the Jews, probably because of the beautiful rural areas where cemetery cites were chosen, until the ghetto era, when burial privileges were seriously curtailed. In the ghetto the cemetery was found at the end of the street as far as possible from any house, in order to honor the ancient custom of burying the dead at least fifty paces from the nearest residence.

A wall was usually erected around the Jewish cemetery for protection against marauders, since the desecration of Jewish graves was very common in the Middle Ages. In sixteenth-century Rome, the government itself confiscated monuments of Jews, using them to build walls around their towns.

In ancient times families were buried together, as they frequently are today. But because of the more restricted areas assigned to Jews in the Middle Ages, the dead were buried in successive rows. Special rows were reserved for men of distinction; suicides and criminals were buried in a separate corner of the cemetery. Until modern times the dead were not usually placed in a coffin, but walls of the graves were boxed with boards. When a learned man passed away, it was customary to use the boards of the bench on which he studied Torah.

For centuries prior to the Middle Ages, tombstones consisted merely of a simple white marker (*tziyyun*), which was eventually replaced for reasons of sentiment with the more elab-

323

orate monuments. The use of inscriptions on the monument was a borrowed custom. Until the beginning of the Christian Era, only artistic symbols, such as the seven-branched candelabrum, were found on Roman Jewish tombs. In the later Middle Ages, the tombstones were etched with symbols identifying the occupation of the deceased—scissors appeared on a tailor's tomb, a violin or harp on the musician's, a lion holding a sword on a doctor's, etc.

The formal unveiling ceremony in which a rabbi is asked to participate and friends are invited to attend is of recent origin. It is nowhere prescribed in Jewish tradition. It was customary merely to erect a tombstone near the first anniversary after death, at which time the simple memorial prayer was recited.

Part XIII

THE LITERARY HERITAGE OF ISRAEL

149

AM HASEFER

עַם הַסֵּפֶר

People of the Book

It is significant that Mohammed is credited with naming the Jews "The People of the Book." From the days of Ezra, the Torah and the books added to it were so intimately a part of the Jewish people that they could not easily conceive of another way of life. They were aware that acceptance of the Book marked the birth of the Hebrew people. Without continued contact with the Book, the Jews instinctively knew that they could not attain self-fulfillment, or even survive as a people. It was a non-Jew then who made explicit a concept that they had long lived by implicitly.

The Torah exempted no one, not even a king of Israel from studying the Book:

> And it shall be, when he sits upon the throne of his kingdom, that he shall write a copy of this law in a book. . . . And it shall be with him, and he shall read therein all the days of his life; that he may learn to fear the Lord his God, to keep all the words of this law and these statutes to do them. [Deut. 17:18–19]

Joshua was likewise instructed to apply himself to the Book: "This book of the law shall not depart from your mouth, but you shall meditate in it day and night, that you may observe to do according to all that is written in it" (Josh. 1:8).

How the people conceived of its dedication to the Book is illustrated by a legend in the Talmud. When the Israelites were assembled at Mount Sinai, an apparition of *The Book* and *The*

Sword appeared before them. A heavenly voice demanded that they make a solemn choice: "You can have one or the other, but not both. If you choose *The Book*, you must renounce *The Sword*. Should you choose *The Sword*, then *The Book* will perish." The Israelites made their most memorable decision. They chose *The Book*. Then God said to Israel: "If you observe what is written in *The Book* you will be delivered from *The Sword*, but should you refuse to observe it, *The Sword* will ultimately destroy you."

The life and destiny of the Jews was formed not only by the Bible but also by the innumerable volumes that were inspired by the Bible. The Jews treated classical books with the warmth and respect that one would show an indispensable companion. A philosopher-poet of the eleventh century, Moses ibn Ezra, in his *Shirat Yisrael* describes a book as "a friend who will cause you no harm and deny you no favor. If you fall upon evil days, it will be a friend in your loneliness, a companion in your exile, a light in darkness, good cheer in your desolation. It will bestow upon you whatever good it can, asking no favor in return. It gives all, it takes nothing."

The Jew, even of the more recent past, did not regard reading merely as a luxury or a leisure activity. It was as necessary to life as eating or sleeping.

In her vivid description of Jewish resistance during the World War II, Marie Syrkin (1949) relates in *Blessed Is the Match* that during their most crucial days the Jews "started furnishing their cave with straw mattresses, blankets and crockery, mats and books." At the time that these men and women struggled for their very lives they formed a children's library to sustain their spirits, their dignity. Their books helped to provide them with courage and hope.

150

TORAH

תּוֹרָה

Literally: Teaching

Torah is frequently translated as the Law or Five Books of Moses. There is no exact translation that accurately conveys the meaning of the word, because it encompasses so much in Jewish thought. The laws of Israel are only one aspect of Torah. The Five Books of Moses or Pentateuch are referred to as the *Torah*, but the *Torah* is not confined to these or even to the twenty-four books that make up the Bible. Torah includes the entire literature and culture of the Jewish people throughout all their years until the present day. It includes the Bible, the Talmud, the Midrash, the writings of the Geonim, the literature of the Jewish philosophers and poets—the entire creative genius of Israel.

Jewish education is also referred to as Torah. Whether studying on one's own or in a formal classroom, the student is engaged in Torah, his most sacred task in life. People have even extended Torah to include the study of general culture and wisdom literature, such as the study of philosophy, primarily because the discipline of study trains the mind and leads to living the ethical life. Usually, however, Torah is confined to the study of Jewish culture.

With the exception of God's name, no word is mentioned as frequently or revered so highly as Torah, mainly because it is associated with the words that God transmitted to Moses at Sinai. Torah is frequently equated with life itself. "It is a tree of life for them that uphold it." "It is our life and the length of our days."

The Jewish attitude toward Torah in general is best reflected in the way that a Torah scroll is regarded—almost as a living being. If desecrated or burned, it is enveloped in a *tallit* and buried in a cemetery. It is mourned with fasting and memorialized by the recitation of *Kaddish*. In times of joy, such as Simhat Torah, it is treated almost as if it were human. Members of the congregation dance with it as if it were a partner. The man called up to the reading of the last section of the Torah is called *"hatan Torah,"* the Torah's bridegroom.

Just as the original Torah was allegedly given to the entire people at Mt. Sinai, so is the study of Torah required of every Jew regardless of his occupation or station in life, his age, or his mental capacity. No excuse was accepted for a community that neglected to teach its young. Judah the Prince stated that the studies of school children may not be interrupted even for the building of the holy Temple. A father was exhorted to make great financial sacrifices to provide his children with the best teacher. The teacher of Torah in turn was accorded the highest respect and reverence, even surpassing the honor due to parents.

The rabbis insisted that without the emphasis on Torah study, the Jewish people could not survive as a group. Belief in God would eventually be renounced. The high standards of morality embodied in the Torah would be neglected and forgotten. However, if Torah study were made a supreme goal, then no external force could ever successfully exterminate Israel. Their survival would be assured, primarily because their determination to preserve the Torah would sustain them physically and spiritually.

151

TALMUD TORAH

תַּלְמוּד תּוֹרָה

The Study of Torah

One of the most ancient passages in the prayer book is the *Shema,* the first paragraph of which is taken from the sixth chapter of Deuteronomy. The basic theme of the paragraph is *Talmud Torah,* for it requires us to express our love for God by constant study "when you lie down and when you rise up." No matter where we are, at home or abroad, we are commanded to engage in Torah study. Furthermore, parents are required to teach Torah to their children through formal education and even in their casual conversation with them.

Torah study was not encouraged merely to sharpen the mind, but primarily as a guide and goal to the moral life. If one takes *Talmud Torah* seriously, he will most probably choose the right moral path. For this reason, the *mitzvah* of *Talmud Torah* outweighs the other commandments. The Mishnah states: "These are the things of which a man enjoys the dividends in this world, while the principal remains for him in the world to come; they are: honoring father and mother, deeds of loving kindness, making peace between a man and his fellow, but *Talmud Torah* is equal to them all."

A person is neither moral nor immoral at birth. Morality can be taught, however, by the training received from parents and teachers, from the study of great source books of morality, all included in the term *Torah.*

Like other Jewish concepts that eventually were concretized into institutions, the *Talmud Torah* was the name given to the elementary religious school provided by the Jewish community, especially for children whose parents could not afford the tuition of a private *heder*. In these schools the teachers were responsible to the officials of the Jewish community and not to the parents of the children.

The *Talmud Torah* was brought to America with the first wave of Jewish immigration from eastern Europe. Here it was the community Hebrew school that served all strata of Jews, not only the underprivileged. One of the main functions of the *Talmud Torah* in this country was to provide higher standards of education and better teachers that could not be obtained by the private *heder*.

In recent years there has been a decline in the number of such schools in the United States. With the growth of new synagogues throughout the country, the synagogue school has become more predominant. However, the *Talmud Torah* still flourishes in a significant number of urban areas that have richly contributed to the cultural and religious progress of American Jewry. They have by no means outlived their usefulness.

152

TORAH LISHMAH

תּוֹרָה לִשְׁמָהּ

Study of Torah for Its Own Sake

Just as the commandments are to be observed without any expectation of reward, so is Torah to be studied for its own sake and not for any material reward. There are many warnings against turning the study of Torah to worldly advantage: "Do not make it (the Torah) a crown to magnify yourself with, nor a hoe to dig with." "He who uses the crown for his own ends forfeits his life."

Great praise is reserved for him who labors in the Torah for its own sake: "The whole world is indebted to him; he is called friend, beloved, a lover of God, a lover of mankind."

This concept may appear strange to many people who think of education in terms of achieving practical goals — a degree or a particular skill to earn a livelihood. The rabbis, however, felt that the privilege and responsibility of Torah study was one of the main purposes of God's placing man on earth. They strongly advocated that in addition to the time spent in study a man should also have an occupation, totally unrelated to his intellectual pursuits, with which he could support himself and his family. Until comparatively recent times a Jew was not permitted to earn a living from teaching Torah to youngsters, nor could he earn a salary from performing rabbinical duties. He studied Torah solely for love of God and for no other motive. "Suppose you say, I am learning Torah that I may get rich, or that I may be called rabbi, or that I may gain reward from God, the teaching of Scripture is, 'To love the Lord your God'; whatever you do, do it only for love."

Although *Torah lishmah* is an ideal in Jewish life, this should not mean that if one has selfish motives for his study of Torah he should cease studying because he has not attained the ideal. The Sages taught that study even with an ulterior motive in mind should not be discouraged. There is hope that in the end, one will come to learn Torah for its own sake. Here the end justifies the means.

153

HUMASH

חֻמָּשׁ

Volume Containing the Five Books of Moses

The word *Humash* is a shortened term for *Hamishah Humshei Torah,* meaning the five books of Moses. Unlike the Torah scroll, it is in book form and is divided into fifty-four titled sections, each called a *sidrah*. As the reader chants from the Torah scroll, the worshipers follow the reading in the *Humash*. Some *Humashim* contain translations and commentaries to which the worshiper may refer as he follows the reading. The prophetic passages are also included in each *Humash* and are found either at the end of each *sidrah* or grouped together at the end of the book. The name of each *sidrah* is usually taken from the opening sentence of the section that is read that week. Thus, the first *sidrah* is called *Bereshit* ("In The Beginning") taken from the first verse of the Torah, "In the beginning God created the heaven and the earth." The third *sidrah* is entitled *Lekh Lekha* ("Go Forth") because in the opening sentence God commands Abram, "Go forth from your father's house."

The first *sidrah* containing the creation story is read on the Sabbath following the festival of Sukkot, after which the reading follows section by section throughout the year until the Sabbath before Sukkot, when the last *sidrah* of the fifth book is read.

Although the division of the Torah into sections is ancient, it was not always divided in the same way as we know it today. Originally the sections read in the synagogue were very brief; there was no rule as to the number of weeks during which the entire Torah had to be completed. In time, however, a fixed cycle for the Torah reading was established. In Palestine a three-year cycle was introduced, within which the Torah had to be read from beginning to end. Eventually the custom of reading an entire *sidrah* every Sabbath took hold, thereby enabling the yearly completion of the Torah. In our day, some synagogues have reintroduced the three-year cycle into their service, in order to abbreviate the service, or to devote more time to the interpretation of the Torah.

154

ASERET HADIBROT

עֲשֶׂרֶת הַדִּבְּרוֹת

Ten Commandments

Known also as the *aseret hadevarim* (Ten Words), the Ten Commandments are referred to more frequently than any other passage in Scriptures. Mentioned for the first time in Exodus and with some variations repeated in Deuteronomy, The Ten Commandments represent the minimal moral requirements of mankind. They are not intended to serve as the sum total of man's moral responsibility. Many other biblical laws are added to these that indicate in greater detail what God requires of man. With the exception of the fourth commandment to observe the Sabbath, none of the commands address themselves to ritual requirements. Yet, the ritual laws mentioned in later passages of the Bible are vital.

In ancient times when the Temple still existed in Jerusalem, the Ten Commandments were recited immediately before the *Shema* as part of the order of worship. With the rise of Christianity, however, the recitation of the Ten Commandments was eliminated. The Talmud explains that the early Christians regarded only these commandments and no others to have been given at Sinai. Their intention was clearly to minimize the importance of the ritual laws in the Bible. It was for this reason that the rabbis abolished the recitation of the Decalogue before the *Shema*. Emphasis was placed on the importance of *tefillin* and *mezuzzah*, mentioned in the first paragraph of the *Shema*, to indicate that the ritual laws were also given at Sinai.

Though the Decalogue was not formally recited in the service any longer, its timeless importance was never questioned by the rabbis. One scholar found in the various phrases of the *Shema* allusions to all the Ten Commandments. For example, "Hear O Israel" reflects the commandment "I am the Lord your God"; "The Lord is One" alludes to the command "You shall have no other gods before Me," etc. Moreover, when the Ten Commandments are read, the congregation is required to stand in order to impress upon them the supreme value of these biblical verses.

The abbreviated Ten Commandments are:

1. I am the Lord your God who brought you out of the land of Egypt.
2. You shall have no other gods before Me.
3. You shall not take the name of the Lord your God in vain.
4. Remember the Sabbath day to keep it holy.
5. Honor your father and your mother.
6. You shall not murder.
7. You shall not commit adultery.
8. You shall not steal.
9. You shall not bear false witness.
10. You shall not covet.

155

TANAKH

תַּנַ"יךְ

The Hebrew Bible

The word *Tanakh* is comprised of three initials representing the divisions of the Hebrew Bible: T-*Torah*, N-*Neviim* or
"Prophets," and KH-*Ketuvim* or "Writings." The Torah includes
the Five Books of Moses, which tells of the origin of the world,
the human race, and the Hebrew nation. The Exodus from
Egypt, culminating in the revelation of the Torah, follows. After
the revelation, most of the remaining pages deal with the moral
and ritual laws that the Israelites were required to adopt upon
entering the new land of Canaan.

The section called *Neviim* or "Prophets" commences with
the era when the Judges ruled Israel; it then traces the history of
Israel's kings, commencing with Saul, and concludes with the
return from Babylonian exile. But most important of all, this
division deals with the teachings of the great prophets of Israel
who brought the word of God to an often erring people. Isaiah,
Jeremiah, Ezekiel, and the Twelve from Hosea to Malachi each
comprise a separate book of the second section.

The *Ketuvim* or "Writings" include the Psalms, prayers
composed over a period of centuries; Proverbs, a collection of
sayings dealing with proper conduct; Job, dealing with the
problem of good and evil; Ecclesiastes; Lamentations; Song of
Songs; and the historical books of Ruth, Esther, Daniel, Ezra,
Nehemiah; and Chronicles.

In each of the three sections of the *Tanakh*, history is
blended with religion and morality. Despite the varieties in style
and content, an obvious unity pervades all the books of the Bible.
God reveals Himself to man and makes His will known to him.

The books included in the Hebrew Bible constitute what is called the "Canon." The Bible was canonized in the second century before the Common Era, though debates about certain books that were included and excluded continued for many years afterward. Those religious books that were excluded from the Canon were known as *Apocrypha*, which means "hidden," because they were prohibited for sacred use and were not permitted to be kept with the other sacred books but instead were placed in a store room for private reading. It is believed that these books were excluded because they lacked the religious intensity of the canonical books, or perhaps did not have the necessary nationalistic appeal. Among these semi-sacred works are the books of the Maccabees, Judith, Tobit, and the Wisdom of Ben Sira.

Jews do not generally speak of the *Tanakh* as the "Old Testament," since they do not share the Christian belief that the Hebrew Bible was merely a prelude to the "New" Testament. In the Christian view, the New Testament represents a more mature development of religious thought. Since Jews do not accept this view, they do not use the terminology that supports it.

156

TEHILLIM

תְּהִילִים

Psalms

The Book of Psalms, *Sefer Tehillim*, is the most widely read of all biblical books. There is hardly an occasion in the religious life of the Jew at which an appropriate psalm is not read. To this day, the daily and Sabbath services consist largely of chapters from the Book of Psalms. In the daily service, Psalms 145–150 are read. Among the psalms recited on the Sabbath are Psalm 19, "The Heavens declare the glory of God"; Psalm 90, "Lord, You have been our dwelling place in all generations"; Psalm 136, "Give thanks unto the Lord for He is good, for His mercy endures forever"; Psalm 33, "Rejoice in the Lord, O you righteous, praise is appropriate for the upright." On the holidays, too, psalms of divine deliverance are recited (Chapters 113–118) and are included under the general title of *Hallel*, meaning "praise."

The Psalms are generally referred to as the Psalms of David, even though Jewish tradition never claimed that King David was author of all of them. In fact, the Book of Psalms ascribes specific chapters to other authors. Thus Psalm 90 is ascribed to Moses; Psalm 72 to Solomon, etc. The Talmud, which claims that David wrote the Psalms with the assistance of ten elders, most probably regarded him as the editor rather than the author of the Book of Psalms, although approximately one-half of the psalms are specifically ascribed to him.

Bible critics are sharply divided on the authorship of the Psalms. Some have claimed that all the Psalms were composed long after the death of King David, even after the exile to Babylonia in 586 B.C.E. This view is not generally held today by most scholars, who claim that many of the Psalms were written prior to the exile and some very possibly during the reign of King David.

The primary reason why the *Tehillim* were chosen to be read on so many different occasions is that they reflect almost every conceivable mood of the group or the individual, ranging from the heights of ecstatic joy to the depths of depression. The Jew finds mirrored in them his own predicament, his own emotional needs, and above all a reaffirmation of faith in God when needed most.

Upon the death of a dear one, he is comforted by the Psalm: "The Lord is my shepherd; I shall not want." When in a mood of doubt concerning the success of the wicked, he finds personal meaning in the words: "For the Lord regards the way of the righteous; But the way of the wicked shall perish." When his heart is filled with the joy of attainment his search for words of gratitude is fulfilled with the words, "Serve the Lord with gladness; Come before His presence with singing. . . . For the Lord is good; His mercy endures forever; And His faithfulness unto all generations." When Israel's future becomes cause for grave concern, he finds reassurance in the Psalm: "When the Lord brought back those that returned to Zion, we were like dreamers. . . . They that sow in tears shall reap in joy." In the Psalms, Heine says, are found "sunrise and sunset, birth and death, promise and fulfillment—the whole drama of humanity."

157

MEGILLAH

מְגִילָה

Scroll

In ancient times all books were read from scrolls. However, a selection of books of the Bible read on special days of the year were grouped together, known as the Five *Megillot*. They are: "The Song of Songs," read on Passover; "Ruth," on Shavuot; "Lamentations," on the Ninth of Av; "Ecclesiastes," on Sukkot; "Esther," on Purim.

Of the Five Scrolls, *Megillat Esther* is the best known. In fact, it is frequently referred to as "The Megillah" because of its continuous popularity over the centuries. Its theme remained ever relevant and meaningful to Jews confronted with enemies similar to Haman, who were bent on destroying the Jews because of their uniqueness. They drew confidence and courage with each reading of the *Megillah*, assuring them that the success of tyrants was temporary.

A unique factor of the *Megillat Esther* is the complete absence of God's name. It is generally agreed, however, that the author's omission was intentional, for he seems at times purposely to avoid mention of God's name. The reason for the omission is not known. Scholars surmise that since it was read on such a happy occasion when many liberties were permitted, the author was concerned that the Divine Name might be profaned by the readers. Perhaps he feared that the *Megillah* would be profaned by the enemies of the Jews, because the story deals with the triumph of Jews over their adversary. Nevertheless, one cannot help but sense God's influence pervading throughout the story. For example, Mordecai requests Esther to reveal her identity to the king so that she may aid them in their hour of crisis. He says, "For if you hold your peace at this time, then relief and deliverance will come to the Jews from another place."

The Song of Songs and Ecclesiastes both became centers of controversy among the rabbinic scholars who debated whether these two books were worthy of inclusion in the sacred literature of the Bible. The former reads like a secular love song without any seeming religious value. However, it was interpreted as an allegory depicting the loving relationship between God and Israel. It tells of Israel's faithfulness to God despite the allurements of Rome and Islam, who sought to woo her away from God. But despite many sufferings, Israel remains steadfast, proclaiming: "I am for my Beloved, and my Beloved is for me." Rabbi Akiba declared that if the other books are holy, the Song of Songs is "holy of holies."

Ecclesiastes portrayed life in terms of meaninglessness. The author experienced everything in life—wealth, wisdom, joy—but nothing gave him satisfaction. He summed up his philosophy with the famous expression, "Vanity of vanities, all is vanity." The Talmud tells of efforts to exclude the book from the canon of Scriptures because its cynical outlook could undermine religious faith. It was included, however, because "its beginning and end are religious teaching."

158

HAFTARAH

הַפְטָרָה

Reading from the Prophets
(literally: Conclusion)

In addition to the regular Torah reading on Sabbaths and Festivals, there is also a reading from the prophets. The literal meaning of the word *Haftarah* is "conclusion" or "dismissal," indicating either that the reading of the Torah for that service has been completed, or possibly that the whole service was concluded, as was the custom at one time. Thus, the congregation was dismissed after the *Haftarah* reading.

We do not know precisely when the prophetic reading was introduced into the synagogue. The Mishnah (completed in 200 C.E.) refers to it as a long-established custom, as does the New Testament. One theory holds that the prophetic reading was introduced during the reign of King Antiochus (ca. 165 B.C.E.). Since he prohibited the reading of the Torah, the Jews substituted a prophetic passage that reminded them of the Torah reading and later continued the custom of reading the *Haftarah* when the Torah reading was reinstituted.

The *Haftarah* selection is usually harmonized with the week's reading from the Torah. On holidays the prophetic selection either refers to the holiday directly or is at least indirectly related to the significance of the special day.

The person who is honored to recite the *Haftarah* is called *Maftir*. He is the last to recite the blessings before and after the final Torah reading. He then waits until the Torah scroll has been raised and rolled before introducing the *Haftarah* with a blessing. After completing the *Haftarah*, he intones four more blessings. The five *Haftarah* blessings express these ideas:

345

1. Gratitude for the Torah and the prophets.
2. God's trustworthiness.
3. A plea for the restoration of the land and people of Israel.
4. A prayer seeking the coming of the Messianic age.
5. Gratitude for the Sabbath or holiday, whichever is being observed at that time.

159

MISHNAH

מִשְׁנָה

Essential Part of the Talmud
(literally: To Rehearse One's Learning)

In addition to the written laws of the Torah, there developed over the centuries oral interpretations of these written laws that were essential to the understanding of the Torah. For example, the Torah did not go into detail concerning the observance of the Sabbath or holidays. What did the Torah mean when it said merely to "afflict your soul" on the Day of Atonement? The oral tradition went into the details of the observances of Yom Kippur, interpreting what the Torah intended to convey. Likewise, the Torah states, "You shall write them upon the doorposts of your house and upon your gates." We are left with no other details from the written law. What is the object to be placed on the doorpost? What should it contain? The interpretations and decisions given by the Sages and transmitted from teacher to pupil were indispensable to understanding the spirit of the written Torah. Without these legal decisions each person who reads the Torah would have created his own interpretation. Afflicting one's soul could have meant inflicting physical punishment on oneself, and writing on the doorpost could have been taken literally.

The Sages who learned these essential laws and transmitted them orally were reluctant to write them down and distribute them to their students, even though they may have kept notes for themselves. It is believed that their reluctance stemmed from the fear that the Oral Law might be regarded as having equal status with the Torah and eventually surpass it.

The Oral Law, however, grew so rapidly with each generation's comments and interpretations that the danger of distorting or forgetting the vast material became very real. No person or group of people could be expected to memorize so much information. At the end of the second century, a daring scholar, Rabbi Judah the Prince, assembled and edited this vast material, which fortunately gained immediate acceptance as the authoritative interpretation of the Bible. It was known as the Mishnah.

Though Rabbi Judah was mainly responsible for the Mishnah as we possess it today, he was greatly indebted to his predecessors who flourished in Palestine and were known as *Tannaim* (teachers). Their interpretations and decisions provided Rabbi Judah with his material. Some of the more prominent *Tannaim* were Hillel, Rabbi Yohanan ben Zakkai, Rabbi Meir, and Rabbi Akiba.

The Mishnah is divided into six sections or Orders, called *Sedarim:* (1) "Seeds," dealing primarily with agricultural laws; (2) "Festivals," relating to the Sabbath and holidays; (3) "Women," including laws of marriage and divorce; (4) "Damages," which includes laws of inheritance, lost property, and usury, in addition to damages caused by a man or his property; (5) "Holy Things," relating to laws of sacrifices, the Temple service, the first born; and (6) "Purities," laws pertaining to ritual cleanliness.

160

PIRKEI AVOT

פִּרְקֵי אָבוֹת

Ethics of the Fathers

Although the *Pirkei Avot* comprises only a very small part
of the Mishnah—one of sixty-three treatises—it is the most
widely quoted. Unlike all the other treatises, it contains no legal
material. It consists exclusively of maxims and epigrams directed to teachers, judges, and laymen that the Sages of the
Mishnah themselves composed or were fond of quoting. It has
aptly been described as a talmudic "Book of Proverbs."

The *Pirkei Avot* is the only treatise that is included in the
Siddur. The five chapters and a sixth, known as the addition of
Rabbi Meir, were in early days read and explained in the syna-
gogue every Sabbath afternoon between *Pesah* and *Shavuot*.
Each Sabbath was devoted to a different *Perek* (chapter). In time
the custom developed to extend the study of these chapters until
Rosh Hashanah. This custom still prevails in most traditional
synagogues.

We are not certain at what date the custom of studying
Pirkei Avot was introduced. Some authorities trace its origin to
the differences between the Sadducees and Pharisees. The Sadducees contended that only the priest could expound the Torah.
The Pharisees maintained that the Sages of the Talmud and not
the priests had been given this authority. The Pharisees therefore deliberately introduced the study of *Pirkei Avot* in public to
support their opinion that they were authorized to be the ex-
pounders of the Torah.

What are some of the values expounded in these chapters by
the Sages? Torah study should become a fixed routine; scholar-

349

ship should be combined with a wordly occupation; man has a duty to be involved in the community; one should respect another's property; prayer requires spontaneity; people should have respect for the law and order of government; there are rewards for fulfilling the commandments; man should develop humility; one must understand the ultimate purpose of learning; there is a need for moderation; envy and excessive ambition are evil, etc.

These sayings were not edited in order to present a consistent position by the Sages. One finds difference of opinion and emphasis—depending on the temperament, the personal philosophy, or the historical conditions that prompted each Sage to expound his lesson. For example, we find both poverty and wealth extolled by different rabbis. This world is given greater importance than the future world by one Sage. Another finds this world merely a prelude to the next. Two Sages differ as to what constitutes the ideals on which the world stands. The student is nowhere required to adopt a particular viewpoint, but he is expected to know what each Sage seeks to teach. The Talmud was unequivocal in its recognition of the value of *Pirkei Avot* as a moral guide: "If one wishes to achieve saintliness, let him carry out the words of the Fathers."

161

GEMARA

גְּמָרָא

The Second Essential Part of the Talmud
(literally: Study)

Just as the Mishnah interprets the laws of Torah by explaining its verses, so does the Gemara interpret the Mishnah. Just as new situations evolved from biblical to Mishnaic times and required elaboration in the Mishnah, so from the years 200 to 500 C.E., when the majority of Jews were in Babylonia rather than Palestine, new situations required even greater clarification of the older laws. The Mishnah and Gemara together form the Talmud.

Unlike the Mishnah, which is written in clear and concise Hebrew, the Gemara is written in Aramaic. Its main editor was Rabbi Ashi, who spent over fifty years collecting the material. The final revision and editing was undertaken by Rabina (d. 500 C.E.). These sages were preceded by the other great minds such as Rav and Samuel, who were the heads of academies in Babylonia. Those responsible for the creation of the Gemara were known as *Amoraim* (Expositors).

Another important difference between the Mishnah and Gemara is that the former is concise and closely knit, whereas the latter records the minutes of long discussions and heated debates, frequently lending itself to free association. The Gemara offers historical data, folklore, medical advice, theology, and sermonic material. Often these are found together on a single page. Only the scholar can discover the relationship between the various topics under discussion; only he can understand why the legal discussion abruptly ends and is followed by an apparently unrelated story.

There are sixty-three volumes of the Babylonian Talmud. Each volume is divided into chapters, usually containing several short *Mishnayot* (pl.). Each Mishnah is separated by pages of Gemara discussion constituting approximately nine-tenths of the whole Talmud.

162

MOREH NEVUKHIM

מוֹרֶה נְבוּכִים

Guide for the Perplexed

Moses Maimonides is best known to Jews for his masterful literary achievements in the area of Jewish law. Nevertheless, his *Moreh Nevukhim,* written in Cairo at the end of the twelfth century, bestowed upon him an added distinction as the most influential Jewish philosopher of his time.

As the title of his work indicates, Maimonides sought to guide the Jew of his day who found it difficult to harmonize his religious beliefs with the current philosophical ideas. He wrote his *Guide* in Arabic and Hebrew characters, since most of the Jews in Islamic countries were more familiar with Arabic than with Hebrew.

Maimonides realized that his *Guide for the Perplexed* could have a harmful effect on masses who were not prepared to accept his emphasis on reason as the path to faith. He claimed that his book was written for one man in ten thousand, and even for the one, he took added care to obscure certain sections in order to withhold "from the multitude the truths required for the knowledge of God." He was convinced that rationalism was not alien to classical Judaism but was natively Jewish, beginning with the Torah.

Of course, the Torah had to be understood in its proper context to appreciate how rational it really is. Maimonides goes to great lengths to show that many words and expressions are to be taken figuratively. Especially anthropomorphic references to God are all explained allegorically. To Maimonides, God is in no way comparable to man. All biblical references to God's organs or emotions are merely figures of speech written "in the language of man." Seriously to attribute any human functions to God was regarded as more sinful than idolatry.

The philosophy of Aristotle enjoyed a great revival in Islamic lands during the Middle Ages. Many intelligent Jews who were influenced by their intellectual environment were equally impressed with Aristotle's brilliant reasoning. Maimonides recognized the formidable challenge of Aristotle to Jewish thought. He greatly admired Aristotle and, in fact, incorporated many of his ideas into his own philosophical system. However, he was not reluctant to take issue with the master of Greek philosophers when he felt that his thought conflicted with the Bible, especially on the question of creation. Maimonides attempts to prove that Aristotle was in error in claiming that the world was eternal. He insists on the biblical account of creation, that the world was created out of nothingness (*creatio ex nihilo*). However, he does not cling to his traditional view out of blind faith in the Bible. He claims that Aristotle's doctrine of the eternity of the world is not convincing. If Aristotle were to have offered sufficient proof, Maimonides would have found a way of reconciling it with the biblical text.

Maimonides also delved into the problems of free will and prophecy. He believed that man was endowed with free will; he had faith in the ability of man to perfect himself by cultivating his intellectual, moral, and spiritual faculties. The prophet is even superior to the philosopher. He is the leader and lawgiver; in him all the conditions of the perfect life are combined: intelligence, imagination, and moral conduct.

Maimonides applies his rational method to explain the origin and meaning of many biblical precepts that were never openly discussed before his time. He offers his theories on animal sacrifices, suggesting that they were merely a divine concession to Israel at a more primitive stage in their history. His interpretation of the dietary laws, circumcision, and the observance of the festivals offer the reader a glimpse of his imaginative mind and his profound understanding of other fields of knowledge— psychology, anthropology, comparative religion.

The *Moreh Nevukhim* evoked bitter controversy among Jews long after the death of its author. Even many who acknowledged the vast erudition and personal piety of Maimonides charged him with heresy. On the other hand, the influence of this one book on Jews and non-Jews alike cannot be fully gauged. Thomas Aquinas, Leibnitz, Spinoza, Mendelssohn, and hundreds of other great minds carefully studied the *Guide* and acknowledged its influence on their thought.

163

TZAVAOT

צַוָּאוֹת

Wills

We usually associate wills exclusively with documents left by the deceased in which they distribute their possessions to survivors. To the Jew, a *tzavaah* (will) has been associated with more than the disposal of property. It has included instructions of moral and spiritual significance left to the survivors who regarded them with utmost seriousness.

Reading the Ethical Wills of ages past has helped us understand a great deal about the values and ideals of the Jewish communities in which they were written. We are able to derive valuable information about social and domestic relationships, customs and traditions, business methods, occupations, and leisure activities from these *tzavaot*. Most striking, however, was the moral sensitivity of these Ethical Wills. The parent was more concerned with leaving an ethical code for his children to follow than with being personally memorialized. For example, many wills left explicit instructions for the giving of charity, the importance of respecting one's fellow man, following sound rules of hygiene and personal appearance, maintaining regular study habits, etc.

Parents were often sensitive to the subject of cleanliness. The famous Judah ibn Tibbon of the twelfth century addresses his son:

> Honor yourself, your household, and your children, by providing proper clothing as far as your means allow, for it is unbecoming in a man, when he is not at work, to go shabbily dressed. Withhold from your stomach, and put it on your back.

One of the oft-quoted passages on the importance of reading is derived from the Ethical Will of the same Judah ibn Tibbon.

> Avoid bad society, but make your books your companions. Let your bookcases and shelves be your gardens and your pleasure grounds. Pluck the fruit that grows therein, gather the roses, the spices, and the myrrh. If your soul be satiate and weary, change from garden to garden, from furrow to furrow, from sight to sight. Then will your desire renew itself, and your soul be satisfied with delight.

The danger of idle hands is expressed in another will of the Middle Ages written to the person's daughters:

> My daughters ought always to be at home and not gadding about. They must not stand at the door (to watch what their neighbors are doing). Most strongly, I beg, most strictly, I command, that the daughters of my home be not, God forbid, without work to do, for idleness leads to sin, but they must spin, or cook, or sew, and be patient and modest in all their ways.

164

HASKALAH

הַשְׂכָּלָה

Enlightenment

The European Age of Enlightenment marks a turning point in Jewish history. Until then Jews were confined almost exclusively to their own groups. They differed from their neighbors, not merely in religion, but also in language, dress, and social customs. But when the leading thinkers of western Europe began calling for a new social order, Jews also began to demand equal rights. They wanted to abolish the degrading laws directed against them. Convinced that the age of emancipation had arrived, they sought to break down the ghetto walls.

The Jews of western Europe embarked on their own Age of Enlightenment. Under the guiding spirit of Moses Mendelssohn (1729–1786), more and more Jews began to participate in the cultural life of Germany. Mendelssohn was intent on bringing the Jews closer to European culture and habits of life. Several of his co-workers began to publish *Ha-Meassef*, a Hebrew magazine that attempted to transmit to Hebrew-reading Jews the thought and literature of the non-Jewish world. The Hebrew language as a modern literary medium sounded artificial after so many centuries of disuse. The publication eventually failed. But at least these founders of the German *Haskalah* made a valiant effort to combine the west European and Hebrew cultures.

From Germany the *Haskalah* moved to Galicia and then to Russia where the *Maskilim* (intellectuals) made every effort to enlighten the masses of Jews in the ways of the world. The basic difference between the Jewish enlightenment in Germany and Russia was the Jewish emphasis of the latter. Most of the east

European *maskilim* defended Jewish cultural values, while simultaneously requesting their fellow Jews to broaden their intellectual and economic life.

Eventually, the Russian *Haskalah* began to produce a small group of poets and novelists who proved to their people that Hebrew could be revived as a living language. The poet, Judah Leib Gordon, and the novelist, Abraham Mapu, were among these pioneers of modern Hebrew literature.

The *Haskalah* movement in Russia dealt with practical approaches to the Jewish problem. It proposed that Jews engage in agriculture and manual trades. It also suggested that secular subjects be included in Jewish schools. Its most valuable contribution, however, was in helping to revive strong feelings of Jewish nationalism, which gave rise to the Zionist movement and ultimately culminated in the establishment of the Jewish State in Israel.

165

MUSAR

מוּסָר

Moral Discipline, Ethics

The word *musar*, when referred to in the Torah, implies a discipline that God imposes on man. Thus in Deuteronomy we read, "Take thought this day that it was not your children, who neither experienced nor witnessed the *lesson (musar)* of the Lord your God – His majesty, His mighty hand, His outstretched arm." In the Book of Proverbs we already begin to see the expression assuming a more general meaning – the moral discipline that is instilled by God and also by the parent: "Hear my son, the *musar* of your father, and forsake not the teaching of your mother." Even self-discipline, the ability to control one's own impulses, is implied by the term *musar* in the Book of Proverbs.

Though the term *musar* is not used extensively in talmudic literature, it is generally understood as self-control, which is essential to ethical conduct. The rabbis were aware that man is endowed with instincts and passions that must be kept under restraint. "The wicked are under the control of their impulses, but the righteous have their impulses under their control," remarked the rabbis; i.e., the former lacked *musar* whereas the latter possessed it.

During the medieval period, the term *musar* gradually came to be associated with the study of ethics that would help to improve relationships among men. A rich literature, dealing almost exclusively with morals and ethics was developed in central Europe, Spain, and Italy. This moralistic literature was generally written in simple, homely style, easily grasped by the masses. It dealt with such topics as family life, relations with Jews and non-Jews, treatment of animals, and care of personal hygiene.

In the nineteenth century, a *Musar* Movement was inaugurated in eastern Europe by Rabbi Israel Salanter, one of the great religious leaders of his day. Fearing that the moral fiber of Jewish communities was being weakened by external influences, Salanter and his followers advocated that the curriculum in the Jewish schools emphasize the study of ethical literature, or *Musar*. A life devoted to contemplation, religious fervor, and self-sacrifice, leading to exemplary ethical conduct, was the primary goal of the *Musarniks*, as they were called.

Some prominent contemporary Jewish educators have vigorously advocated that the emphasis on *musar* permeate the curriculum of Religious Schools. Especially today, when the need for moral direction among youth is greater than ever, it would be wise to expose the student to the vast resources of moral literature that have been virtually ignored in modern Jewish education. It cannot be denied that the Bible and Talmud are our greatest repositories of moral teachings, but in addition to these main sources, many more recent works of Jewish literature can offer the searching student rich and relevant material for classroom discussion.

Certainly the informal *musar* discussions between teacher and pupil dealing with some of the critical moral problems of our time should be explored in the classroom. Even if the more formal lesson is delayed until another session, the classroom time shall have been most wisely spent if the student will later associate his Religious School with his quest for moral values.

166

LESHON HAKODESH

לְשׁוֹן הַקֹּדֶשׁ

The Holy Tongue

The Hebrew language was the spoken language of the Jews for only a brief period in their history. For many centuries they spoke the languages of the majority groups with whom they lived. They spoke Aramaic, Greek, Arabic, Spanish as they now speak English in America.

When Hebrew ceased to be the spoken language of the Jews, it became the sacred language of prayer and study, known as *leshon hakodesh*. The Talmud refers to the "holy tongue" to distinguish it from the secular languages spoken by the people. Maimonides writes that the reason for calling Hebrew *leshon hakodesh* is that it contains no indecent words or expressions. "It only hints at them, as if to indicate that these things should not be mentioned, and should therefore have no names. . . ."

What is most surprising is that the Hebrew language was never forgotten, despite the fact that it was not the spoken tongue for many centuries. Fortunately, many Hebrew words and idioms were preserved in the Jewish vernacular for Hebrew prayers, even though Jewish law permits one to pray "in whatever language he understands," which includes the most basic prayers—the *Shema* and *Amidah*. The only exception to the rule was the Jewish community of Alexandria in Egypt, which dispensed with the sacred language in its religious life. Even the Torah was read in Greek and all the prayers similarly in translation. Solomon Schechter has appropriately described Alexandrian Jewry:

"The result was death. It withered away, and ended in total apostasy from Judaism."

The use of Hebrew, though restricted, nevertheless, kept alive the vigor of a people scattered in exile. Another people driven from its home for almost two thousand years would have long forgotten its relationship with its former land. Not so the Jewish people. The holy tongue kept alive the dream of a restored Zion and also kept world Jewry united. All Jews speaking the same language felt that they were members of a living people bound to their brothers wherever they might be.

The use of modern Hebrew as a living tongue encountered bitter opposition in the early days of the Zionist movement. The ultrapious especially considered it sacrilegious to use Hebrew in daily conversation. Much of the controversy has now subsided; Hebrew has become the national language of Israel. New words and expressions are being coined daily to meet the urgent demands of the modern state. The use of Hebrew as a spoken language does not mean that it can no longer be referred to as *leshon hakodesh*. The Bible is still the most important source from which modern Hebrew words are derived. Moreover, the life of holiness is not restricted to the synagogue. It can be experienced in the marketplace, in the office, and on the sports field as well. The revival of an ancient language enhances rather than detracts from its sanctity.

Part XIV

THE COMMUNITY OF ISRAEL AND THE LAND OF ISRAEL

167

KLAL YISRAEL

כְּלָל יִשְׂרָאֵל

Community of Israel

Centuries ago the rabbis emphasized the intimate partnership between God, Torah, and the community of Israel. Judaism could not be properly understood without the inclusion of these three concepts.

The community of Israel is known by several names: *Klal Yisrael, Knesset Yisrael,* and *Am Yisrael,* all suggesting the indisoluble partnership among all members of the Jewish community throughout the world. They are bound together by a common tradition inherited from the past, a common concern and way of life in the present and the awareness of a similar destiny in the future.

The Sages expressed their most bitter criticism against the Jew who denied his relationship with *Klal Yisrael.* In the *Haggadah,* he is identified with the *Rasha,* the wicked son, who, by excluding himself from the community, virtually denies the existence of God.

Many attempts have been made to define the Jewish people, but with little success. The Jews have been called a race, a religion, a nation, etc. All of these definitions are inadequate. Race implies common physical characteristics—a condition not met by all Jews. Though the religion is closely identified with Jewish people, the Jews are not merely a religious group in the sense that Protestants or Catholics are. Atheists, even, are not excluded from the Jewish community. Nationhood implies common political allegiance to a particular country—again a condition not met by all Jews.

It is precisely because the Jews cannot be defined by any of the usual terms applied to other collective groups that any definition borrowed from another language remains inadequate. For this reason, Jews prefer to describe the Jewish group with an authentic Hebrew expression, either by the biblical term *Am* (people), or by the later names, *Knesset Yisrael* or *Klal Yisrael*.

Dr. Solomon Schechter referred to *Klal Yisrael* as "catholic Israel," implying a universal people. Schechter never fully explained all the ramifications of this imaginative term; nevertheless, it made a powerful impact on the Jewish community. Henrietta Szold (1958) elaborated on Schechter's phrase in a speech before the New York Council of Jewish Women:

> The supremacy of catholic Israel differs from and is more than the solidarity of Jews. Solidarity means that each Jew stands ready to suffer with every other Jew, to succor him with the superabundance of prosperity, defend him against the aspersions of prejudice, espouse him when he is maligned . . .
>
> Allegiance to catholic Israel requires such sacrifices, such lessons got by heart, such emotions translated into effective action – and it requires much more. The duty of the Jew tingling with the consciousness of catholic Israel extends beyond his outcast brother to the prosperous. He is not patron, but fellow aspirant. He seeks to understand mental conditions as well as physical needs. . . . His obligation grows out of whole-souled belief in a mission waiting to be performed by Israel – Israel scattered or Israel nationalized. . . . [p. 112]

168

KEHILLAH

קְהִילָה

Self-governing Jewish Community

In premodern times most European Jews belonged to self-contained Jewish communities. Self-government was granted to these Jewish communities primarily because it made the collection of taxes easier for the state. The Jews in turn were eager to unify the community, and wherever possible, to form a federation of several Jewish communities. They needed unity to protect themselves from their enemies. But just as important to them was the opportunity to apply the Jewish law to their daily lives, which was possible only in an autonomous Jewish community.

The most highly developed *kehillah* in the Middle Ages was formed in Poland during the sixteenth century and was known as the Council of Four Lands. Four provinces had their own separate councils and chose representatives to the supreme Council of Four Lands, which governed the internal affairs of most Polish Jews.

The tasks of the Council were varied. It served as a judicial body hearing differences between individuals and communities, or between two communities. It established schools and talmudical academies in every town and set down rules for instruction. It ordered the strict enforcement of the moral law in accordance with rabbinic tradition. It also enforced the laws of the state even though they were not always favorable to Jews.

In more recent times, *kehillot* existed in German communities until the Nazi period, but not with the same legal force as their medieval counterparts. In fact, New York City was a more or less united community until 1835. Each synagogue was authorized to be called a *kahal*. But secessions brought about a multiplicity of synagogues, and gradually the state stepped in to enact its own laws on marriage and burial, and later on other matters once exclusively in the hands of the Jewish community.

In 1909 a serious attempt was made to form a permanent *kehillah* in New York City. Jewish leaders under the leadership of Dr. Judah L. Magnes realized the need for a democratically elected representative body that would turn its attention to many problems facing the Jews of New York. During its first years, the *kehillah* established an arbitration court for religious disputes, a bureau of Jewish education, and a welfare bureau. It also attempted to deal with the problems of *kashrut*.

After a few years, however, the *kehillah* failed because of internal conflicts and the lack of power to enforce its decisions. The only tangible result was the establishment of the Bureau of Jewish Education, which continued to function after the *kehillah* attempt failed.

In recent years, many Jewish communities in the United States have formed Jewish Community Councils. These represent the first successful attempt to establish an organization representing all Jewish groups in a particular community. The rise of these councils came about, in large part, because of the need for centralizing campaigns for funds needed to help the Jews in Europe and Israel. Many of these local councils are affiliated with a National Council of Federations and Welfare Funds, which exercises influence in areas of fund-raising, allocation of funds, and community organization. Also under the aegis of the Council, the National Community Relations Advisory Council (NCRAC) was set up to avoid duplication of funds and energies in defending Jewish rights.

Although great strides have been made in the past few decades to organize American Jewry locally and nationally, many areas are still woefully neglected. Especially in the area of Jewish education, where standards are sorely lacking, is the need for coordination greater than ever. In a democratic society,

American Jews can never expect to establish a European type of *kehillah* with the same degree of self-government and enforcement assuring strength and cohesiveness. However, they can still work toward a well-organized Jewish community with a vital social structure to provide much needed status and dignity.

169

SHTADLAN

שְׁתַּדְלָן

Advocate of the Jewish Community
(literally: One Who Tries)

Starting in the sixteenth century, the Jewish communities of Poland relied heavily on the efforts of their officially appointed ambassador who would protect their interests and guard their welfare. The *shtadlan* qualified for his post by virtue of his wealth, business connections, personality, his thorough knowledge of the Polish language, and his ability to practice the art of diplomacy.

The Polish Jews were well aware that powerful enemies were prepared to seize every opportunity to hurt Jewish interests. They knew that every meeting of the Polish parliament presented possible crises for them. The *shtadlan* lived in the capital where he could visit influential noblemen, and by appealing to their reason and sense of justice, convert them to friends and supporters of the Jewish community. When he failed to avert the passage of an anti-Jewish law, he would even appeal to the king to seek moderation. If all his efforts failed, he could at least warn his fellow-Jews of the dangers ahead.

The presence of this back-door diplomat or lobbyist was not an unmixed blessing for the Jews. He was frequently carried away by his influence. At times his selfish interests prompted him to work against his fellow Jews. He would discourage the entry of Jewish exiles into his country if he felt that they threatened to compete with his business interests. Likewise, his personal problems with the court would have a harmful effect on the Jewish community at large.

Though the official *shtadlan* disappeared in Europe in the second half of the eighteenth century, American Jews also had a few prominent leaders who used their influence to intercede on behalf of their brethren. Louis Marshall has been referred to as the last of the great *shtadlanim* in American life. He was instrumental in abrogating a commercial treaty between the United States and Russia when the latter discriminated against Jews. He forced Henry Ford to retract his anti-Semitic articles in his newspaper, the *Dearborn Independent*. Marshall was also successful in eliciting an apology from Ford for his sponsoring of the circulation of the English translation of the infamous *Protocols of the Elders of Zion in the United States.*

Though American Jews no longer rely on single individuals to plead their cause, as a rule, presidents still have Jewish advisers who help to guide them on issues affecting the Jewish community. However, they are not recognized by the Jewish community as official spokesmen, nor are they expected to intercede on its behalf.

170

ERETZ YISRAEL

אֶרֶץ יִשְׂרָאֵל

Land of Israel

One of the greatest miracles of Jewish history has undoubtedly been the unbroken tie between the Jewish people and the Land of Israel. In rabbinic Hebrew *Haaretz*, the Land, signified the Holy Land while every other country was *Hutz Laaretz*, outside the Land. *Ha'ir*, the City, signified Jerusalem, which the Sages fondly called the very center of the earth. These were not just figures of speech. Palestine was the umbilical cord of Jewish life. It was The Land, the pivot about which all religious life revolved.

Even after the destruction of the Second Temple and the exile of Jewry from the land, its holiness remained intact. The rabbis of the Talmud enacted this doctrine into law:

> One may compel his entire household to go with him to the Land of Israel, but none may be compelled to leave it. . . . Living in the Land of Israel equals the performance of all the commandments of the Torah. . . . A man may enter into a contract (verbally, with a non-Jew) for the purpose of acquiring a house in the Land of Israel, even on the Sabbath (on which day such a transaction is usually forbidden).

Much of the content of medieval Jewish literature reflects the pain of separation from *Eretz Yisrael*. Not only in France and Germany, where Jews suffered many disadvantage, was the hope of return expressed, but even in enlightened Spain where Jews attained high positions in the world of affairs. Jewish poets yearned for their homeland. Their successes in Spain reminded them either of their past, which was gone, or of the glory of their future. Yehuda Halevi, the most celebrated of the Jewish poets, was impatient with the *galut* (exile) in spite of all the recognition he received in Spain:

> Israel, helpless doves given over into a
>   land of pits and deserts, arise!
> This is not your rightful residence.
> Return to your place of comfort, to the
>   borders of your land.

Halevi was faithful to his convictions and left for the Land of Israel. The arduous journey was a moving experience for him despite the dangers of travel in those days. Throughout the voyage he was guided by a light from Zion. On approaching the land, his poetry became even loftier, and the poems about his journey comprise some of the greatest writing in Jewish literature.

There were always individual Jews, some unknown, others renowned, who returned to *Eretz Yisrael*. Still others bemoaned the fate that prevented them from fulfilling the *mitzvah* of living in the Holy Land. Palestine was never completely bereft of at least a small community of Jews, despite the most difficult hardships under which they lived.

With the emergence of political Zionism, the hopes of world Jewry quickened. *Eretz Yisrael* was no longer the object of dreams and prayers alone. The masses of European and American Jews who did not intend to settle in Palestine themselves nevertheless contributed toward its development with a spirit of zeal and unprecedented urgency. Theodor Herzl's enthusiasm ignited a spark that became a consuming flame. Zionism became synonymous with the coming of the Messianic Age. A new state would emerge in the forseeable future that would live by the highest ideals of social justice and cultural creativity.

Anyone who is aware of this long, indissoluble partnership between the Jewish people and the Land of Israel can understand why the establishment of the State of Israel in 1948 represent the most significant event in modern Jewish history.

171

GALUT

גָּלוּת

Exile

The term expressing the condition of the Jews outside their own land and scattered among the peoples of the world is called *galut*. It is especially associated with the oppression and persecution that have accompanied the homelessness of the Jew since the destruction of the Second Temple in the year 70 C.E. until the establishment of the State of Israel in 1948.

Galut implies compulsory banishment of the Jews from their homeland. It is not synonymous with the term Diaspora or dispersion, which includes any Jewish community outside of *Eretz Yisrael*, even those where Jews may have settled voluntarily and were relatively secure.

In spite of their bitter exile, the Jews surprisingly did not place the blame upon those who banished them from their homeland. They recalled the words of the prophets who warned them before their first expulsion from Palestine in 586 B.C.E. that their own sins would be responsible for their exile.

They likewise accepted the responsibility for the second exile and even incorporated a prayer in their liturgy that reads: "Because of our sins we are exiled from our land and removed far away from our country."

A very relevant question has arisen since the recent establishment of the State of Israel: What of those Jews who have chosen to remain outside of Israel? Are they still regarded as living in *galut* despite their freedom to return? Some voices in Israel maintain that the Jew can never live a normal Jewish life in the diaspora, no matter how democratic the society. They contend that a minority group always lives with a sense of insecurity and is subject to the whims of the majority. Furthermore, a Jewish minority does not have the same opportunities for self-development as those living in a natural Jewish environment.

On the other hand, there are Jews, many of whom are staunch Zionists, who deny that they are living in *galut*. They contend that Jews living in democratic countries such as the United States are not merely tolerated by the non-Jewish majority, but are secure partners possessing equal rights and responsibilities, in spite of their small number.

Actually, *galut* is more than a locality. It is more a state of mind than a geographical place. There are some Jews living outside of Israel who are in *galut* and others who are not. Those who deny or belittle their Jewishness because they are overly sensitive to the reaction of non-Jews, those who resort to slavish imitation of the majority, are very much in *galut*. But those who are proud of their heritage and do not compromise their convictions are justified in denying that they are *galut* Jews.

172

KIBBUTZ GALUYOT

קִבּוּץ גָּלֻיּוֹת

Ingathering of the Exiles

One of the most miraculous events that was attributed to the coming of the Messiah was that he would bring an end to the miseries of the Jews throughout the dispersion; he would gather the people from the four corners of the earth and return them to their ancient homeland, where they would be restored once again to a great nation. For centuries prior to the advent of political Zionism, most Jews faithfully waited for the Messiah to bring about the miraculous return of all dispersed Jews. To this day, some of the opponents of political Zionism, among the extremely Orthodox element, still cling to the hope that the Messiah will fulfill his appointed task by supernatural means.

Meanwhile, the *Kibbutz Galuyot* began on the day that the State of Israel came into being. Its gates swung open for every Jew who wanted to enter. Israel's Declaration of Independence stated: "The State of Israel will be open to the immigration of Jews from all countries of their dispersion."

The great ingathering eclipsed all previous immigrations. Jews came from fifty-two countries. Survivors of European death camps were reunited with their relatives in Israel. They arrived from Morocco, Tunisia, and other parts of North Africa. They left their homes in India, Pakistan, and Persia to start life anew in the Land of Israel.

The most dramatic single episode of *Kibbutz Galuyot* was known as "Operation Magic Carpet"–the airborne evacuation of over 50,000 Yemenite Jews to Israel in 1949. Thirty thousand were transported within a five-month period. The Yemenites trace their origin to the destruction of the First Temple. They

379

attributed their suffering to divine punishment for not having heeded the call of Ezra to return and help rebuild the Temple in the fifth century B.C.E. Until their emigration they lived degraded lives in segregated ghettos. They were not permitted to ride a camel or horse and had to dismount even from a donkey if a Moslem passed by. They were forbidden to wear robes or to carry defensive weapons. All but a small number were incredibly poor and undernourished.

Yet throughout their exile the Yemenites never lost their religious faith, nor did they renounce their belief in the ultimate return to Zion. Every boy attended a religious school, studying the Torah in the original Hebrew as well as in Aramaic and Arabic translations. Since there was never more than one book to a class, they were able to read upside-down or sideways. Amidst their poverty, they remained industrious and clean. They brought with them to Israel their artistic tradition of song, poetry, and dance, which has made a strong impact on Israeli culture.

On the first day of Hanukkah 1959, the one-millionth person entered Israel. The special event was transformed into a national holiday celebrated with singing and dancing in the streets of the cities, in the *kibbutzim*, in the army camps, and in the newly built towns. Today in 1988, Israel's population numbers approximately 4.2 million. Yet, *Kibbutz Galuyot* was far from completion. Israel has continued to prepare for and welcome new citizens from any part of the world where Jews have sought to establish a new home. About 7,000 Ethiopian Jews had emigrated to Israel before 1984, and between November 1984 and March 1985 another 14,000 were rescued by Operation Moses in response to widespread famine in Ethiopia.

173

KIBBUTZ

קִבּוּץ

Collective

One of the outstanding achievements of modern-day Israel has been its experiment in group living. The history of the *kibbutz* began in 1909 when Degania was founded. In spite of the difficulties of attracting new members and retaining young adults born on these *kibbutzim,* several hundred are still operative; they represent various political and religious ideologies. Observers have come from all parts of the world to study the inner life and accomplishments of the *kibbutznik.* A number of developing nations have attempted to establish their own collectives based on the model of the *kibbutz* in Israel.

The *kibbutz* was born of ideological belief and economic necessity. The second wave of immigrants who came to Palestine from eastern Europe after 1902 had participated in the bitter struggle against Czarism in Russia. They were infused with both Socialist and Zionist ideals. Their interest in the latter brought them to Palestine, despite the most difficult economic conditions, with the intention of participating in the building of a Jewish homeland.

However, when they sought employment with adequate wages in the existing colonies, they found that they could not compete with the experienced Arab peasants who made no demands on their employers. Out of their frustration a handful of intellectual immigrants formed a small collective *(kevutzah).* They were determined to perform all the work themselves without exploiting cheap Arab labor. Thus the first *kibbutz* was founded. It served as a model for all other collectives that were to follow.

As was mentioned above, most of the *kibbutzim* represent various ideologies. There are those which follow socialist principles; some follow Marxist principles, and others are affiliated with Hapoel Hamizrachi, the labor wing of the Orthodox Mizrachi movement. Even the extreme Orthodox Jews have their *kibbutzim*.

Despite their wide political and religious differences, most collectives function in a similar manner. Each *kibbutz* is a self-governing group that collectively accepts or rejects applicants for admission. Once the applicant is accepted, he is required to conform with all the standards of the group. Even though he is not punished for infractions, he is subject to moral pressure from his fellow workers and may be requested to leave. Should he decide to leave for personal reasons, he must be prepared to surrender his material possessions.

The government of each *kibbutz* is usually comprised of a general assembly, made up of every adult member, several administrators, and working committees to deal with such problems as health, education, and welfare. Meetings are held weekly and a majority vote is decisive on all questions. Generally over half the members of a *kibbutz* are actively engaged in some aspect of the government of the group.

Since the women are required to work in the fields and factories, they are not expected to assume the normal responsibilities of a houswife. Community kitchens, dining rooms, and laundries relieve them of most household chores. Even their children are cared for by others. Some Kibbutz children live together in special quarters and are returned to their parents after school for several hours together, but afterwards return to their own dormitories for the night.

It is difficult to ascertain whether these co-operatives will continue to exist indefinitely. Many problems may affect their future, such as the lack of higher educational facilities and the normal desire to be rewarded financially as an incentive for hard work. Some *kibbutzim* have already combined free enterprise with their socialist ideology. Although the number of "dropouts" has not threatened the future of the kibbutz movement, the establishment of new collectives has not kept pace with the country's population increase. Whatever its future will be, the *kibbutz*, nevertheless, will have made an indelible contribution to Israel's development and welfare.

174

KEREN KAYEMET LEYISRAEL

קֶרֶן קַיֶּמֶת לְיִשְׂרָאֵל

Jewish National Fund

The problem of financing the colonization of Palestine was uppermost in Theodor Herzl's mind. He first conceived of the "Jewish Colonial Trust" to be the financial instrument. Herzl negotiated with important financiers but met with apathetic postponements. He then sought a different approach, turning to the masses of sympathetic Jews. Shares were offered at the equivalent of five dollars and could be paid in installments. This plan met with greater success than former attempts to raise funds. The Second Zionist Congress then decided officially to establish the Jewish Colonial Trust, the first national bank that would further support the Zionist cause.

The most significant fund-raising instrument, however, was developed in 1901–the *Keren Kayemet Leyisrael*, or Jewish National Fund (JNF). It was first proposed in a brief telegram addressed to a conference of Zionists in 1884 and was signed by professor of mathematics Hermann Schapira of Heidelberg, Germany. The telegram suggested that the Jewish people establish a fund to purchase land in Palestine, financed by small donations. Schapira presented his proposal again in 1887 at the First Zionist Congress. As revised and finally adopted in 1901, the JNF was inspired by biblical agricultural law. It provided that the land to be purchased could never be sold or mortgaged and would remain the permanent property of the Jewish people. It could only be leased at nominal rental for a period of not more than forty-nine years and then returned to its owner, just as the Bible prescribed the law of the Jubilee.

In its early period the *Keren Kayemet* was the Zionist

colonizing agency and its land-buying instrument. Some of the first colonies were founded with JNF assistance, which included the supplying of livestock and farm equipment. The JNF provided hundreds of thousands of acres for agricultural settlements. The land is worked by its owners since the policy of JNF prohibits hired labor except in hardship cases. It has installed water supply systems and carried out vast drainage programs on its land holdings. As part of its afforestation program it has planted millions of trees in forests and beautified many roads with shade trees. Many housing units were erected on JNF land; plots for schools, public buildings, and hospitals have also been supplied by *Keren Kayemet.*

The JNF is governed by a board of directors elected by the General Council of the World Zionist Organization. Its main office is in Jerusalem, but its funds come from all parts of the world. Contributions are raised primarily by the familiar blue-and-white coin boxes, tree certificates, and Golden Book inscriptions.

175

KNESSET

כְּנֶסֶת

Israeli Parliament

In 1949 the first parliament of the new Jewish state met in a movie house in Tel Aviv. The representatives took their seats and recalled the history of the Zionist movement from the time that Theodor Herzl convened the First Zionist Congress in Basle, Switzerland. Israel's first prime minister, David Ben-Gurion, was installed, and the functions of the *Knesset* were then defined to assure an orderly and representative government.

The *Knesset* (a biblical word meaning assembly) is a single House of one hundred and twenty members. Its members are elected by secret ballot. Unlike the American system of election, which is based on congressional districts, Israel abides by the system of proportional representation. Each political party may submit a list of candidates with as many as 120 names. It will then receive the number of seats in Parliament proportionate to the percentage of the total national vote. For example, if a party gets ten per cent of the votes, it would then receive ten per cent of the 120 seats. The first twelve persons appearing on its list would then be elected to office.

Under this system, the *Knesset* is divided among more than a dozen parties. Every government must rely on a coalition of several parties. The opposition consists of unrelated groups from extreme right to extreme left. The one advantage to this system is that the demands of each party, no matter how small, must be heard if their support is to be counted upon.

After a national election, the President, who has limited political powers, meets with the leaders of each party before calling on one of them to form a government. The head of the largest single party is most likely to become the prime minister, who is the most active and influential leader in the country. The major party must then begin negotiations with the smaller parties to form a coalition that will give them a majority in the *Knesset.*

The following parties are just some of the parties represented in the present*Knesset:*

Mapai, the Israel Labor Party, which is moderately socialist; *Mapam,* a Labor Party more extreme in its socialist views; *Herut,* a rightest, more militant group than the other major parties in Israel. The Religious Parties comprise four distinct religious groupings: *Mizrachi, Poalei Mizrachi, Agudat Yisrael,* and *Poalei Agudat Yisrael.*

There is also the Liberal Party, formed in 1961 through the merger of the General Zionists and Progressives. *Achdut Avodah* represents a view somewhere between *Mapai* and *Mapam.* There are some Communists, and there are the *Mapai*-affiliated Arab groups.

Part XV

JEWISH LAW AND AUTHORITY

176

HALAKHAH

הֲלָכָה

Jewish Law, Rule of Right Conduct
(literally: The Path)

Halakhah as a specific term is a legal decision on a religious or civil problem proposed by a rabbinical authority in conformity with God's will. As a general term it connotes all the legal material found in rabbinic literature.

Since the Torah could not have anticipated all the new problems of a more complex society, the talmudic authorities sought to render binding decisions on all current problems in the spirit of the original Torah. The *halakhah* covered almost every area of life, not merely for the individual but for the community as well, including the civil and criminal laws by which the Jewish community lived.

No single authority was competent to render a binding decision of Jewish law, however revered he might be. He could declare what he thought the *halakhah* should be on a given question, but his opinion never became law until it was accepted by the majority of the academy. After its acceptance it then became a legal guide for the entire Jewish community. The *halakhah* was accepted by the masses because they trusted their leaders as able interpreters of God's will.

The Jewish system of law served a two-fold purpose: It was the most potent means of unifying the Jewish community in an often alien environment, and it provided the individual Jew with a means of consciously serving God by observing His laws.

Non-Jewish critics have frequently criticized the emphasis on law in Judaism. They have claimed that the *halakhah* was an

391

iron-clad system never subject to change. But these critics have not understood the nature of Jewish law. Laws that were fixed by one assembly could be repealed if necessary by another group, if they surpassed the former in numbers or wisdom. Just as a rabbinic law in some instances modified a biblical law, so a new rabbinic law occasionally modified an older rabbinic law, if conditions warranted change. The rabbis were most sensitive about imposing laws on a community that were too difficult to follow.

Other critics claimed that the *halakhah* encouraged blind obedience to the law. Charges of religious hypocrisy were also leveled against followers of the law. However, the formulators of the *halakhah* clearly indicated that by blindly fulfilling the letter of the law, a Jew could not serve God. To perform the act without the intention of serving God was meaningless.

A goodly number of Jews, especially those who look upon the law as divine, continue to observe the *halakhah* scrupulously, despite the fact that religious authorities cannot enforce compliance. Others are more selective and prefer to observe only those laws that have meaning for themselves or are deemed essential to Jewish survival. However, even those who question the necessity of observing Jewish law today would probably concede that Jewish survival would have been impossible in the past were it not for the general acceptance of the *halakhah* by the Jewish community.

177

SHULHAN ARUKH

שֻׁלְחָן עָרוּךְ

The Code of Jewish Law

One of the most authoritative Jewish works ever written was composed in the sixteenth century by Joseph Karo. He gave it the name *Shulhan Arukh*—The Prepared Table. In it he systematized the involved and often confusing laws of Judaism so lengthily debated in the Talmud. The *Shulhan Arukh* makes it possible for the average student to learn the final decision on almost any legal or ritual question without following all the discussion leading up to the decision.

The *Shulhan Arukh* consists of four sections: *Orah Hayyim* (The Way of Life), dealing with the laws of the festivals and prayers; *Yoreh Deah* (The Guide to Knowledge), dealing with the dietary laws, mourning practices, vows, etc.; *Even Haezer* (The Rock of Help), dealing with marriage and divorce; and *Hoshen Mishpat* (The Breastplate of Judgment), covering civil and criminal laws.

Although it gained immediate acceptance among many communities, Karo's Code was challenged by scholars in central and eastern Europe. Those scholars felt that the author frequently represented the Sephardic rather than the Ashkenazic viewpoint and that he was partial to the Spanish and African schools of law. Rabbi Moses Isserles of Cracow studied Karo's decisions carefully, then added and modified some of those decisions in his commentary representing the Ashkenazic viewpoint. To the "Prepared Table" of Karo he supplemented his "Tablecloth" *(Mappah)*. Karo and Isserles appear together in standard editions of the *Shulhan Arukh;* both are necessasy for a comprehensive understanding of practices of the total Jewish community.

To this day, Orthodox Jews are committed to the decisions of the *Shulhan Arukh,* regarding it with utmost reverence as their handbook of Jewish practice. Many Conservative Jews also seek direction from Karo's Code of Jewish Law but claim that it does not carry the same authority as it did at one time. It is their opinion that Jewish law must be permitted to develop in order to meet current situations.

There is no question that the common recognition of the *Shulhan Arukh* as the authoritative code of practice served as a unifying force among most Jews for three and a half centuries. The *Kitzur Shulhan Arukh,* an abridged version of the original Code, was consulted regularly in the Jewish home, reminding Jews throughout the world that their common acceptance of Jewish law was necessary to their survival as a people.

178

MINHAG

מִנְהָג

Custom, Public Practice

Many customs and usages were never originally prescribed by Jewish law but were observed so scrupulously by certain Jewish groups that they later assumed the importance of law and were rarely questioned by pious Jews. Such *minhagim* (pl.) are covering the head, breaking the glass at weddings, reciting *Yizkor* on the last day of major festivals, etc.

The rabbis showed great respect for community practices. When undecided about a legal decision, they would frequently accept the *minhag* (practice) that prevailed among members of the community as authoritative. The Talmud advised to "go forth and see what the community is accustomed to do, and then act accordingly." This was taken to be an act of faith in the people who were probably following an ancient law, the source of which was not known to the modern court but was evidently handed down by word of mouth from generation to generation. Of course, when the rabbis spoke of the strength of custom in deciding law they did not mean that the customs of uninterested or uneducated Jews would be the determining factor. Only the customs of the pious and the scholarly would carry sufficient weight to become law.

Custom was generally so highly regarded that the Talmud charges: "One must not change the custom." Or, "If you come into a city, guide yourself according to its custom." Often quoted is the statement recorded in the Palestinian Talmud that custom can sometimes abolish a law. It has been indicated, however, that this statement deals with civil rather than religious matters. The

Mishnah states: If one hires laborers to work early or to work late, he has no right to compel them to do so where the custom is not to work early or not to work late; where the custom is to provide them with food, he should give it to them, and where sweets are customarily provided, he should provide them. Everything should follow the custom of the land."

179

MINHAG SEFARAD

מִנְהַג סְפָרַד

The Custom among Sephardic Jews

Although the name *Sefarad* is found in the Bible, in the Middle Ages it came to be identified with the Iberian Peninsula, which is unrelated to the biblical territory. The Jews who were expelled from Spain (1492) and Portugal (1498) were known as *Sephardim*. Their descendants also, who were spread to various parts of the globe, were called by the same name. They brought to their new homes customs and traditions that to this day distinguish them from the Ashkenazic Jews who emanate from Germany and eastern Europe. Though there are fewer Sephardic Jews than Ashkenazic Jews, their customs are no less valid. They have never been regarded as a sect, like the Samaritans in Israel, whose status as authentic Jews has been questioned for centuries.

One of the most obvious differences between *Sephardim* and *Ashkenazim* is found in the pronunciation of the Hebrew and in the liturgy. The *Sephardim* claim that their pronunciation of Hebrew and their liturgy are derived from the perod of the *Geonim* who led the great academies of Babylonia until the center of Jewish life shifted to Spain. The text of their prayer book is based on the *Siddur* of Amram, a distinguished Babylonian *Gaon*.

The order of prayers, the customs and traditions of the Sephardic Jews, are known as *Minhag Sefarad*, as distinguished in various particulars from the *Minhag Ashkenaz*. Examples of Sephardic custom are:

1. The naming of a child after a living parent or grandparent, unlike the *Ashkenazim,* who name children only after the deceased.
2. The reciting of the *Kol Nidre* in the manner of a simple prayer. Among the *Ashkenazim,* the *Hazzan* alone chants it aloud. The *Kol Nidre* found its way into the Sephardic prayer book long after its adoption by the *Ashkenazim.*

Unlike the Bible, whose text did not change after a certain date, the Sephardic and Ashkenazic prayer books borrowed freely from each other, revealing the interdependence of the two communities. The mere fact that the *Hasidim* of eighteenth-century Galicia, Ukraine, and Poland—all *Ashkenazim*—adopted the Sephardic text of prayer is an indication of the give-and-take among the various groupings of Jews.

Sephardic communities today are found principally in Turkey, Greece, North Africa, Israel, England, Latin America, and the United States. Like the Yiddish-speaking Ashkenazic Jews, the *Sephardim,* too, speak a group language or vernacular, known as Ladino. It is written in Hebrew characters and consists primarily of Castilian, mixed with many Hebrew idioms and expressions. It is also studded with Turkish, Arabic, and Greek words.

180

DIN

דִּין

Judgment, Justice, Legal Decision

The original meaning of *Din* was probably "judgment." One of the names for Rosh Hashanah is *Yom Hadin,* the Day of Judgment, when the fate of the individual is judged by God.

Din is more frequently identified with the concept of justice. The *Bet Din* is a court of justice and a *din Torah* is a trial held according to the principles of Jewish law and justice. The rabbis repeatedly extol the society whose courts insist on justice and whose officials enforce justice to protect human rights. Imperfect justice was preferred to no justice at all. Jews were exhorted to accept the overly harsh laws of the Romans rather than to live under a government without laws.

> And you have made men as the fishes of the sea, as the creeping things that have no ruler over them. [*Habakkuk* 1:14]

> Why were people compared to the fishes of the sea? Because in the case of the fishes of the sea, athe larger one swallows the smaller one; so, too, in the case of men: were it not for the fear of government, the stronger would swallow the weaker. [*Avodah Zarah* 46]

When a judge renders a decision in accordance with the law of the Torah, he is imitating the justice of God, for one of His attributes is that He is just. While the judge should not waver in his execution of justice, especially when two litigants come before him—for an act of mercy to one party may be an act of injustice to the other—the layman is expected to imitate the

399

other attribute of God—His mercy. The people are required to go beyond the line of strict justice *(lifnim meshurat hadin)* and to live in accordance with those greater ideals that the court cannot enforce. In his relations with his fellow man, a person should be guided by compassion and trust rather than by the literalness of justice.

It is quite natural for the term *din* to assume the meaning of the law, the legal decision. When one asks, "What is the *din?*" he expects an incisive answer, the final decision on either a civil or religious problem discussed in the Jewish codes.

181

DIN TORAH

דִּין תּוֹרָה

Arbitration of a Private Dispute
(literally: Law of the Torah)

As early as Mishnaic times, courts of three persons were provided to judge private disputes. Each party was asked to choose an arbiter, and the two arbiters chose a third who presided. If the regular court was in session at that place, the parties could not demand that the decision of the arbitration court be followed, but they would frequently submit themselves voluntarily to the decision of the arbitration court.

In the Middle Ages, the rabbi of the community was usually the head of the court of arbitration. The main function of the court was to persuade the two disputing parties to accept its decision. The advantage of a small court to decide on personal disputes was clearly to prevent a public airing of differences.

Until the dissolution of the eastern European Jewish communities, the community rabbi was considered the highest legal authority, by virtue of his learning and piety. When a dispute arose between two parties in a legal or religious matter, they would submit to a *din Torah* before the rabbi, who would make his decision in accordance with the sacred law. Hence the term *din Torah* (Law of the Torah). If the community were large, the rabbi would have an assistant, called a *dayan* (judge), who assisted him in his religious and legal cases. If the town were too small to support a rabbi, there would be only a *dayan*. Some large cities had several rabbis with their assistants.

The rabbi's authority was not absolute. His verdict could be appealed if one of the litigants was dissatisfied. On occasion they would submit their case before a second rabbi, or occasionally they would finally take their case to the government court, though this course was seldom taken.

The custom of submitting personal grievances to a rabbi has still survived in certain Orthodox Jewish communities. If a dispute arises between two observant Jews who are opposed to bringing their differences to a civil court, one summons the other to a *din Torah* before their rabbi, who is asked to judge between them, but only according to Jewish law and tradition.

An outgrowth of older arbitration courts are the Jewish Conciliation Courts of America that have been formed in several larger Jewish communities. Varied cases are brought before them, such as difficulties in domestic relations, complaints of aged parents against their children, etc. At these sessions sit three judges: a rabbi, a jurist, and a businessman. There are no technicalities of procedure and no court fees or lawyers involved. The litigants present their case in person and in most instances accept the decision of the court without rancor. Unlike the parties who submit to a *din Torah*, the litigants are not necessarily traditional Jews and do not seek a decision based on Jewish law. Like their ancestors, however, they prefer to settle their disputes out of court to avoid unnecessary publicity among brethren.

182

SEMIKHAH

סְמִיכָה

Ordination
(Literally: Laying of the Hands)

The ancient practice of ordaining religious leaders by "laying of the hands" upon them is traced to the Bible, which records that Moses ordained Joshua in this manner. This became the accepted manner of ordaining scholars until the Hadrianic persecutions (135 C.E.) when the death penalty was decreed for anyone participating in the ordination ceremony. It was thereafter decided to ordain merely by bestowing the title rabbi. After the Roman oppression eased, some returned to the former method of ordination, but by the Middle Ages the placing of the hands completely disappeared as a symbol of ordination.

In the talmudic age, only scholars living in Palestine could have conferred on them the title *Rabbi*. Similarly, the ordaining rabbi had to be from Palestine. It was not necessary, however, for both of them to be together at the time of the ordination. Ordination was known to have been given by letter or messenger. Ordination was usually sanctioned by a board of three rabbis, except in times of emergency, when one was sufficient.

Scholars residing in Babylonia were called *Rav* instead of *Rabbi*. Some Babylonians went to study in Palestine for the purpose of receiving ordination, but subsequently the Palestinian leaders decided not to ordain any scholar who did not intend to remain in Palestine.

Studies have shown that ordination continued in Palestine until the end of the eleventh century, when the Crusaders pillaged Jerusalem. Attempts were made to revive the custom when a group of brilliant students settled in Safed in the sixteenth century. Following the suggestion of Maimonides that if all the scholars of Palestine agreed to ordain a scholar, the process of ordination could be renewed, Jacob Berab convened twenty-five outstanding scholars who ordained him. After being ordained, he in turn ordained others, among them the famous Joseph Karo, compiler of the *Shulhan Arukh*. After a bitter controversy with the main rabbi of Jerusalem who refused to consent to Berab's activity, the whole movement lost impetus and subsequently died out.

In modern times, Orthodox rabbis issue to the rabbinate a certificate of admission, which is formally called *Heter Horaah* or more figuratively, *Semikhah*. It is presented to the candidate following a thorough examination in the field of Jewish law by one or more outstanding talmudic authorities. In effect, the title permits the student to render an authoritative decision on ritual matters. The majority of rabbis in America today, including the Orthodox, receive ordination from a rabbinical school after completing a prescribed course of studies consisting of several Hebraic courses, in addition to Jewish law. Only the Orthodox, however, must pass a special examination showing thorough acquaintance with the laws of the *Shulhan Arukh* and its commentaries.

183

TAKKANAH

תַּקָּנָה

Enactment, Improvement

During the talmudic and medieval ages authorities enacted many new ordinances that were not found previously in the Bible and yet were legally binding on the Jewish community.

Examples of *takkanot* enacted in the days of the Mishnah are: (1) a man must support his children while they are minors; (2) a gift of more than one-fifth of one's property for charity is forbidden; (3) a father must deal gently with his son until the age of twelve; after that age he may be strict with him; (4) one who attacks an old man must pay one pound of gold for the injury.

The rabbis never enacted *takkanot* arbitrarily. Every enactment was seriously regarded, since it represented change, and occasionally a break with older practices. But they recognized the growing needs of the Jewish community in a more complex society. Their new contacts with the Gentile world, the more complicated problems involving commerce and court laws demanded bold action to deal with contemporary needs. Every *takkanah* was to be an improvement over the existing practice and yet could not move away from the intent or spirit of the biblical law.

Some of their enactments were specifically geared to improving the order of the world *(Tikkun Haolam)* or to promote peace *(Darkei Shalom)*. Examples of the former are: (1) if one divorces a wife for reasons of immorality, he must not take her back again; (2) one should not pay an excessive sum of ransom to redeem a prisoner. Examples of the latter are: (1) one's cistern nearest to the river is to be filled first; (2) the non-Jew may share in the harvest given to the poor.

405

During the Middle Ages, *takkanot* could be drawn up by the laymen of the community, but never without the rabbi's consent. When a *takkanah* was passed, it was proclaimed in the synagogue on a weekday, after public notice had been given, and it was held that unless a formal protest was immediately expressed, every individual was bound to honor the enactment. The most far-reaching *takkanot* in medieval Europe were promulgated by the great scholar, Rabbenu Gershom (965–1028). Among the *takkanot* attributed to him are: (1) polygamy is not allowed; (2) people must respect the privacy of mail; (3) the owner of a private synagogue may not refuse admission to a worshiper because of a personal grievance; (4) a divorce may not be forced upon a woman; (5) if absence or poverty makes it impossible for a man to support his wife, the community must provide for her; (6) one who is summoned to court by a messenger must attend.

Special *takkanot* were enacted in Poland as late as the seventeenth and eighteenth centuries, and the authority of the rabbinate was unequivocally accepted by the Jewish community. In more recent times, however, as the legal authority of the rabbi declined, the *takkanah* was seldom invoked. The traditionalist has had to rely instead on the principle, "When in doubt the more severe opinion prevails."

184

SHEELOT UTESHUVOT

שְׁאֵלוֹת וּתְשׁוּבוֹת

Responsa Literature
(literally: Questions and Answers)

After the Talmud was completed in Babylonia (ca. 500 C.E.), the *Geonim* became the undisputed authorities of Jewish law and were recognized as the direct successors of those scholars who developed the Talmud. The Jews living outside of Babylonia looked to the *Geonim* as their final authority and sent questions in writing from every land where Jews were settled. The *Geonim* encouraged this not only because they wanted to preserve a universal respect for Jewish law, but also because each inquiry was usually accompanied by a contribution to maintain their academies.

The questions that were asked of the *Geonim* and their answers were known as *Sheelot Uteshuvot* (Responsa). Most of this valuable correspondence has been lost, but hundreds have been recovered, thus forming a great literature of Jewish laws-by-correspondence. Since Cairo represented the crossroads between the East and West, it became a natural distribution point for the answers sent to western countries, such as Morocco and Spain. These answers were often copied in Cairo and a copy kept there for the records. Hence, when Solomon Schechter made his great *Geniza* discovery in a Cairo synagogue room before the turn of the century, one of his greatest finds consisted of a hoard of Gaonic Responsa.

Many of the problems directed to the *Geonim* dealt with questions of Jewish custom and proper procedure of worship. Other responsa sought clarification of difficult talmudic passages that only the Babylonian scholars could unravel.

407

Eventually the western Jewish communities developed their own great talmudic authorities. Spain, North Africa, France, and Germany became centers of Jewish learning. More and more questions were addressed to the local authorities who surpassed the Babylonians in scholarship. In time, the answers given to questions became very elaborate essays and were preserved by the authors so that their students could thoroughly study them and refer to them if they were confronted with similar questions.

A study of the questions and answers yields priceless information about the social customs, moral standards, and the problems confronting Jewish communities at the time that the responsa were written. From the hundreds of Responsa written by Rabbi Meir of Rothenburg, the leading scholar of his era, we are able to derive a clearer picture of the medieval Jewish community in Germany. There are, for example, many inquiries addressed to Rabbi Meir concerning the lending of money to non-Jews, one of the chief occupations of the Jews at that time. Questions dealing with forced conversions and heavy taxation reveal a clearer picture of the persecutions and expulsion of Jews. The inner life of the Jew is better understood from the many Responsa dealing with pawning and the sale of books, which show the high value placed upon books even by poverty-stricken Jews. Many inquiries addressed to Rabbi Meir deal with the relations of teachers to parents who engaged them. One cannot help being impressed with the high position education held for the Jews. Inquiries about commercial cases indicate that German Jews in Rabbi Meir's day were engaged in export and import businesses.

More important, however, than the historical information that the *Sheelot* and *Teshuvot* yielded were the valuable legal decisions that the great scholars handed down and the spirit in which they were written. Decisions were given on many questions that could not have been anticipated in previous centuries. New social problems or new inventions required the serious attention of the greatest scholars to determine how the pious Jew could adapt to change and at the same time maintain the Jewish law. It was through this question–answer method continuing through the modern times that the vitality of Jewish law was preserved.

185

SEYAG LATORAH

סְיָג לַתּוֹרָה

Protective Fence for the Torah

One of the sayings ascribed to the men of the Great Assembly is "Make a fence for the Torah," which explains why the Sages set up so many regulations and enactments. They wanted to protect the Torah with cautionary rules to halt a man before he could get within breaking distance of the biblical law. The Talmud justifies these added regulations by citing the biblical verse, "Therefore shall you keep what I have given you to keep," which is interpreted to mean: Add protection to what I have already given you as protection.

The clearest example of precautionary laws enacted to protect the principal law is the prohibition of handling certain objects on the Sabbath. The rabbis prohibited even the handling of money, work tools, or candlesticks on the Sabbath. Even though the original intention was not to use them, the rabbis reasoned that one could possibly forget the holiness of the day once these objects were being handled. They referred to these objects as *muktzeh*—"stored away" or "off limits."

It is clear to the student of Jewish law that the rabbis did not seek to set up arbitrary laws merely to impose added hardships on the Jew. In fact, they frequently suspended or set aside certain biblical laws when the times demanded it. For example, they enthusiastically accepted the legal fiction called *Prozbul*, devised by Hillel. The biblical law required all loans to be canceled at the beginning of every seventh year (Deuteronomy 15:1–3). Hillel recognized the impracticability of such a law. No matter how distressed a man might be, lenders would not make a loan in the fifth or sixth year knowing that it would soon be canceled. Hillel's enactment gave legal protection to the lender by enabling him to reclaim his loan at any time he desired.

Fences were also set up by the rabbis to protect moral injunctions in the Torah. The Torah instructs that storekeepers use proper weights and measures, but, as time went on, storekeepers were instructed in other methods of fair dealing not explicitly named in the Bible. The rabbis recognized other ways of exploiting the customer that were not anticipated in the less complex era of the Bible. Their fences, therefore, served the additional purpose of keeping the biblical law applicable to a changing society.

A Jewish moralist interpreted the expression, "Set up a fence," to derive an ethical lesson: make a fence about your words the way God made a fence about His words. This rather obscure passage has been applied in the following way: "Let every man take care that what he says shall not be too difficult for his listeners to understand, especially when he speaks words of the Torah; let him take care to speak of them only at the proper time, in the proper idiom, in the proper place, and under proper circumstances, both as regards himself and as regards his listeners."

186

PIKKUAH NEFESH

פִּקּוּחַ נֶפֶשׁ

A Life in Danger

The preservation of human life takes precedence over all the other commandments in Judaism. The Talmud emphasizes this principle by citing the verse from Leviticus: "You shall therefore keep my statutes . . . which if a man do, *he shall live by them.*" The rabbis add: "*That he shall live by them,* and not that he shall die by them."

When life is involved, all Sabbath laws may be suspended to safeguard the health of the individual, the principle being *pikkuah nefesh doheh Shabbat*—life in danger takes precedence over the Sabbath.

One is not merely permitted—one is required to disregard a law that conflicts with life or health. "It is a religious precept to desecrate the Sabbath for any person afflicted with an illness that may prove dangerous; he who is zealous is praiseworthy while he who asks questions sheds blood."

This duty to ignore the law, if necessary, to safeguard health is also stressed in connection with fasting on Yom Kippur. A sick person is obliged to break the fast. Neither the patient nor those attending him need atone when performing such acts that are forbidden under normal circumstances.

In spite of the virtue of observing the fast, it is not virtuous to observe laws at the risk of one's life. Such conduct is regarded as foolish, even as sinful. The Sages described this stubbornness as a "piety of madness."

Pikkuah nefesh was not only confined to serious crises in health. The victims of religious persecution who lived under the constant threat of death were also guided by the principle of *pikkuah nefesh*. They, too, were cautioned against sacrificing their lives in order to observe the Sabbath and festivals. There were exceptions, to be sure, when martyrdom was considered a greater virtue than surrendering one's principles. Generally, however, the Jew was encouraged to accept temporary indignity and choose life, to live in misery, rather than to die in glory.

REFERENCES

Ahad Ha-am (1912). *Selected Essays by Ahad Ha-am*. Translated from Hebrew by Leon Simon. Philadelphia: Jewish Publication Society.

Birnbaum, P., ed. (1957). *A Treasury of Judaism*. New York: Hebrew Publishing Co.

Fromm, E. (1967). *The Heart of Man*. New York: Harper & Row.

Garfiel, E. (1958). *Service of the Heart—A Guide to the Jewish Prayer Book*. New York: Thomas Yoseloff (for the United Synagogue of America).

Glueckel of Hameln (1719). *The Memoirs of Glueckel of Hameln*. Translated by M. Lowenthal. New York: Schocken (1977).

Gordis, R. (1956). *Judaism for the Modern Age*.

Gordon, A. D. (1938). *Selected Essays*. Translated by Frances Burnce. New York: New York League for Labor Palestine.

Hertzberg, A., ed. (1971). *The Zionist Idea*. New York: Atheneum (paperback). Originally published, Philadelphia: Jewish Publication Society, 1959.

Heschel, A. (1954). *Man's Quest for God*. New York: Charles Scribner's Sons.

Jacob, B. (1974). *Genesis*. Edited and translated from German by Ernest and Walter Jacob. New York: KTAV.

Pallière, A. (1925). *The Unknown Sanctuary: A Piligrimage from Rome to Israel*. Translated by Louise Waterman Wise. New York: Bloch.

Schechter, S. (1909). *Some Aspects of Rabbinic Theology*. New York: Macmillan. (Newer version, *Aspects of Rabbinic Theology*. New York: Schocken, 1961.)

Zangwill, I. (1892). *Children of the Ghetto.* Philadelphia: Jewish Publication Society.

Zborowski, M., and Herzog, E. (1962). *Life is with People. The Culture of the Shtetl.* New York: Schocken (first Schocken paperback edition).

INDEX